THE JOURNEY TO A FULFILLING AND MEANINGFUL LIFE

Wisdom for Personal Growth,
Fulfillment, and Financial Well-being

Elijah M. James, Ph. D.

Copyright © 2024 Elijah James
All rights reserved

No part of this book may be reproduced in any form or by any electronic or mechanical means, without permission in writing from the publisher.

Canadian Cataloguing in Publication Data
James, Elijah M.
A Journey to a Fulfilling and Meaningful Life

ISBN 978-1-0690086-2-6

EJ Publishing
663 White Plains Road
Hammonds Plains
Nova Scotia, Canada. B4B 1W7

It is with deep gratitude that I dedicate this book to my friend and colleague of many years, Mrs. Veronica Martin-Batson. Your life is a true embodiment of the principles shared within these pages—purpose, love, wisdom, and grace. Your unwavering commitment to living a life of meaning, and your ability to inspire others to do the same, have been a constant source of encouragement to me.

May this book honour the path you have walked and continue to walk, and may it touch the lives of others as profoundly as you have touched mine.

Table of Contents

Preface 1

Acknowledgments 5

INTRODUCTION 7
The Purpose of This Book 7
The Journey of Self-Improvement 7
How to Use This Book 8

PART I MASTERING THE MIND 11

CHAPTER 1 THE POWER OF THOUGHT 12
The Bible Says 12
Introduction 13
Sayings about the Power of Thought 15
Understanding the Role of Mindset 18
Developing Positive Thinking Habits 19
Overcoming Negative Thought Patterns 20
Conclusion 21

CHAPTER 2 EMOTIONAL INTELLIGENCE 27
The Bible Says 27
Introduction 29
Sayings about Emotional Intelligence 31
Understanding Emotional Intelligence 35
Recognizing and Managing Your Emotions 36
Building Empathy and Understanding Others 37
Cultivating Emotional Resilience 38
Applying Emotional Intelligence to Everyday Life 39
Conclusion 40

CHAPTER 3 MINDFULNESS AND PRESENCE 47
The Bible Says 47
Introduction 49

Sayings about Mindfulness and Presence...........................51
Understanding Mindfulness 55
Practicing Mindfulness in Daily Life 56
The Power of Presence..57
Mindfulness and Emotional Regulation 58
Mindfulness and Cognitive Functioning 59
Conclusion...60

PART II NURTURING THE BODY 67

CHAPTER 4 THE FOUNDATIONS OF PHYSICAL HEALTH 68

The Bible Says 68
Introduction..70
Sayings about Physical Health 72
The Importance of Physical Health 76
Nutrition: Fueling Your Body 76
Exercise and Physical Activity 78
Sleep and Recovery 79
Preventive Health Care...80
Conclusion...81

CHAPTER 5 BUILDING HEALTHY HABITS.............. 89

The Bible Says 89
Introduction..91
Sayings about Building Healthy Habits 93
Creating a Sustainable Wellness Routine 95
Overcoming Obstacles to Physical Health..........................97
The Connection Between Body and Mind 98
Conclusion...99

CHAPTER 6 STRESS MANAGEMENT AND RELAXATION 107

The Bible Says 107
Introduction..110
Sayings about Stress Management..................................112
Understanding the Sources of Stress 114
Practical Techniques for Managing Stress 114

The Importance of Relaxation 115
Integrating Stress Management into Daily Life 116
Conclusion 117

PART III STRENGTHENING RELATIONSHIPS 125

CHAPTER 7 BUILDING STRONG RELATIONSHIPS 126

The Bible Says 126
Introduction 128
Sayings about Building Strong Relationships 131
The Importance of Healthy Communication 132
Nurturing Love and Compassion 133
Resolving Conflicts with Grace 134
Conclusion 136

CHAPTER 8 CULTIVATING COMMUNITY AND CONNECTION 143

The Bible Says 143
Introduction 146
Sayings about Cultivating Community and Connection 147
The Power of Social Support Networks 149
Building and Maintaining Friendships 150
Contributing Positively to Society 151
Conclusion 153

CHAPTER 9 THE ROLE OF SERVICE AND KINDNESS 161

The Bible Says 161
Introduction 164
Sayings about Service and Kindness 165
Giving Back: The Benefits of Altruism 168
Small Acts of Kindness 170
Creating a Legacy of Compassion 171
Conclusion 172

PART IV FINDING PURPOSE AND FULFILLMENT . 181

CHAPTER 10 DISCOVERING YOUR LIFE'S PURPOSE 182

The Bible Says 182
Introduction 186
Sayings about Discovering Your Life's Purpose 188
The Quest for Meaning and Direction 190
Aligning Your Life with Your Values 191
Pursuing Passion and Purpose 193
Conclusion 195

CHAPTER 11 SETTING AND ACHIEVING GOALS .. 204

The Bible Says 204
Introduction 207
Sayings about Setting and Achieving Goals 208
The Science of Goal Setting 213
Overcoming Procrastination and Self-Doubt 216
Celebrating Milestones and Successes 219
Conclusion 221

CHAPTER 12 LIVING A BALANCED AND FULFILLED LIFE 229

The Bible Says 229
Introduction 230
Sayings about Living a Balanced and Fulfilled Life 232
Balancing Work, Family, and Personal Growth 236
Finding Joy in Simple Pleasures 238
Creating a Life of Contentment and Fulfillment 240
Conclusion 241

PART V FINANCIAL WELL-BEING AND ECONOMIC EMPOWERMENT 249

CHAPTER 13 UNDERSTANDING PERSONAL FINANCE 250

The Bible Says 250
Introduction 254

Sayings about Personal Finance 255
The Basics of Budgeting and Saving 257
Managing Debt and Building Credit 258
Planning for Major Life Expenses 260
Conclusion.. 262

CHAPTER 14 INVESTING FOR THE FUTURE 270

The Bible Says 270
Introduction 272
Sayings about Investing 274
The Fundamentals of Investing 276
Diversifying Your Investment Portfolio 279
Retirement Planning and Financial Independence 281
Conclusion.. 283

CHAPTER 15 ECONOMIC LITERACY AND DECISION-MAKING 292

The Bible Says 292
Introduction 293
Sayings about Economic Literacy 295
Analyzing Economic Data 297
Making Informed Economic Decisions 300
The Role of Economic Awareness in Life Planning 301
Conclusion.. 304

PART VI SPIRITUAL GROWTH AND INNER PEACE 311

CHAPTER 16 EXPLORING SPIRITUALITY 312

The Bible Says 312
Introduction 313
Sayings about Spirituality 315
Understanding the Role of Spirituality in Life 317
Different Paths to Spiritual Fulfillment 318
The Connection Between Spirituality and Happiness 321
Conclusion.. 322

CHAPTER 17 DEVELOPING INNER PEACE 329

The Bible Says 329

Introduction 332
Sayings about Developing Inner Peace 334
The Practice of Meditation and Reflection........................336
Letting Go of Fear and Anxiety 337
Embracing Forgiveness and Gratitude 339
Conclusion..340

CHAPTER 18 THE ART OF LETTING GO 348
The Bible Says 348
Introduction..352
Sayings about Letting Go 355
Releasing Control and Surrendering to Life 358
Accepting Change and Impermanence.............................359
Finding Freedom in Detachment 360
Conclusion..362

CONCLUSION 371
Reflecting on the Journey...371
Continuous Growth and Lifelong Learning.......................372
Final Thoughts and Encouragement 373

Riddles.. 375

Glossary of Terms 379

Preface

In a world filled with endless distractions, fleeting pleasures, and constant noise, the quest for a meaningful life has become more crucial than ever. We are all travelers on this journey, each of us seeking a path that leads to fulfillment, purpose, and inner peace. Yet, amid the rush of daily life, it's easy to lose sight of what truly matters, to forget that the most important journey we undertake is not measured in miles or achievements, but in the depth of our souls.

The Journey to a Fulfilling and Meaningful Life is born out of a deep reflection on what it means to live a life of substance, one that resonates with the core of our being. It is a guide for those who yearn for more than just success, more than mere survival—it is for those who long to leave a lasting imprint on the world, and to find contentment within themselves.

This book is not a manual filled with rigid rules or a blueprint for happiness. Instead, it is a collection of insights, reflections, and practices that can help you carve out your own path to meaning. It draws on timeless wisdom, contemporary psychology, and the lived experiences of people who have found their way to lives rich in purpose and significance.

Included in each chapter is a life story that offers readers a relatable and human connection to the concepts being discussed. These life stories transform abstract ideas into tangible experiences, providing real-world examples that illustrate the principles in action. By sharing personal journeys and challenges, these life stories inspire and encourage readers, making the lessons more impactful and memorable. They create an emotional resonance, showing how others have navigated similar paths, and offer a sense of hope, guidance, and deeper understanding.

At the end of each chapter, you'll find suggestions for reflection and exercises that are intended to deepen your understanding of the topics covered. These are tools meant to support your personal journey, helping you apply what you've learned to your daily life. Take your time with these exercises, returning to them whenever you need to refresh your perspective or revisit certain areas of growth.

Each chapter invites you to explore different facets of a meaningful life—from discovering your true purpose to cultivating deep connections with others, from embracing challenges as opportunities for growth to finding joy in the simplicity of the present moment. The journey outlined in these pages is one of self-discovery, personal growth, and spiritual awakening.

As you embark on this journey, remember that the path to a meaningful life is not a straight line, nor is it the same for everyone. It is a personal and ever-evolving process, shaped by your values, passions, and experiences. There will be moments of doubt and uncertainty, but there will also be moments of profound clarity and joy. It is in walking this path that you will find not only what you are looking for, but also who you truly are.

PREFACE

I invite you to take these words to heart, to engage deeply with the ideas presented here, and to embark on your own journey towards a life of meaning. May this book serve as a companion on your path, offering guidance, inspiration, and encouragement as you navigate the complexities of life with a renewed sense of purpose and direction.

Word-search Puzzles

The word-search puzzles at the end of the chapters in *The Journey to a Fulfilling and Meaningful Life* serve multiple functions, enhancing both engagement and reflection for readers:

Reinforcing Key Concepts: The word search can help reinforce the chapter's main ideas by incorporating essential terms, concepts, or themes covered in the book. This offers a fun and interactive way for readers to review and internalize what they've read.

Encouraging Mindfulness: The process of completing a word search requires focus and attention, promoting mindfulness. This activity aligns with the book's theme of self-reflection, encouraging readers to slow down and contemplate the messages of each chapter.

Promoting Active Engagement: Rather than passively reading, the puzzle invites readers to actively participate, enhancing their engagement with the content. This can make the experience of the journey more enjoyable and memorable.

Providing a Mental Break: After delving into sometimes deep or complex subjects, the word search offers a light, relaxing activity. It provides a brief mental break while still keeping readers connected to the chapter's themes.

Fostering Personal Reflection: Some readers may find that while searching for the words, they reflect more deeply on the chapter's content, sparking personal insights and connections with the material.

Overall, these puzzles can serve as a creative tool for reinforcing learning while aligning with the book's holistic approach to living a meaningful life.

With each step you take, may you find the meaning you seek, and may your life become a testament to the power of living with intention, compassion, and grace.

Welcome to the journey.

Acknowledgments

About thirty years ago, I had a discussion with one of my close friends. The topic was "The Good Life". That discussion opened my eyes to a different perspective of the meaning of life. I promised my friend then that I would one day write a book about a fulfilling life. I thank you, V, for your invaluable contribution.

Writing *The Journey to a Fulfilling and Meaningful Life* has been a deeply rewarding journey, and I am grateful for the support, inspiration, and encouragement I have received along the way. This book would not have been possible without the influence of many remarkable individuals who have helped shape my thoughts and life experiences.

To my dear friends, who have walked alongside me through both the highs and lows, thank you for your companionship, wisdom, and encouragement. Your conversations, perspectives, and life stories have enriched the pages of this book, and I am deeply thankful for your presence in my life.

A special thank you to the mentors and teachers who have guided me over the years, offering valuable insights on personal growth, mindfulness, and living a purposeful life. Your lessons have deeply influenced the heart of this book, and I am forever grateful for your guidance.

To my readers, I am profoundly thankful for your interest in this work. Whether you are just beginning your journey of self-discovery or have been on the path for some time, I hope that this book serves as a source of encouragement, insight, and hope. Your willingness to explore the deeper meaning of life is inspiring, and I am honored to share these reflections with you.

Lastly, to the Divine presence that guides all our lives, thank You for the grace, peace, and wisdom that continually lead us on the path toward a meaningful existence. This book is, above all, a reflection of that journey and the lessons learned along the way.

With heartfelt gratitude,

Elijah James

INTRODUCTION

The Purpose of This Book

Life, in its many twists and turns, often leaves us searching for meaning and fulfillment. In a fast-paced world where the pursuit of success, material wealth, and outward appearances can overshadow what truly matters, many of us feel disconnected from a deeper sense of purpose. The aim of *The Journey to a Fulfilling and Meaningful Life* is to offer a roadmap for discovering that purpose, helping you find a greater sense of alignment between your inner self and the life you live.

This book is not just about success in the traditional sense, but about creating a life that feels truly fulfilling—one that balances personal growth, emotional well-being, strong relationships, and spiritual depth. It's about realizing that a meaningful life is defined not by what we achieve but by how we connect with ourselves, others, and the world around us. Through each chapter, you'll explore key aspects of personal development, relationships, health, and spirituality, and learn how to bring these elements together to live with greater intention and contentment.

The Journey of Self-Improvement

Self-improvement is not a one-time event; it's an ongoing journey. This book is designed to guide you along that path, helping you build self-awareness and adopt practices that will support your long-term well-being. Along the way, you'll learn how to cultivate emotional intelligence, nurture mindfulness, foster meaningful relationships, and embrace change with courage and grace.

Each chapter builds on the previous, offering insights and practical tools to help you grow in every area of your life. From learning how to better manage your emotions to embracing the importance of spiritual growth, the journey of self-improvement is woven throughout this book, encouraging you to reflect on your personal goals and experiences while offering new perspectives on how to live more fully and authentically.

How to Use This Book

The Journey to a Fulfilling and Meaningful Life is designed to be both a guide and a companion on your journey. You can choose to read it from start to finish, allowing each chapter to build upon the previous one, or you can dive into specific sections that speak to your immediate needs. Whether you are working on building stronger relationships, improving your physical health, or exploring spiritual practices, each chapter offers practical advice, reflective questions, and actionable steps to help you apply the lessons to your own life.

At the beginning of each chapter, you will find Bible verses to support you and deepen your understanding as you reflect on the topics covered. These verses are meant to support your personal journey to a fulfilling and meaningful life. Take your time with the verses, returning to them whenever you need to refresh your perspective or revisit certain areas of growth.

INTRODUCTION

This book is not about providing quick fixes or one-size-fits-all solutions. Instead, it invites you to embark on a thoughtful, deliberate path toward a more meaningful life—one rooted in awareness, gratitude, love, and personal fulfillment. Wherever you are on your journey, this book aims to provide encouragement, wisdom, and practical guidance to help you live with purpose and intention.

PART I
MASTERING THE MIND

CHAPTER 1
THE POWER OF THOUGHT

What you think affects your behavior, and
your behavior defines who you are.

The Bible Says

Trust in the Lord with all your heart and lean not on your own understanding. **(Proverbs 3:5)**

Take captive every thought and make it obedient to Christ. **(2 Corinthians 10:5)**

You were taught, with regard to your former way of life, to put off your old self, which is being corrupted by its deceitful desires; to be made new in the attitude of your minds; and to put on the new self, created to be like God in true righteousness and holiness. **(Ephesians 4:22-24)**

Whatever is true, whatever is noble, whatever is right, whatever is pure, whatever is lovely, whatever is admirable—if anything is excellent or praiseworthy— think about such things. **(Philippians 4:8)**

Set your mind on things above, not earthly things. **(Colossian 3:2)**

Do not conform to the pattern of this world, but be transformed by the renewing of your mind. Then you will be able to test and approve what God's will is —his good, pleasing and perfect will. **Romans 12:2**

Therefore, with minds that are alert and fully sober, set your hope on the grace to be brought to you when Jesus Christ is revealed at his coming. **1Peter 1:13.**

Introduction

The mind is one of the most powerful tools we possess, shaping not only our perception of the world but also the outcomes we experience in life. Our thoughts have the ability to influence our emotions, decisions, and actions, often determining the trajectory of our personal and professional journeys. Whether we recognize it or not, the patterns of thinking we adopt can build us up or hold us back, create opportunities or generate obstacles. In this chapter, we will explore the profound impact that thoughts have on our lives, the science behind the mind's influence, and how cultivating positive, constructive thinking can lead to transformation. Understanding the power of thought is the first step toward unlocking new potential and shaping a future that aligns with our deepest aspirations.

Life Story

As a child, Maya had always dreamed of becoming a doctor. Her fascination with helping others and her natural curiosity about the human body fueled her ambition. But as she grew older, life's obstacles began to cloud her path. Struggling financially and surrounded by doubt from those who believed her dreams were too big, Maya began to question her potential. The weight of others' opinions made her feel as if her goal was slipping further away.

However, one day, everything changed. She came across a story of a lady who, despite impossible odds, achieved her dream by transforming her mindset. Inspired, Maya decided to shift her focus. She began to harness the power of her thoughts, replacing fear and doubt with determination and belief. Every morning, she visualized herself achieving her dream. She sought out opportunities, worked tirelessly, and allowed her positive thoughts to guide her actions.

Years later, Maya stood proudly in her white coat, a symbol of the doctor she had always envisioned herself becoming. Reflecting on her journey, she realized that the key to her success was not just hard work, but the power of her thoughts. By choosing to believe in herself, even when the world doubted her, she unlocked her full potential.

Maya's story is a testament to the transformative power of thought. How we choose to think can shape our reality, unlock our potential, and set us on the path to achieving our dreams.

Sayings about the Power of Thought

The purpose of reading sayings about the power of thought is to inspire reflection on the influence that our thoughts have on our lives. These sayings often highlight the connection between mindset and outcomes, encouraging individuals to cultivate positive, focused thinking to shape their experiences. By reflecting on such wisdom, people are reminded that their thoughts can:

Shape their reality: Thoughts influence emotions, decisions, and actions, thus shaping one's life.

Boost self-awareness: Encourages mindfulness and intentionality in how they think, promoting growth.

Empower personal change: Inspires the belief that changing one's thoughts can change one's circumstances.

Promote positivity: Offers motivation to focus on optimistic and constructive thoughts for well-being.

Deepen understanding: Provides insight into the power of thought in overcoming challenges, achieving goals, and maintaining inner peace.

Ultimately, reading such sayings serves as a reminder that thoughts are powerful tools for personal development and life transformation.

Here are some sayings about the power of thought.

Thoughts have power; thoughts are energy. And you can make your world or break it by your own thinking.
Susan L. Taylor

If you realized how powerful your thoughts are, you would never think a negative thought.
Peace Pilgrim

A man is but the product of his thoughts what he thinks, he becomes.
Mahatma Gandhi

The world we have created is a product of our thinking.
Albert Einstein

All feelings derive and become alive, whether negative or positive, from the power of Thought.
Sydney Banks

As a single footstep will not make a path on the earth, so a single thought will not make a pathway in the mind. To make a deep physical path, we walk again and again. To make a deep mental path, we must think over and over the kind of thoughts we wish to dominate our lives.
Henry David Thoreau

Man's greatness lies in his power of thought.
Blaise Pascal

It is true if you believe it to be true.
Louise Hay

Imagination is more important than knowledge.
Albert Einstein

Thoughts are things; they have tremendous power. Thoughts of doubt and fear are pathways to failure.
Bryan Adams

The most common way people give up their power is by thinking they don't have any.
Alice Walker

The greatest discovery of all time is that a person can change his future by merely changing his attitude.
Oprah Winfrey

The greatest force is derived from the power of thought. The finer the element, the more powerful it is. The silent power of thought influences people even at a distance, because mind is one as well as many. The universe is a cobweb; minds are spiders.
Swami Vivekananda

Mind is the creator of everything. You should therefore guide it to create only good. If you cling to a certain thought with dynamic will power, it finally assumes a tangible outward form. When you are able to employ your will always for constructive purposes, you become the controller of your destiny.
Paramahansa Yogananda

You and I are not what we eat; we are what we think.
Walter Inglis Anderson

The Law of Attraction attracts to you everything you need, according to the nature of your thought life.
Joseph Murphy

Nurture your mind with great thoughts
Benjamin Disraeli

Thought creates character.
Annie Besant

If you can dream it, you can achieve it.
Zig Ziglar

As a single footstep will not make a path on the earth, so a single thought will not make a pathway in the mind.
Henry David Thoreau

Positive anything is better than negative nothing.
Elbert Hubbard

I have about concluded that wealth is a state of mind, and that anyone can acquire a wealthy state of mind by thinking rich thoughts.
Andrew Young

If you can dream it, you can make it so.
Belva Davis

Just as a physicist has to examine the telescope and galvanometer with which he is working; has to get a clear conception of what he can attain with them, and how they may deceive him; so, too, it seemed to me necessary to investigate likewise the capabilities of our power of thought.
Hermann von Helmholtz

We do not yet trust the unknown power of thoughts.
Ralph Waldo Emerson

Source: TOP 25 POWER OF THOUGHT QUOTES (of 80) | A-Z Quotes (azquotes.com)

Understanding the Role of Mindset

The Science Behind Mindset and Success

The concept of mindset has gained significant attention in recent years, largely because of the groundbreaking work of psychologist Carol Dweck. Her research reveals that mindset is a critical factor in determining success. According to Dweck, our mindset shapes how we perceive challenges, respond to setbacks, and ultimately, achieve our goals. The brain is malleable, and the way we think can influence our ability to grow and adapt. Scientific studies have shown that individuals with a positive and growth-oriented mindset are more likely to succeed because they view challenges as opportunities for learning rather than insurmountable obstacles.

Fixed vs. Growth Mindsets

Dweck's research highlights two primary types of mindsets: fixed and growth. Individuals with a fixed mindset believe that their abilities and intelligence are static and cannot be changed. This belief can lead to a fear of failure, avoidance of challenges, and a tendency to give up easily. In contrast, those with a growth mindset believe that their abilities can be developed through effort, learning, and persistence. This mindset encourages resilience, a love for learning, and an openness to new experiences. By cultivating a growth mindset, individuals can unlock their potential and achieve greater success in various aspects of life.

Developing Positive Thinking Habits

Daily Practices for Positive Thinking

Developing positive thinking habits requires consistent practice. Daily rituals such as gratitude journaling, where individuals write down things they are thankful for, can significantly boost positive thinking. Starting the day with positive affirmations—statements that reinforce one's values, strengths, and capabilities—can set a constructive tone for the day. Mindfulness meditation is another powerful tool, helping individuals stay present and focused, reducing stress, and fostering a positive outlook. Regularly engaging in these practices helps rewire the brain to focus on positivity, making it easier to navigate life's challenges with a constructive mindset.

Reframing Negative Thoughts

Reframing is a cognitive technique that involves changing the way we perceive and respond to negative thoughts. Instead of allowing negative thoughts to dominate our mindset, reframing helps us see them from a different perspective. For example, instead of viewing a mistake as a failure, we can reframe it as a learning opportunity. This shift in perspective not only reduces the emotional impact of negative thoughts but also encourages growth and resilience. By actively practicing reframing, we can transform our thinking patterns and develop a more positive and empowering mindset.

Overcoming Negative Thought Patterns

Identifying Self-Sabotaging Thoughts

Negative thought patterns, often referred to as cognitive distortions, can sabotage our success and well-being. These patterns include all-or-nothing thinking, overgeneralization, and catastrophizing, where individuals expect the worst possible outcome. Identifying these self-sabotaging thoughts is the first step in overcoming them. Self-awareness is key; by paying attention to our thoughts and recognizing when they are irrational or overly negative, we can begin to challenge and change them. Keeping a thought journal can be an effective way to track and identify these patterns, allowing for greater insight and control over our thinking.

Strategies for Cognitive Restructuring

Cognitive restructuring is a therapeutic technique used to challenge and alter negative thought patterns. This process involves questioning the validity of negative thoughts and replacing them with more balanced and rational ones. For example, if you catch yourself thinking, "I'll never be successful," you can challenge this by asking, "Is this thought based on facts or assumptions? What evidence do I have to support or refute this belief?" Over time, consistently practicing cognitive restructuring can help break the cycle of negative thinking, leading to a more positive and resilient mindset.

Conclusion

The power of thought cannot be overstated. Our mindset shapes our reality, influencing how we perceive challenges and achieve success. By understanding the difference between fixed and growth mindsets, developing positive thinking habits, and overcoming negative thought patterns, we can harness the power of thought to lead a meaningful and fulfilling life.

Exercise

Reflecting on Your Thoughts

Take some time to engage in the following reflective exercise. It will help you explore the role of your thoughts in shaping your life and guide you toward cultivating a more positive and empowered mindset.

Step 1: Thought Awareness

1. **Set aside 10-15 minutes** in a quiet space where you won't be disturbed.

2. Take a notebook or journal and write down the thoughts that have been recurring in your mind lately. These could be related to work, relationships, health, or any other area of life.

   Are they positive or negative?
   Do they uplift you or weigh you down?

3. As you write, observe any patterns. Do you tend to focus more on fears, doubts, or negative self-talk, or are your thoughts empowering and constructive?

Step 2: Reframing Negative Thoughts

1. Select two or three recurring negative thoughts from your list.

2. Ask yourself, **What is the underlying belief behind this thought?**

4. For example, if you often think, "I'm not good enough," the underlying belief might be a lack of self-confidence.

3. Now, **reframe each negative thought into a positive or constructive one.**

Instead of "I'm not good enough," try, "I'm continually growing, and every challenge is an opportunity for me to learn and improve."

Step 3: Thought Alignment with Goals

1. Think about one personal or professional goal you are currently pursuing.
2. Reflect on how your thoughts support or hinder your progress toward that goal.

   Are your thoughts aligned with the outcome you desire?
   What changes can you make in your thinking to better support your goal?

3. Write down one positive thought or affirmation that will help keep you focused on achieving this goal. Practice repeating this affirmation daily.

Step 4: Visualization Exercise

1. Close your eyes and take a few deep breaths. Imagine yourself living the life you desire, where your thoughts are positive and empowering.
2. **Visualize yourself overcoming challenges with ease** and embracing opportunities with confidence.
3. After spending a few moments in this visualization, open your eyes and write down how you felt during the exercise. What changes did you notice in your mindset?

Step 5: Daily Practice

Commit to spending 5-10 minutes each day reviewing your thoughts and practicing positive thinking. By becoming aware of your mental patterns and consciously reframing negative thoughts, you can harness the power of thought to create a more meaningful and fulfilling life.

CHAPTER 1
WORDSEARCH

	1	2	3	4	5	6	7	8	9	10	11	12	13	14	15	16	17	18	19	20
1	F	T	F	M	H	U	C	I	U	Q	E	F	L	G	P	K	V	M	U	O
2	T	X	L	E	Z	X	W	G	D	L	H	R	B	F	T	D	E	L	Z	A
3	L	F	U	D	W	X	S	C	Z	P	C	C	U	E	Y	D	J	V	J	K
4	A	D	C	U	X	K	E	H	E	N	D	I	S	T	D	K	G	H	L	O
5	N	E	R	T	V	S	U	W	S	L	J	D	G	X	R	G	W	R	Z	M
6	P	X	O	I	N	D	N	H	U	R	N	E	D	O	F	U	P	Z	N	K
7	E	N	L	T	W	M	K	M	W	I	X	G	N	D	B	I	N	O	G	K
8	R	K	R	T	Y	U	D	F	M	G	M	T	N	M	U	Z	I	A	L	L
9	S	L	Q	A	A	C	X	X	R	C	K	Y	P	R	Y	T	E	P	Y	M
10	P	S	R	E	F	R	A	N	I	N	G	F	T	O	A	H	W	X	F	W
11	E	D	P	O	S	I	T	I	V	E	T	H	I	N	K	I	N	G	O	G
12	C	U	F	E	C	Y	M	S	X	A	F	U	I	F	I	X	M	V	F	M
13	T	V	I	O	X	D	G	A	S	Z	J	G	Z	T	R	H	S	P	M	M
14	I	G	H	I	G	C	E	G	J	F	A	I	J	V	T	C	T	B	X	R
15	V	M	U	D	Y	C	K	D	A	M	P	E	R	C	E	P	T	I	O	N
16	E	V	Z	N	G	N	I	Z	I	H	P	O	T	S	A	T	A	C	Z	N
17	O	D	F	E	Y	G	Q	P	M	K	E	Y	C	I	W	N	E	G	V	B
18	W	E	U	G	L	U	V	Z	T	B	Z	T	R	C	U	B	E	F	D	K
19	V	Y	G	J	B	N	E	X	A	F	X	M	Y	C	S	Y	N	T	J	E
20	Q	C	P	E	G	Z	Y	L	F	I	D	A	T	R	Z	R	U	Z	P	T

ATTITUDE   MINDSET   PERSPECTIVE

CATASTOPHIZING   NURTURE   POSITIVE THINKING

IMAGINATION   PERCEPTION   REFRANING

THE JOURNEY TO A FULFILLING AND MEANINGFUL LIFE

ANSWER

	1	2	3	4	5	6	7	8	9	10	11	12	13	14	15	16	17	18	19	20
1	F	T	F	M	H	U	C	I	U	Q	E	F	L	G	P	K	V	M	U	O
2	T	X	L	E	Z	X	W	G	D	L	H	R	B	F	T	D	E	L	Z	A
3	L	F	U	D	W	X	S	C	Z	P	C	C	U	E	Y	D	J	V	J	K
4	A	D	C	U	X	K	E	H	E	N	D	I	S	T	D	K	G	H	L	O
5	N	E	R	T	V	S	U	W	S	L	J	D	G	X	R	G	W	R	Z	M
6	P	X	O	I	N	D	N	H	U	R	N	E	D	O	F	U	P	Z	N	K
7	E	N	L	T	W	M	K	M	W	I	X	G	N	D	B	I	N	O	G	K
8	R	K	R	T	Y	U	D	F	M	G	M	T	N	M	U	Z	I	A	L	L
9	S	L	Q	A	A	C	X	X	R	C	K	Y	P	R	Y	T	E	P	Y	M
10	P	S	R	E	F	R	A	N	I	N	G	F	T	O	A	H	W	X	F	W
11	E	D	P	O	S	I	T	I	V	E	T	H	I	N	K	I	N	G	O	G
12	C	U	F	E	C	Y	M	S	X	A	F	U	I	F	I	X	M	V	F	M
13	T	V	I	O	X	D	G	A	S	Z	J	G	Z	T	R	H	S	P	M	M
14	I	G	H	I	G	C	E	G	J	F	A	I	J	V	T	C	T	B	X	R
15	V	M	U	D	Y	C	K	D	A	M	P	E	R	C	E	P	T	I	O	N
16	E	V	Z	N	G	N	I	Z	I	H	P	O	T	S	A	T	A	C	Z	N
17	O	D	F	E	Y	G	Q	P	M	K	E	Y	C	I	W	N	E	G	V	B
18	W	E	U	G	L	U	V	Z	T	B	Z	T	R	C	U	B	E	F	D	K
19	V	Y	G	J	B	N	E	X	A	F	X	M	Y	C	S	Y	N	T	J	E
20	Q	C	P	E	G	Z	Y	L	F	I	D	A	T	R	Z	R	U	Z	P	T

ATTITUDE 9:4   MINDSE 8:9T   PERSPECTIVE 6:1
CATASTOPHIZING   NURTURE 7:17   POSITIVE
16:18   THINKING 11:3
IMAGINATION   PERCEPTION   REFRANING 10:3
16:9   15:11

CHAPTER 2
EMOTIONAL INTELLIGENCE

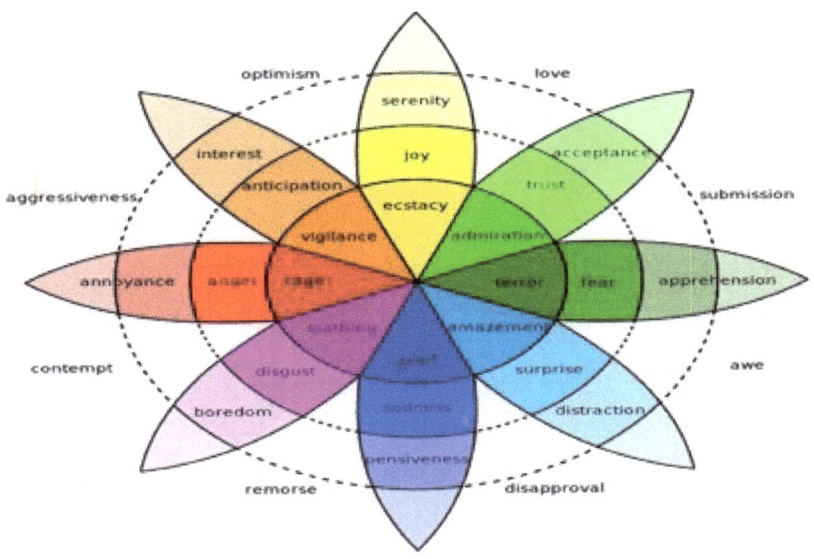

Can you understand and manage your own emotions?

The Bible Says

Be careful for nothing; but in every thing by prayer and supplication with thanksgiving let your requests be made known unto God. And the peace of God, which passeth all understanding, shall keep your hearts and minds through Christ Jesus. — **(Philippians 4:6-7)**

And be ye kind one to another, tenderhearted, forgiving one another, even as God for Christ's sake hath forgiven you. — **(Ephesians 4:32)**

But the fruit of the Spirit is love, joy, peace, longsuffering, gentleness, goodness, faith, Meekness, temperance: against such there is no law. — **(Galatians 5:22-23)**

Wherefore, my beloved brethren, let every man be swift to hear, slow to speak, slow to wrath: For the wrath of man worketh not the righteousness of God. — **(James 1:19-20)**

Put on therefore, as the elect of God, holy and beloved, bowels of mercies, kindness, humbleness of mind, meekness, longsuffering; — **(Colossians 3:12)**

With all lowliness and meekness, with longsuffering, forbearing one another in love; — **(Ephesians 4:2)**

Let nothing be done through strife or vainglory; but in lowliness of mind let each esteem other better than themselves. Look not every man on his own things, but every man also on the things of others. — **(Philippians 2:3-4)**

A soft answer turneth away wrath: but grievous words stir up anger. — **(Proverbs 15:1)**

Be ye angry, and sin not: let not the sun go down upon your wrath: — **(Ephesians 4:26)**

But he giveth more grace. Wherefore he saith, God resisteth the proud, but giveth grace unto the humble. — **(James 4:6)**

A fool uttereth all his mind: but a wise man keepeth it in till afterwards. — **(Proverbs 29:11)**

But the wisdom that is from above is first pure, then peaceable, gentle, and easy to be intreated, full of mercy and good fruits, without partiality, and without hypocrisy. **— (James 3:17)**

Let all bitterness, and wrath, and anger, and clamour, and evil speaking, be put away from you, with all malice: **— (Ephesians 4:31)**

He that hath no rule over his own spirit is like a city that is broken down, and without walls. **— (Proverbs 25:28)**

He that is slow to anger is better than the mighty; and he that ruleth his spirit than he that taketh a city. **— (Proverbs 16:32)**

Make no friendship with an angry man; and with a furious man thou shalt not go: **— (Proverbs 22:24)**

Introduction

In today's fast-paced world, success is often measured by tangible achievements—degrees earned, promotions secured, and wealth accumulated. While these accomplishments are important, they tell only part of the story. Beneath the surface of outward success lies a skill that is just as critical but often overlooked: emotional intelligence. Unlike traditional forms of intelligence, which are measured by IQ tests or academic performance, emotional intelligence is the ability to understand and manage your own emotions, as well as recognize and influence the emotions of others.

Emotional intelligence, often referred to as EQ, is foundational to building strong relationships, making sound decisions, and navigating the complexities of both personal and professional life. In fact, research consistently shows that individuals with high emotional intelligence tend to be more successful, not just in their careers but in all areas of life. This is because they can regulate their emotions under stress, empathize with others, and communicate effectively—all of which are essential for thriving in an interconnected world.

In this chapter, we will explore the key components of emotional intelligence and why it is so essential for personal and professional development. We will delve into practical ways to enhance your EQ, from becoming more self-aware to improving your emotional regulation and empathy. As you read on, you will come to see that emotional intelligence is not just a skill to be learned but a way of being that can transform how you approach life's challenges, relationships, and opportunities.

Understanding and cultivating emotional intelligence is a lifelong journey, one that holds the potential to unlock deeper fulfillment and success in all that you do. Let's begin by exploring the core elements of EQ and how they influence your daily life.

Life Story

Peter was known for his quick temper. As a successful manager, he was brilliant at solving problems, but he struggled to connect with his team. His harsh criticism and emotional outbursts left his employees feeling undervalued and afraid to approach him. Though his intentions were good, Peter's lack of emotional control began to take a toll on the team's morale, and eventually, productivity suffered.

One day, after a particularly heated meeting, a colleague pulled him aside and gently said, "Peter, you're a great leader, but your emotions are standing in the way of your success." Initially defensive, Peter took a step back and reflected on his actions. It was a turning point for him.

Determined to improve, he began reading about emotional intelligence and learned that being in tune with one's emotions—and the emotions of others—was just as important as intellectual ability. He started practicing self-awareness, paying attention to his feelings before they overwhelmed him. Instead of reacting in anger, he paused, considered his response, and learned to listen more carefully to his team. Over time, he became more empathetic, better at managing conflicts, and more open to feedback.

A year later, Peter's office had transformed. His team was thriving, and the atmosphere was collaborative and positive. His new approach to leadership—rooted in emotional intelligence—had not only improved his relationships but also his effectiveness as a manager.

Peter's journey shows that emotional intelligence is crucial for personal and professional growth. It's not just about being smart; it's about being emotionally aware, managing your emotions, and understanding how they impact those around you. In the end, emotional intelligence can be the key to lasting success and deeper connections with others.

Sayings about Emotional Intelligence

Here are some views about emotional intelligence to give you an idea of how others view this concept. They may help you to understand emotions in yourself and others, thus helping you to better manage your relationships and increase your overall happiness in life and at work.

When our emotional health is in a bad state, so is our level of self-esteem. We have to slow down and deal with what is troubling us, so that we can enjoy the simple joy of being happy and at peace with ourselves. **--Jess C. Scott**

Every time we allow someone to move us with anger, we teach them to be angry. **-- Barry Neil Kaufman**

Our feelings are not there to be cast out or conquered. They're there to be engaged and expressed with imagination and intelligence. **-- T.K. Coleman**

It isn't stress that makes us fall--it's how we respond to stressful events. **-- Wayde Goodall**

Use pain as a stepping stone, not a camp ground. **-- Alan Cohen**

We are dangerous when we are not conscious of our responsibility for how we behave, think, and feel. **-- Marshall B. Rosenberg**

We cannot tell what may happen to us in the strange medley of life. But we can decide what happens in us-- how we can take it, what we do with it--and that is what really counts in the end. **-- Joseph Fort Newton**

When awareness is brought to an emotion, power is brought to your life. **-- Tara Meyer Robson**

"It is very important to understand that emotional intelligence is not the opposite of intelligence, it is not the triumph of heart over head - it is the unique intersection of both." **- David Caruso**

Where we have strong emotions, we're liable to fool ourselves. **-- Carl Sagan**

The secret of contentment is knowing how to enjoy what you have, and to be able to lose all desire for things beyond your reach. -- **Lin Yutang**

Man's main task in life is to give birth to himself, to become what he potentially is. The most important product of his effort is his own personality. -- **Erich Fromm**

Experience is not what happens to you -- it's how you interpret what happens to you. -- **Aldous Huxley**

Experiencing one's self in a conscious manner--that is, gaining self-knowledge--is an integral part of learning. -- **Joshua M. Freedman**

Feelings are not supposed to be logical. Dangerous is the man who has rationalized his emotions. -- **David Borenstein**

For news of the heart, ask the face. -- West African saying

He who spends time regretting the past loses the present and risks the future. -- **Quevedo**

Holding on to anger is like grasping a hot coal with the intent of throwing it at someone else: you are the one who gets burned. -- **Buddha**

Realize that now, in this moment of time, you are creating. You are creating your next moment based on what you are feeling and thinking. That is what's real. -- **Doc Childre**

Revenge has no more quenching effect on emotions than salt water has on thirst. -- **Walter Weckler**

The essential difference between emotion and reason is that emotion leads to action while reason leads to conclusions. -- **Donald Calne**

There is only one corner of the universe you can be certain of improving... and that's your own self. -- **Aldous Huxley**

You can conquer almost any fear if you will only make up your mind to do so. For remember, fear doesn't exist anywhere except in the mind. -- **Dale Carnegie**

The secret of genius is to carry the spirit of the child into old age, which means never losing your enthusiasm. -- **Alous Huxley**

When you listen with empathy to another person, you give that person psychological air. -- **Stephen R. Covey**

Be not disturbed at being misunderstood; be disturbed rather at not being understanding. -- **Chinese proverb**

Change happens in the boiler room of our emotions -- so find out how to light their fires. -- **Jeff Dewar**

Forgiveness does not change the past, but it does enlarge the future. -- **Paul Boese**

Fall seven times, stand up eight. -- **Australian Aboriginal proverb**

"When awareness is brought to an emotion, power is brought to your life." - **Tara Meyer Robson**

The most important educational goal is learning to learn. -- **Aristotle**

Questions are the creative acts of intelligence. -- **Plato**

The greatest discovery of my generation is that human beings can alter their lives by altering their attitudes of mind. -- **William James**

Source: 33 Quotes on Emotional Intelligence to Boost Your Overall Happiness | Inc.com

Understanding Emotional Intelligence

The Importance of Emotional Awareness

Emotional intelligence (EI) is the ability to recognize, understand, and manage our own emotions, as well as recognize, understand, and influence the emotions of others. The foundation of EI lies in emotional awareness, which requires us to be attuned to our feelings, understand the impact they have on our thoughts and behaviours, and recognize how these emotions can influence our decision-making. Emotional awareness helps us navigate complex social environments and enhances our ability to interact effectively with others.

Components of Emotional Intelligence

EI comprises several key components:

Self-awareness: The ability to recognize and understand one's own emotions.

Self-regulation: The capacity to manage emotions in a healthy and productive manner.

Motivation: The inner drive to pursue goals with energy and persistence, even in the face of challenges.

Empathy: The ability to understand and share the feelings of others.

Social skills: The ability to manage relationships and build networks effectively.

These components work together to form the basis of emotional intelligence, enabling individuals to lead more successful and fulfilling lives.

Recognizing and Managing Your Emotions

The Role of Self-Awareness

Self-awareness is the cornerstone of emotional intelligence. It involves being conscious of our emotional states, understanding the triggers that influence our emotions, and recognizing how these emotions affect our behaviour and interactions with others. By developing self-awareness, we can gain greater control over our emotional responses and make more informed decisions in various aspects of life.

Strategies for Managing Emotions

Managing emotions effectively requires a combination of self-awareness and self-regulation. Some strategies include:

Mindfulness practices: Techniques such as meditation and deep breathing can help individuals stay present and reduce emotional reactivity.

Cognitive restructuring: This involves challenging and changing negative thought patterns that contribute to emotional distress.

Healthy coping mechanisms: Engaging in activities like exercise, journaling, or talking to a trusted friend can provide a healthy outlet for emotions.

By implementing these strategies, individuals can enhance their emotional regulation skills, leading to improved mental and emotional well-being.

Building Empathy and Understanding Others

The Importance of Empathy

Empathy is a crucial aspect of emotional intelligence. It involves the ability to understand and share the emotions of others, allowing for deeper connections and more effective communication. Empathy enables us to see situations from others' perspectives, fostering compassion and understanding in our interactions.

Techniques for Developing Empathy

To build empathy, individuals can:

Practice active listening: Fully engage with others during conversations, showing genuine interest and withholding judgment.

Seek diverse perspectives: Make an effort to understand different viewpoints and experiences, especially those that differ from yours.

Reflect on your own emotions: By understanding your emotional experiences, you can better relate to the emotions of others.

Developing empathy requires intentional effort, but it is essential for building meaningful relationships and navigating social interactions effectively.

Empathy in Action

Empathy can be applied in various contexts, from personal relationships to professional environments. In the workplace, for example, empathetic leaders are more likely to build trust, improve team dynamics, and foster a positive organizational culture. In personal relationships, empathy strengthens connections and enhances communication, leading to more fulfilling interactions.

Cultivating Emotional Resilience

Understanding Emotional Resilience

Emotional resilience refers to the ability to adapt to and recover from stress, adversity, and challenges. It is a vital component of emotional intelligence, as it determines how well we can cope with difficulties and maintain emotional stability. Resilient individuals are not immune to negative emotions, but they possess the skills and mindset to bounce back from setbacks.

Building Emotional Resilience

To cultivate emotional resilience, individuals can:

Develop a positive mindset: Focus on solutions and opportunities rather than dwelling on problems and obstacles.

Strengthen social connections: Build a support network of friends, family, and colleagues who can provide emotional support during difficult times.

Practice self-care: Engage in activities that promote physical, mental, and emotional well-being, such as regular exercise, healthy eating, and adequate sleep.

These practices help build the mental and emotional fortitude needed to cope effectively with life's challenges.

The Role of Adaptability in Resilience

Adaptability is a key factor in emotional resilience. It involves being flexible and open to change, recognizing that challenges are an inevitable part of life, and being willing to adjust your thoughts, behaviors, and strategies in response to new circumstances. Cultivating adaptability allows individuals to handle change with less stress and greater confidence, ultimately enhancing their ability to recover from setbacks and thrive in the face of adversity.

Applying Emotional Intelligence to Everyday Life

Improving Personal Relationships

Emotional intelligence plays a critical role in the quality of our personal relationships. By recognizing and managing our emotions, and by empathizing with others, we can create deeper, more meaningful connections with those around us. This leads to more satisfying and fulfilling relationships, both personally and professionally.

Enhancing Professional Success

In the workplace, emotional intelligence is often a key differentiator between good and great leaders. Those who are emotionally intelligent are better able to manage teams, navigate complex social dynamics, and make informed decisions that consider the emotional well-being of their employees. This not only improves workplace morale but also leads to better overall performance.

Living a Balanced and Fulfilled Life

Ultimately, emotional intelligence contributes to a balanced and fulfilled life. By mastering the skills of emotional awareness, empathy, resilience, and adaptability, individuals can manage the complexities of life with greater ease, leading to more success, happiness, and a sense of purpose.

Conclusion

Emotional intelligence is a powerful tool that influences every aspect of our lives. By understanding and managing our own emotions, building empathy and understanding others, and cultivating emotional resilience, we can enhance our personal and professional lives. The development of these skills is an ongoing process, but with dedication and practice, the benefits are profound and long-lasting.

Exercise

Strengthening Your Emotional Intelligence

Take time to engage in the following exercise. This will help you practice self-awareness, empathy, and emotional regulation, key components of emotional intelligence that can improve your relationships and decision-making.

Step 1: Self-Awareness Check

1. **Set aside 10-15 minutes** in a quiet, reflective space.
2. Think about a recent situation where you experienced a strong emotion, whether positive or negative.

   What emotion did you feel?
   How did you react to it?

3. Write down your thoughts, focusing on the following:

   What triggered the emotion?
   Did you understand why you felt that way at the time?
   Looking back, do you think your reaction was appropriate?

4. Reflect on how this experience may have affected your actions or decisions. Recognizing these patterns helps build emotional self-awareness.

Step 2: Practicing Empathy

1. Think about a recent interaction you had where someone shared his/her feelings or perspective with you.

How did you respond to them?
Did you take time to fully understand their emotions?

2. In your journal, write down how you think the other person might have felt during the conversation. Ask yourself:
    - **Did I listen actively and without judgment?**
    - **Did I show empathy, or was I more focused on my own perspective?**

3. Reflect on how you could improve your empathetic response in future interactions, practicing truly "walking in someone else's shoes."

Step 3: Emotional Regulation in Practice

1. Identify an emotion that tends to get the better of you—whether it's anger, frustration, anxiety, or stress.

2. Think about the last time you experienced this emotion. How did it affect your behavior and interactions with others?

3. Now, develop a **coping strategy** that you can use the next time you feel this emotion:

    Breathing exercises (slow, deep breaths to calm down)
    Taking a brief pause before responding in difficult situations
    Positive self-talk to remind yourself of the bigger picture

4. Write down your action plan for how you will regulate this emotion the next time it arises. Keep this plan in a place where you can easily review it during stressful moments.

Step 4: Building Emotional Awareness in Relationships

1. Pick a relationship (personal or professional) where you feel emotional intelligence could improve.

2. Ask yourself the following questions:

   How well do I understand this person's emotions and needs?

   Am I effectively communicating my own emotions in this relationship?

   What can I do to foster a deeper emotional connection with this person?

3. Write down one or two specific actions you can take to enhance emotional intelligence in this relationship, whether it's by practicing active listening, being more patient, or expressing your own feelings more clearly.

Step 5: Emotional Intelligence in Decision-Making

1. Think of a recent decision you made that involved emotions, either yours or someone else's.

2. Reflect on how emotions influenced your decision:

   Were they helpful or did they cloud your judgment?

   Could a greater awareness of your emotions have led to a different decision?

3. Write down one lesson you've learned about how emotions can impact decision-making, and how emotional intelligence can help you make more balanced, informed choices in the future.

Step 6: Daily Emotional Intelligence Practice

Commit to practicing emotional intelligence daily by:

- **Checking in with your emotions regularly**
- **Pausing to reflect before reacting in emotionally charged situations**
- **Listening to others with empathy and openness**

By strengthening these habits, you will become more emotionally aware and able to navigate relationships and life's challenges with greater wisdom and clarity.

CHAPTER 2
WORDSEARCH

	1	2	3	4	5	6	7	8	9	10	11	12	13	14	15	16	17	18	19	20	21	22	23	24	25
1	F	H	W	X	T	W	P	Q	A	A	Q	U	W	P	K	E	L	K	O	H	N	S	Z	E	G
2	X	G	T	E	A	R	O	U	G	Q	P	V	V	R	T	X	I	C	E	R	P	C	I	Q	Y
3	W	J	L	U	M	Q	H	C	H	G	O	K	T	V	U	D	J	X	Z	I	V	H	X	J	R
4	C	S	T	F	Y	O	U	Q	K	S	E	H	A	I	S	A	B	C	H	L	O	Y	B	K	M
5	G	H	V	G	W	N	T	Q	J	H	T	D	C	X	R	B	T	S	H	B	N	F	M	K	D
6	F	I	Y	K	S	G	R	I	Z	G	V	K	D	P	G	T	N	M	M	N	Y	P	O	A	U
7	J	S	V	X	Y	I	J	R	O	R	H	F	C	M	Z	O	N	G	Z	H	K	U	S	N	X
8	O	V	R	G	T	C	V	O	F	N	J	P	J	H	I	F	C	F	W	P	I	S	E	V	W
9	P	N	H	J	N	Z	L	O	O	U	A	Z	H	T	M	A	V	D	K	V	B	D	L	K	W
10	B	L	Z	F	R	I	I	L	A	K	R	L	A	Z	D	E	O	H	W	N	R	R	F	V	K
11	H	E	A	C	I	R	L	H	C	E	I	L	I	A	M	B	M	Q	H	Y	V	E	C	E	B
12	X	N	T	A	R	J	G	A	S	V	E	A	P	N	Z	V	K	P	D	U	B	H	A	S	J
13	B	H	J	H	S	V	Y	I	N	R	C	T	D	J	T	G	H	L	A	Y	B	Z	R	J	P
14	J	G	Y	Q	U	W	L	N	E	R	A	F	B	N	U	E	P	T	O	T	K	J	E	X	V
15	S	B	M	I	V	I	U	Q	L	B	U	L	U	G	U	M	L	J	R	L	H	Q	Q	M	T
16	N	G	X	Y	E	W	L	U	I	O	B	O	R	Q	G	S	S	L	P	C	K	Y	P	S	R
17	I	R	U	N	S	R	R	L	I	C	S	X	J	E	P	T	U	E	I	R	H	K	N	M	E
18	P	Z	C	A	U	C	I	T	E	U	I	D	S	U	U	P	U	D	B	G	C	R	Z	Q	I
19	Y	E	D	X	H	T	W	B	I	Y	P	X	U	T	M	H	L	K	V	Z	E	G	Q	R	M
20	Y	J	I	S	Y	X	P	T	J	E	Y	U	X	D	N	R	N	N	S	M	J	N	R	U	C
21	H	M	C	D	F	R	Z	T	I	T	Q	J	M	O	T	I	V	A	T	I	O	N	C	K	M
22	I	D	P	I	X	L	B	L	S	L	I	H	X	V	J	K	G	L	A	E	P	O	C	E	L
23	R	E	F	L	E	C	T	I	O	N	L	J	F	F	J	C	V	F	M	P	I	Q	Z	L	X
24	H	N	K	C	N	I	E	N	S	P	R	N	P	L	R	Z	U	L	D	B	L	S	K	Y	M
25	W	V	K	Z	Y	C	H	G	J	F	V	Q	R	J	N	G	K	D	V	D	R	D	R	N	I

ADAPTABILITY JOURNALING RELATIONSHIPS
EMOTIONAL MOTIVATION RESILIENCE
INTELLIGENCE
EMPATHY REFLECTION SELF CARE

THE JOURNEY TO A FULFILLING AND MEANINGFUL LIFE

ANSWER

	1	2	3	4	5	6	7	8	9	10	11	12	13	14	15	16	17	18	19	20	21	22	23	24	25
1	F	H	W	X	T	W	P	Q	A	A	Q	U	W	P	K	E	L	K	O	H	N	S	Z	E	G
2	X	G	T	E	A	R	O	U	G	Q	P	V	V	R	T	X	I	C	E	R	P	C	I	Q	Y
3	W	J	L	U	M	Q	H	C	H	G	O	K	T	V	U	D	J	X	Z	I	V	H	X	J	R
4	C	S	T	F	Y	O	U	Q	K	S	E	H	A	I	S	A	B	C	H	L	O	Y	B	K	M
5	G	H	V	G	W	N	T	Q	J	H	T	D	C	X	R	B	T	S	H	B	N	F	M	K	D
6	F	I	Y	K	S	G	R	I	Z	G	V	K	D	P	G	T	N	M	M	N	Y	P	O	A	U
7	J	S	V	X	Y	I	J	R	O	R	H	F	C	M	Z	O	N	G	Z	H	K	U	S	N	X
8	O	V	R	G	T	C	V	O	F	N	J	P	J	H	I	F	C	F	W	P	I	S	E	V	W
9	P	N	H	J	N	Z	L	O	O	U	A	Z	H	T	M	A	V	D	K	V	B	D	L	K	W
10	B	L	Z	F	R	I	I	L	A	K	R	L	A	Z	D	E	O	H	W	N	R	R	F	V	K
11	H	E	A	C	I	R	L	H	C	E	I	L	I	A	M	B	M	Q	H	Y	V	E	C	E	B
12	X	N	T	A	R	J	G	A	S	V	E	A	P	N	Z	V	K	P	D	U	B	H	A	S	J
13	B	H	J	H	S	V	Y	I	N	R	C	T	D	J	T	G	H	L	A	Y	B	Z	R	J	P
14	J	G	Y	Q	U	W	L	N	E	R	A	F	B	N	U	E	P	T	O	T	K	J	E	X	V
15	S	B	M	I	V	I	U	Q	L	B	U	L	U	G	U	M	L	J	R	L	H	Q	Q	M	T
16	N	G	X	Y	E	W	L	U	I	O	B	O	R	Q	G	S	S	L	P	C	K	Y	P	S	R
17	I	R	U	N	S	R	R	L	I	C	S	X	J	E	P	T	U	E	I	R	H	K	N	M	E
18	P	Z	C	A	U	C	I	T	E	U	I	D	S	U	U	P	U	D	B	G	C	R	Z	Q	I
19	Y	E	D	X	H	T	W	B	I	Y	P	X	U	T	M	H	L	K	V	Z	E	G	Q	R	M
20	Y	J	I	S	Y	X	P	T	J	E	Y	U	X	D	N	R	N	N	S	M	J	N	R	U	C
21	H	M	C	D	F	R	Z	T	I	T	Q	J	M	O	T	I	V	A	T	I	O	N	C	K	M
22	I	D	P	I	X	L	B	L	S	L	I	H	X	V	J	K	G	L	A	E	P	O	C	E	L
23	R	E	F	L	E	C	T	I	O	N	L	J	F	F	J	C	V	F	M	P	I	Q	Z	L	X
24	H	N	K	C	N	I	E	N	S	P	R	N	P	L	R	Z	U	L	D	B	L	S	K	Y	M
25	W	V	K	Z	Y	C	H	G	J	F	V	Q	R	J	N	G	K	D	V	D	R	D	R	N	I

ADAPTABILITY 9:16

EMOTIONAL INTELLIGENCE 2:4

EMPATHY 10:16

JOURNALING 17:13

MOTIVATION 21:13

REFLECTION 23:1

RELATIONSHIPS 13:10

RESILIENCE 10:11

SELF CARE 7:23

CHAPTER 3
MINDFULNESS AND PRESENCE

The practice of fully engaging with the here and now is one of the keys to a meaningful life.

The Bible Says

What is man, that thou art mindful of him? And the son of man, that thou visitest him? — **Psalm 8:4 (KJV)**

Finally, brothers and sisters, whatever is true, whatever is noble, whatever is right, whatever is pure, whatever is lovely, whatever is admirable—if anything is excellent or praiseworthy—think about such things. — **Philippians 4:8 (NIV)**

Fix these words of mine in your hearts and minds; tie them as symbols on your hands and bind them on your foreheads. — **Deuteronomy 11:18 (NIV)**

You shall love the Lord your God with all your heart, with all your soul, and with all your mind. — **Matthew 22:37 (ESV)**

To set the mind on the flesh is death, but to set the mind on the Spirit is life and peace. — **Romans 8:6 (ESV)**

Be thankful, singing to God with gratitude in your hearts. And whatever you do, whether in word or deed, do it all in the name of the Lord Christ Jesus, giving thanks to God the Father through him. — **Colossians 3:15–17 (NIV)**

Do not be anxious about anything, but in every situation, by prayer and petition, present your requests to God with thanksgiving. — **Philippians 4:6 (NIV)**

That the Lord may establish his word that he spoke concerning me, saying, "If your sons pay close attention to their way, to walk before me in faithfulness with all their heart and with all their soul, you shall not lack a man on the throne of Israel." — **1 Kings 2:4 (ESV)**

My son, pay attention to what I say; turn your ear to my words. Do not let them out of your sight. Keep them in your heart, for they are life to those who find them and health to one's whole body. — **Proverbs 4:20–22 (NIV)**

Be careful, then, how you live—not as the unwise but as the wise, making the most of every opportunity because the days are evil. Therefore, do not be foolish, but understand what the Lord's will is. — **Ephesians 5:15–17 (NIV)**

Pray diligently. Stay alert, with your eyes wide open in gratitude. — **Colossians 4:2 (MSG)**

You will keep in perfect peace all who trust in you and all whose thoughts are fixed on you. — **Isaiah 26:3 (NLT)**

Keep this Book of the Law always on your lips; meditate on it day and night so that you may be careful to do everything written in it. — **Joshua 1:8 (NIV)**

I will remember the deeds of the LORD; yes, I will remember your miracles of long ago. I will consider all your works and ponder all your mighty deeds. — **Psalm 77:11-12 (NIV)**

I will meditate on your precepts and fix my eyes on your ways. I will delight in your statutes, and I will not forget your word. — **Psalm 119:15-16 (ESV)**

Introduction

In a world filled with constant distractions and the pressures of daily life, the ability to remain present in the moment has become increasingly elusive. Our minds are often preoccupied with past regrets or future anxieties, leaving little room for the richness of the present. However, there is immense power in cultivating mindfulness—the practice of fully engaging with the here and now.

Mindfulness is more than just a trend; it is a way of living that brings clarity, calm, and a deeper sense of connection to the world around us. When we practice mindfulness, we learn to observe our thoughts and emotions without judgment, allowing us to respond to life's challenges with greater awareness and intentionality. This practice of being present enhances not only our mental and emotional well-being but also the quality of our relationships, work, and personal growth.

In this chapter, we will explore the foundational principles of mindfulness and its transformative impact on our lives. We will examine the benefits of being fully present, the challenges that come with distractions, and practical ways to incorporate mindfulness into your daily routine. By embracing the present moment, you will discover a greater sense of peace, balance, and fulfillment.

Whether you are new to mindfulness or looking to deepen your practice, this chapter will guide you through the essential steps to becoming more aware, grounded, and present in every aspect of your life. Let's begin the journey toward a more mindful and enriched existence.

Life Story

Hilda had always prided herself on her ability to juggle multiple tasks at once. As a mother of two with a demanding job, she was constantly on the go. Her days were filled with meetings, errands, and endless to-do lists. Yet, despite her efforts, she often felt disconnected—both from her work and her family. She'd find herself at the dinner table, physically present but mentally miles away, worrying about tomorrow's deadlines or the emails she needed to respond to.

One evening, as Hilda's young daughter shared an exciting story from school, she realized she hadn't heard a word. Her daughter's face fell when she noticed Hilda was lost in her phone again. The guilt hit her hard. That night, Hilda decided something had to change. She couldn't continue living life on autopilot.

The next day, Hilda began practicing mindfulness. At first, it was difficult. She set small goals—five minutes of meditation in the morning, focusing on her breathing during stressful moments, and most importantly, being fully present with her family. Gradually, Hilda noticed a shift. She started to savor the little moments: the warmth of her morning coffee, the laughter of her children, and the sound of birds outside her window. Her mind no longer raced ahead to the future, and she found joy in the present moment.

Months later, Hilda was calmer, more focused, and deeply connected to the people and things she valued most. Her relationships improved, her stress levels decreased, and she found greater satisfaction in both her work and personal life.

Hilda's story illustrates the transformative power of mindfulness and presence. By learning to be fully engaged in the here and now, we can break free from the constant noise of life, find peace in the present, and reconnect with what truly matters.

Sayings about Mindfulness and Presence

The following quotes about mindfulness and presence will help to deepen your understanding of these principles and enlighten your path to a meaningful life.

"Mindfulness is about being fully awake in our lives. It is about perceiving the exquisite vividness of each moment. We also gain immediate access to our own powerful inner resources for insight, transformation, and healing." – **Jon Kabat-Zinn**

"You practice mindfulness, on the one hand, to be calm and peaceful. On the other hand, as you practice mindfulness and live a life of peace, you inspire hope for a future of peace." – **Thich Nhat Hanh**

"Mindfulness can help people of any age. That's because we become what we think." – **Goldie Hawn**

"Mindfulness has helped me succeed in almost every dimension of my life. By stopping regularly to look inward and become aware of my mental state, I stay connected to the source of my actions and thoughts and can guide them with considerably more intention." – **Dustin Moskovitz**

"All work done mindfully rounds us out, helps complete us as persons." – **Marsha Sinetar**

"It takes a little bit of mindfulness and a little bit of attention to others to be a good listener, which helps cultivate emotional nurturing and engagement." – **Deepak Chopra**

"Yoga is about compassion and generosity towards others. It means being mindful of the world around us." – **Christy Turlington**

"The key to creating the mental space before responding is mindfulness. Mindfulness is a way of being present: paying attention to and accepting what is happening in our lives. It helps us to be aware of and step away from our automatic and habitual reactions to our everyday experiences." – **Elizabeth Thornton**

"I find mindfulness helps me participate in my religion more wholeheartedly. ... Whatever your religion is, it can enhance the experience of participating in that religion." – **Tim Ryan**

"Mindfulness is a quality that's always there. It's an illusion that there's a meditation and post-meditation

period, which I always find amusing, because you're either mindful or you're not." – **Richard Gere**

"To see a world in a grain of sand and heaven in a wild flower, hold infinity in the palm of your hand and eternity in an hour." – **William Blake**

"A mind is like a parachute. It doesn't work if it isn't open." – **Frank Zappa**

"Mindfulness is the aware, balanced acceptance of the present experience. It isn't more complicated than that. It is opening to or receiving the present moment, pleasant or unpleasant, just as it is, without either clinging to it or rejecting it." – **Sylvia Boorstein**

"Life is a dance. Mindfulness is witnessing that dance." – **Amit Ray**

"Mindfulness is simply being aware of what is happening right now without wishing it were different; enjoying the pleasant without holding on when it changes (which it will); being with the unpleasant without fearing it will always be this way (which it won't)." – **James Baraz**

"Mindfulness isn't difficult, we just need to remember to do it." – **Sharon Salzberg**

"Always hold fast to the present. Every situation, indeed every moment, is of infinite value, for it is the representative of a whole eternity." – **Johann Wolfgang von Goethe**

"The practice of mindfulness begins in the small, remote cave of your unconscious mind and blossoms with the sunlight of your conscious life, reaching far beyond the people and places you can see." – **Earon Davis**

"The most precious gift we can offer others is our presence. When mindfulness embraces those we love, they will bloom like flowers." – **Thich Nhat Hanh**

"Training your mind to be in the present moment is the #1 key to making healthier choices." – **Susan Albers**

"Mindfulness means paying attention to how things are in any given moment, however they are, rather than as we want them to be." – **Mark Williams**

"Mindful eating is a way to become reacquainted with the guidance of our internal nutritionist." – **Jan Chozen Bays**

"Mindfulness gives you time. Time gives you choices. Choices, skillfully made, lead to freedom. You don't have to be swept away by your feeling. You can respond with wisdom and kindness rather than habit and reactivity." – **Bhante Henepola Gunaratana**

"The great benefit of practicing mindfulness ... is presence of mind within a storm of emotions." – **Phillip Moffitt**

"The goal of mindfulness is to become fully aware of the thoughts one is having, and of the emotions one is experiencing." – **Larry Shapiro**

"You have a treasure within you that is infinitely greater than anything the world can offer." – **Eckhart Tolle**

"Mindfulness meditation should be more than just watching what you are doing. What you really need to watch is your motivation." – **Lama Zopa Rinpoche**

"Every time we become aware of a thought, as opposed to being lost in a thought, we experience that opening of the mind." – **Joseph Goldstein**

"Be mindful of your self-talk. It's a conversation with the universe." – **David James Lees**

"Who looks inside, awakens." – **Carl Jung**

"When we contemplate the whole globe as one great dewdrop, striped and dotted with continents and islands, flying through space with other stars all singing and shining together as one, the whole universe appears as an infinite storm of beauty." – **John Muir**

"There are only two ways to live your life. One is as though nothing is a miracle. The other is as though everything is a miracle." – **Albert Einstein**

"On life's journey, faith is nourishment, virtuous deeds are a shelter, wisdom is the light by day and right mindfulness is the protection by night. If a man lives a pure life, nothing can destroy him." – **Buddha**

"Be happy in the moment; that's enough. Each moment is all we need, not more." – **Mother Teresa**

Source: https://wellbeing.gmu.edu/famous-quotes-on-mindfulness-and-well-being/

Understanding Mindfulness
What is Mindfulness?

Mindfulness is the practice of being fully present in the moment, with an open and non-judgmental awareness of your thoughts, feelings, and surroundings. It involves consciously paying attention to the present rather than dwelling on the past or worrying about the future. By cultivating mindfulness, individuals can develop a deeper connection with themselves and their environment, leading to enhanced well-being and a greater sense of inner peace.

The Origins and Benefits of Mindfulness

Rooted in ancient meditation practices, particularly within Buddhism, mindfulness has gained widespread recognition for its mental, emotional, and physical benefits. Modern scientific research supports mindfulness as a powerful tool for reducing stress, improving concentration, and enhancing emotional regulation. By integrating mindfulness into daily life, individuals can experience greater clarity, improved decision-making, and a heightened sense of fulfillment.

Practicing Mindfulness in Daily Life

Mindful Breathing

One of the simplest and most effective ways to cultivate mindfulness is through mindful breathing. This practice involves focusing on the breath as it enters and leaves the body, helping to anchor the mind in the present moment. Mindful breathing can be practiced anywhere and at any time, making it a versatile tool for reducing stress and promoting relaxation.

Mindful Eating

Mindful eating encourages individuals to slow down and fully engage with the experience of eating. By paying attention to the taste, texture, and aroma of food, as well as the body's hunger and fullness cues, mindful eating fosters a healthier relationship with food and can prevent overeating. This practice also enhances the enjoyment of meals and contributes to overall well-being.

Mindful Movement

Mindful movement practices, such as yoga, tai chi, and walking meditation, combine physical activity with mindfulness. These practices involve paying attention to the sensations and movements of the body, promoting physical and mental harmony. Mindful movement can be a powerful way to connect with the body, reduce stress, and improve overall health.

Incorporating Mindfulness into Routine Activities

Mindfulness can be woven into everyday tasks, such as washing dishes, brushing teeth, or walking. By bringing full attention to these activities, individuals can transform mundane moments into opportunities for mindfulness practice. This approach helps to cultivate a more mindful lifestyle, where presence and awareness are consistently nurtured.

The Power of Presence

Why Presence Matters

Presence refers to the quality of being fully engaged and attentive in the current moment. It is closely linked to mindfulness and is essential for building strong relationships, making informed decisions, and living a meaningful life. When we are present, we are better able to connect with others, appreciate the richness of life's experiences, and respond effectively to challenges.

Overcoming Distractions

In today's fast-paced, technology-driven world, distractions are abundant. The constant barrage of notifications, emails, and social media can pull our attention away from the present moment. Overcoming these distractions requires a conscious effort to prioritize presence. Strategies such as setting boundaries with technology, practicing digital detoxes, and creating designated times for focused work can help individuals reclaim their attention and be more present in their daily lives.

The Role of Presence in Relationships

Presence is a critical component of healthy relationships. When we are fully present with others, we show that we value their thoughts, feelings, and experiences. This fosters deeper connections and strengthens emotional bonds. Whether in personal or professional relationships, practicing presence can lead to more meaningful interactions and improved communication.

Mindfulness and Emotional Regulation

Mindfulness as a Tool for Managing Emotions

Mindfulness can play a significant role in emotional regulation by helping individuals observe their emotions without being overwhelmed by them. Through mindfulness, people learn to recognize and accept their feelings without judgment, creating space between their emotions and their reactions. This practice enhances emotional resilience and enables more thoughtful responses to challenging situations.

Cultivating Emotional Balance

Emotional balance involves maintaining a stable and positive emotional state, even in the face of adversity. Mindfulness supports emotional balance by promoting awareness of the fluctuations in our emotional landscape and encouraging a non-reactive approach to emotions. Techniques such as mindful breathing, body scanning, and loving-kindness meditation can be particularly effective in fostering emotional balance.

Reducing Stress and Anxiety through Mindfulness

Mindfulness has been shown to reduce stress and anxiety by shifting focus away from worry and rumination and toward the present moment. Regular mindfulness practice can lower cortisol levels, the body's primary stress hormone, and improve overall mental health. By cultivating mindfulness, individuals can develop a greater sense of calm and equanimity, even in stressful situations.

Mindfulness and Cognitive Functioning

Enhancing Focus and Concentration

Mindfulness has been proven to improve focus and concentration by training the mind to stay anchored in the present moment. This can lead to enhanced productivity, better decision-making, and a greater ability to complete tasks efficiently. Mindfulness practices such as focused attention meditation and mindful breathing are particularly beneficial for boosting cognitive performance.

Mindfulness and Memory

Mindfulness also positively impacts memory by encouraging individuals to engage fully with their experiences, leading to better encoding and recall of information. Studies have shown that mindfulness can enhance both short-term and long-term memory, making it a valuable tool for students, professionals, and anyone looking to improve his or her cognitive abilities.

Creativity and Mindfulness

Creativity flourishes when the mind is calm, open, and free from distractions. Mindfulness fosters these conditions by quieting the noise of the mind and allowing creative ideas to emerge naturally. Techniques such as open-monitoring meditation, where attention is not focused on a specific object but remains open to whatever arises, can be particularly effective in enhancing creativity.

Conclusion

Mindfulness and presence are powerful tools for enhancing every aspect of life, from emotional well-being to cognitive functioning. By cultivating mindfulness through practices such as mindful breathing, mindful movement, and presence in daily activities, individuals can develop a deeper connection with themselves and their environment. This, in turn, leads to greater clarity, emotional resilience, and a more fulfilling life. The journey toward mindfulness is ongoing, but the rewards are profound and life-changing.

Exercise

Mindfulness and Presence

Do the following exercise to help you integrate mindfulness into your daily life. This will deepen your ability to stay present in the moment, reduce distractions, and enhance your overall sense of calm and awareness.

Step 1: Mindful Breathing

1. Find a quiet space where you won't be interrupted. Sit comfortably with your back straight and your feet grounded on the floor.

2. Close your eyes and focus on your breathing. Breathe in slowly through your nose for a count of four, hold for a count of four, and exhale gently through your mouth for a count of four.

3. Continue this breathing pattern for 3-5 minutes. If your mind starts to wander, gently bring your focus back to your breath.

4. After you've completed this mindful breathing exercise, write down how you felt:

   Did you notice any difference in your state of mind?

   Were you able to stay present, or did your mind wander often?

   How did it feel to focus solely on your breath?

Step 2: Mindful Observation

1. Choose an object in your surroundings—something simple, like a leaf, a cup, or a pen.

2. Spend 2-3 minutes observing this object with your full attention. Notice its shape, color,

texture, and any small details that you might normally overlook.

3. As you observe, let go of any judgments or labels. Simply notice the object as it is.

4. Reflect on this experience in your journal:

   Did it feel natural or challenging to stay focused on the object?

   What did you notice about the object that you hadn't observed before?

   How did this practice affect your overall sense of presence?

Step 3: Practicing Mindfulness in Everyday Activities

1. Choose a simple daily activity, such as eating, brushing your teeth, or walking, and make a conscious effort to do it mindfully. For this exercise, focus on **eating mindfully:**

   When eating your next meal, turn off all distractions (TV, phone, etc.) and focus solely on the experience of eating.

   Pay attention to the taste, texture, and aroma of the food.

   Notice the movements of your hands and mouth as you eat. Take your time and savor each bite.

2. After the meal, reflect in your journal:

   How did it feel to eat mindfully compared to your usual way of eating?

   Did you notice anything new about the food or the experience?

Were you able to stay present throughout the meal?

Step 4: Mindfulness in Conversations

1. During your next conversation, whether in person or over the phone, practice **mindful listening:**

   Focus entirely on what the other person is saying, without thinking about how you'll respond or getting distracted by your own thoughts.

   Notice the speaker's tone, words, and emotions, and try to fully understand their perspective.

   Avoid interrupting or finishing their sentences.

2. After the conversation, reflect on the following questions:

   Did you notice any differences in how you experienced the conversation?

   How did the other person respond to your mindful presence?

   Were you able to stay focused and attentive, or did you find your mind wandering?

Step 5: Creating a Daily Mindfulness Practice

1. Dedicate a few minutes each day to practice mindfulness. It could be through mindful breathing, observing your surroundings, or simply being fully present in your daily activities.

2. In your journal, set a goal for how you will integrate mindfulness into your routine:

   Will you start with 5 minutes of mindful breathing each morning?

Can you practice mindful eating during one meal per day?

How will you remind yourself to stay present during conversations or activities?

3. At the end of each day, briefly write down how these practices made you feel. Over time, this daily practice will help you cultivate a greater sense of presence, calm, and clarity in your life.

Step 6: Reflection on Presence

1. At the end of the week, look back at your journal entries and reflect on your mindfulness journey:

   What changes have you noticed in your ability to stay present?

   Has practicing mindfulness affected your emotional well-being, stress levels, or interactions with others?

   What challenges have you faced, and how can you overcome them to deepen your practice?

By consistently practicing mindfulness, you will enhance your awareness and presence, leading to a more fulfilling and peaceful life.

CHAPTER 3
WORDSEARCH

	1	2	3	4	5	6	7	8	9	10	11	12	13	14	15
1	E	J	D	D	W	M	Q	E	S	K	U	C	J	L	S
2	C	D	X	V	Y	T	I	V	I	T	A	E	R	C	T
3	N	H	I	J	H	V	V	X	M	G	P	X	N	H	R
4	A	T	T	S	S	U	C	O	F	H	M	E	F	P	E
5	L	F	S	E	T	Y	D	F	C	I	I	P	M	O	S
6	A	Y	F	O	C	R	B	B	N	Q	B	E	I	B	S
7	B	R	T	V	O	K	A	D	H	B	D	E	D	L	S
8	M	O	E	J	P	M	F	C	O	I	C	Q	Q	Y	Z
9	F	M	S	K	L	U	Q	U	T	N	J	E	Z	P	Q
10	B	E	I	I	L	K	S	A	E	I	I	Z	N	M	I
11	A	M	Y	N	Z	F	T	S	R	W	O	R	A	J	O
12	Q	Z	E	Z	P	I	E	J	N	Z	F	N	G	H	A
13	O	S	N	L	O	R	J	L	U	C	K	X	S	L	J
14	S	C	L	N	P	L	I	O	E	Q	Y	R	T	N	X
15	E	I	E	X	V	L	Z	A	Y	T	E	I	X	N	A

ANXIETY FOCUS PRESENCE
BALANCE MEDITATION STRESS
CREATIVITY MEMORY
DISTRACTIONS MINDFULNESS

THE JOURNEY TO A FULFILLING AND MEANINGFUL LIFE

ANSWER

	1	2	3	4	5	6	7	8	9	10	11	12	13	14	15
1	E	J	D	D	W	M	Q	E	S	K	U	C	J	L	S
2	C	D	X	V	Y	T	I	V	I	T	A	E	R	C	T
3	N	H	I	J	H	V	V	X	M	G	P	X	N	H	R
4	A	T	T	S	S	U	C	O	F	H	M	E	F	P	E
5	L	F	S	E	T	Y	D	F	C	I	I	P	M	O	S
6	A	Y	F	O	C	R	B	B	N	Q	B	E	I	B	S
7	B	R	T	V	O	K	A	D	H	B	D	E	D	L	S
8	M	O	E	J	P	M	F	C	O	I	C	Q	Q	Y	Z
9	F	M	S	K	L	U	Q	U	T	N	J	E	Z	P	Q
10	B	E	I	I	L	K	S	A	E	I	I	Z	N	M	I
11	A	M	Y	N	Z	F	T	S	R	W	O	R	A	J	O
12	Q	Z	E	Z	P	I	E	J	N	Z	F	N	G	H	A
13	O	S	N	L	O	R	J	L	U	C	K	X	S	L	J
14	S	C	L	N	P	L	I	O	E	Q	Y	R	T	N	X
15	E	I	E	X	V	L	Z	A	Y	T	E	I	X	N	A

ANXIETY 15:15   FOCUS 4:9   PRESENCE 14:5
BALANCE 7:1   MEDITATION 5:13   STRESS 1:15
CREATIVITY 2:14   MEMORY 11:2
DISTRACTIONS 2:2   MINDFULNESS 4:11

PART II
NURTURING
THE BODY

CHAPTER 4
THE FOUNDATIONS OF PHYSICAL HEALTH

It is difficult to envision a fulfilling and meaningful life in the absence of physical health.

The Bible Says

What? know ye not that your body is the temple of the Holy Ghost which is in you, which ye have of God, and ye are not your own? **1 Corinthians 6:19-20**

Beloved, I wish above all things that thou mayest prosper and be in health, even as thy soul prospereth. **3 John 1:2**

If any man defile the temple of God, him shall God destroy; for the temple of God is holy, which temple ye are. **1 Corinthians 3:17**

Whether therefore ye eat, or drink, or whatsoever ye do, do all to the glory of God. **1 Corinthians 10:31**

For bodily exercise profiteth little: but godliness is profitable unto all things, having promise of the life that now is, and of that which is to come. **1 Timothy 4:8**

A merry heart doeth good like a medicine: but a broken spirit drieth the bones. **Proverbs 17:22**

For ye are bought with a price: therefore glorify God in your body, and in your spirit, which are God's. **1 Corinthians 6:20**

And said, If thou wilt diligently hearken to the voice of the LORD thy God, and wilt do that which is right in his sight, and wilt give ear to his commandments, and keep all his statutes, I will put none of these diseases upon thee, which I have brought upon the Egyptians: for I am the LORD that healeth thee. **Exodus 15:26**

I beseech you therefore, brethren, by the mercies of God, that ye present your bodies a living sacrifice, holy, acceptable unto God, which is your reasonable service. **Romans 12:1-2**

I will praise thee; for I am fearfully and wonderfully made: marvellous are thy works; and that my soul knoweth right well. **Psalms 139:14**

Know ye not that ye are the temple of God, and that the Spirit of God dwelleth in you? **1 Corinthians 3:16**

Wine is a mocker, strong drink is raging: and whosoever is deceived thereby is not wise. **Proverbs 20:1**

And be not drunk with wine, wherein is excess; but be filled with the Spirit; **Ephesians 5:18**

Introduction

Our physical health serves as the foundation upon which the rest of our well-being is built. It affects how we feel, think, and perform daily, influencing everything from our emotional state to our ability to pursue personal and professional goals. Yet, in the midst of busy lives, the importance of maintaining good physical health is often overlooked or taken for granted.

Physical health is not merely the absence of illness; it encompasses a holistic approach that includes proper nutrition, regular exercise, adequate rest, and attention to our body's needs. By cultivating healthy habits, we not only improve our physical vitality but also enhance our mental clarity, emotional balance, and overall quality of life.

This chapter will explore the key elements of physical health and why they are essential for long-term well-being. We will dive into the importance of balanced nutrition, the role of exercise in maintaining strength and flexibility, and the impact of sleep on our bodies and minds. Additionally, we will discuss the importance of listening to your body's signals and taking proactive steps toward maintaining your health, rather than simply reacting to illness.

Achieving and sustaining physical health is a lifelong commitment that requires intention and consistency. As you read on, you will gain practical insights and actionable strategies to improve your physical health and build a strong foundation for living a full and vibrant life.

Life Story

David had always been a hard worker, dedicating long hours to his career. Over time, though, his commitment to work began to take a toll on his body. Skipping meals, sitting at a desk for hours on end, and neglecting exercise had become his norm. At 45, David found himself feeling sluggish, constantly fatigued, and dealing with frequent back pain.

One afternoon, after climbing a single flight of stairs left him winded, David decided to visit his doctor. The doctor's words were sobering: "You're at risk for serious health problems if you don't start taking care of your body." It was a wake-up call. For years, David had prioritized everything but his health, and now it was catching up to him.

Determined to make a change, David started small. He incorporated daily walks into his routine, swapped fast food for nutritious home-cooked meals, and made a conscious effort to get more sleep. He also signed up for yoga to help with his flexibility and posture. As the weeks went by, he began to notice a difference. His energy levels increased, his back pain lessened, and he felt more focused and alert at work.

Six months later, David felt like a new person. The simple decision to prioritize his physical health not only improved his body but his overall quality of life. His productivity soared, his mood lifted, and he had more energy to enjoy time with his family.

David's journey underscores the importance of building a strong foundation for physical health. By making mindful choices—whether it's moving your body, eating well, or getting enough rest—you can transform not just your physical well-being, but every aspect of your life. A healthy body truly is the cornerstone of a balanced, fulfilling life.

Sayings about Physical Health

These quotes emphasize the importance of physical health.

Exercise is the key not only to physical health but to peace of mind.
Nelson Mandela

Physical fitness is not only one of the most important keys to a healthy body, it is the basis of dynamic and creative intellectual activity.
John F. Kennedy

Lack of activity destroys the good condition of every human being
Plato

Taking care of your mental and physical health is just as important as any career move or responsibility.
Mireille Guiliano

Health is a state of complete harmony of the body, mind and spirit. When one is free from physical disabilities and mental distractions, the gates of the soul open.
B.K.S. Iyengar

Physical fitness can neither be acquired by wishful thinking nor by outright purchase.
Joseph Pilates

Health is worth more than learning.
Thomas Jefferson

If you always put limit on everything you do, physical or anything else. It will spread into your work and into your life. There are no limits. There are only plateaus, and you must not stay there, you must go beyond them.
Bruce Lee

The doctor of the future will no longer treat the human frame with drugs, but rather will cure and prevent disease with nutrition.
Thomas A. Edison

Meditation will change your life for the better, enhance your physical health, improve your sleep, and help you achieve your goals, both material and spiritual.
Deepak Chopra

As far as physical health goes, I try to eat in a balanced way, sleep enough, and stay active.
Maria Canals Barrera

Research has shown that a simple act of kindness directed toward another improves the functioning of the immune system and stimulates the production of serotonin in both the recipient of the kindness and the person extending the kindness. Kindness extended, received or observed beneficially impacts the physical health and feelings of everyone involved.
Wayne Dyer

Quite literally, your gut is the epicenter of your mental and physical health. If you want better immunity, efficient digestion, improved clarity and balance, focus on rebuilding your gut health
Kris Carr

A vigorous five-mile walk will do more good for an unhappy but otherwise healthy adult than all the medicine and psychology in the world.
Paul Dudley White

I can make choices that make me happy, and it will ripple and benefit my kids, my husband, and my physical health. That's hard for women to own; we're not taught to do that.
Michelle Obama

Physical health doesn't exist apart from the health of other things. Health ultimately involves the community, and the community ultimately involves the place and natural life of that place, so that real health is harmony with the world.
Wendell Berry

Leave all the afternoon for exercise and recreation, which are as necessary as reading. I will rather say more necessary because health is worth more than learning.
Thomas Jefferson

Never continue in a job you don't enjoy. If you're happy in what you're doing, you'll like yourself, you'll have inner peace. And if you have that, along with physical health, you will have had more success than you could possibly have imagined.
Johnny Carson

Even with mental health as well as physical health, it's about taking responsibility and knowing that you're part of the solution always.
Mariel Hemingway

Scientists are coming to recognise the effects of the mind on physical health. The sense of relaxation associated

with inner peace involves not only being physically at ease. If you are nagged by worry or seething with anger, you're not really relaxed. The key to relaxation is peace of mind. The relaxation gained from alcohol, drugs or just listening to music may seem attractive, but it doesn't last.
Dalai Lama

The voice collects and translates your bad physical health, your emotional worries, your personal troubles.
Placido Domingo

We know a great deal more about the causes of physical disease than we do about the causes of physical health.
M. Scott Peck

Care for life and physical health, with due regard for the needs of others and the common good, is concomitant with respect for human dignity.
Salvatore J. Cordileone

We have a largely materialistic lifestyle characterized by a materialistic culture. However, this only provides us with temporary, sensory satisfaction, whereas long-term satisfaction is based not on the senses but on the mind. That's where real tranquility is to be found. And peace of mind turns out to be a significant factor in our physical health too.
Dalai Lama

Source: https://www.azquotes.com/quotes/topics/physical-health.html

The Importance of Physical Health

Why Physical Health Matters

Physical health is the cornerstone of a meaningful and fulfilling life. It directly influences our energy levels, mental clarity, emotional stability, and overall quality of life. When we prioritize our physical health, we equip ourselves with the strength and vitality needed to pursue our goals, nurture our relationships, and enjoy life's experiences to the fullest. Understanding the significance of physical health is the first step toward building a lifestyle that supports long-term well-being.

The Interconnection of Body, Mind, and Spirit

Physical health is not an isolated aspect of our existence; it is deeply interconnected with our mental and spiritual well-being. A healthy body supports a clear and focused mind, while a calm and balanced mind contributes to better physical health. Moreover, when we take care of our physical health, we are better able to engage in spiritual practices, fostering a sense of inner peace and fulfillment. Recognizing this interconnection allows us to approach health holistically, considering all aspects of our being.

Nutrition: Fueling Your Body

The Role of a Balanced Diet

Nutrition is a foundational pillar of physical health. A balanced diet provides the essential nutrients our bodies need to function optimally. This includes macronutrients like carbohydrates, proteins, and fats, as well as micronutrients such as vitamins and minerals. By consuming a variety of whole, unprocessed foods, we can ensure that our bodies receive the nutrients necessary for energy production, immune function, and overall vitality.

Understanding Macronutrients

Macronutrients are the primary building blocks of our diet and provide the energy needed for daily activities. Carbohydrates are the body's main source of energy, proteins are crucial for tissue repair and muscle growth, and fats play a key role in hormone production and nutrient absorption. Understanding the role of each macronutrient helps us make informed choices about our diet and tailor it to our individual needs.

The Importance of Micronutrients

Micronutrients, though needed in smaller amounts, are equally vital for health. Vitamins such as A, C, D, and E, along with minerals like calcium, magnesium, and iron, support a wide range of bodily functions, from bone health to immune support. A diet rich in fruits, vegetables, lean proteins, and whole grains ensures that we obtain these essential micronutrients, helping to prevent deficiencies and promote overall well-being.

Hydration and Its Impact on Health

Water is the most essential nutrient for life. It plays a crucial role in regulating body temperature, supporting digestion, transporting nutrients, and eliminating waste. Staying adequately hydrated is key to maintaining energy levels, cognitive function, and physical performance. Incorporating water-rich foods and making a habit of drinking water throughout the day are simple yet effective ways to ensure proper hydration.

Exercise and Physical Activity

The Benefits of Regular Exercise

Regular physical activity is one of the most effective ways to improve and maintain physical health. Exercise strengthens the heart, improves lung capacity, boosts circulation, and enhances muscle tone and flexibility. Additionally, it has profound mental health benefits, such as reducing stress, improving mood, and enhancing cognitive function. Whether through aerobic activities like running and swimming, strength training, or flexibility exercises like yoga, incorporating regular exercise into your routine is essential for overall health.

Types of Exercise: Aerobic, Strength, and Flexibility

A well-rounded exercise regimen includes three key components: aerobic exercise, strength training, and flexibility exercises. Aerobic activities, such as walking, cycling, and dancing, improve cardiovascular health and endurance. Strength training, which includes activities like weightlifting and bodyweight exercises, builds muscle mass and bone density. Flexibility exercises, such as stretching and yoga, enhance joint mobility and prevent injuries. By balancing these different types of exercise, we can achieve comprehensive physical fitness.

Incorporating Movement into Daily Life

While structured exercise routines are important, incorporating movement into daily life is equally crucial. Simple practices like taking the stairs instead of the elevator, walking or cycling to work, and engaging in active hobbies like gardening or dancing can significantly contribute to overall physical activity levels. The key is to find enjoyable ways to move throughout the day, making physical activity a natural and integrated part of your lifestyle.

Sleep and Recovery

The Role of Sleep in Physical Health

Sleep is a vital component of physical health, as it allows the body to repair and regenerate. During sleep, muscles recover, the immune system strengthens, and the brain processes and consolidates memories. Adequate sleep is essential for cognitive function, emotional regulation, and physical performance. Chronic sleep deprivation, on the other hand, can lead to a host of health issues, including weakened immunity, weight gain, and increased risk of chronic diseases.

Strategies for Improving Sleep Quality

Improving sleep quality involves establishing healthy sleep habits, such as maintaining a consistent sleep schedule, creating a relaxing bedtime routine, and optimizing the sleep environment. Reducing exposure to screens before bed, limiting caffeine intake, and ensuring a dark, quiet, and cool bedroom can all contribute to better sleep. By prioritizing sleep and implementing these strategies, individuals can enhance their overall health and well-being.

The Importance of Rest and Recovery

In addition to sleep, rest and recovery are critical for physical health. This includes taking time to relax and unwind after periods of intense activity, allowing the body to recover and prevent burnout. Active recovery practices, such as stretching, foam rolling, and gentle movement, can help alleviate muscle soreness and improve flexibility. Recognizing the importance of rest and recovery helps maintain balance and ensures sustainable long-term health.

Preventive Health Care

Regular Health Screenings

Preventive health care involves taking proactive steps to maintain health and prevent illness. Regular health screenings, such as blood pressure checks, cholesterol tests, and cancer screenings, allow for early detection of potential health issues. Early intervention can significantly improve outcomes and reduce the risk of serious conditions. By staying informed about recommended screenings and scheduling regular check-ups, individuals can take charge of their health and prevent complications.

Vaccinations and Immunizations

Vaccinations are a key component of preventive health care, protecting individuals and communities from infectious diseases. Keeping up with recommended vaccinations, such as the flu shot and other age-appropriate immunizations, is crucial for maintaining health and preventing the spread of disease. Understanding the importance of vaccinations and staying up-to-date with immunization schedules is an essential part of a comprehensive health strategy.

Developing a Relationship with Health Care Providers

Building a strong, trusting relationship with healthcare providers is vital for effective preventive care. Regular visits to a primary care physician, open communication about health concerns, and following medical advice are important aspects of managing health. A collaborative approach with health care providers can help individuals make informed decisions about their health and receive the necessary support for maintaining well-being.

Conclusion

Physical health is the foundation upon which all other aspects of life are built. By prioritizing nutrition, exercise, sleep, and preventive care, we can create a strong and resilient body that supports our goals, relationships, and overall quality of life. Understanding the importance of physical health and taking proactive steps to nurture it is essential for living a meaningful and fulfilling life. Through consistent effort and mindful choices, we can lay the groundwork for a lifetime of health and vitality.

Exercise

Strengthening the Foundations of Physical Health

Use the following exercise to assess and enhance your commitment to a healthier lifestyle. This exercise will guide you through a personal evaluation and help you create a plan for improving your physical health.

Step 1: Assess Your Current Physical Health

Take a moment to reflect on your current physical health. In your journal or a notebook, answer the following questions honestly:

- **How would you rate your overall physical health?** (Poor, Fair, Good, Excellent)
- **What is your current level of physical activity?** (Sedentary, Light, Moderate, Active)
- **How consistent are you with eating a balanced and nutritious diet?**
- **Do you get enough restful sleep each night?** (Yes/No, Hours per night)
- **What habits or activities do you currently engage in that contribute to or detract from your health?**

By identifying where you stand, you'll gain clarity on areas that need improvement.

Step 2: Set SMART Health Goals

Using the insights from your self-assessment, set 2-3 **SMART goals** related to your physical health. SMART goals are:

- **Specific** – Clearly define what you want to achieve.

- **Measurable** – Make sure you can track your progress.
- **Achievable** – Ensure the goal is realistic and within reach.
- **Relevant** – Align the goal with your overall health and lifestyle priorities.
- **Time-bound** – Set a deadline or time frame for achieving the goal.

Examples of SMART goals might be:

- "I will walk for 30 minutes five days a week for the next month."
- "I will reduce my sugar intake by cutting out sugary drinks for the next four weeks."
- "I will aim to get 7-8 hours of sleep each night for the next 30 days."

Write down your goals and display them somewhere visible to keep yourself accountable.

Step 3: Create an Action Plan for Wellness

To build the foundations of good health, consistency is key. Develop an action plan to incorporate healthy habits into your daily routine. Consider the following areas:

- **Physical Activity:** What form of exercise will you commit to, and how often will you engage in it? (e.g., walking, running, yoga, strength training)
- **Nutrition:** How can you improve your eating habits? Will you include more vegetables, reduce processed foods, or eat smaller, more balanced meals?

- **Sleep:** What steps will you take to improve your sleep hygiene? (e.g., creating a bedtime routine, limiting screen time before bed)
- **Stress Management:** How will you manage stress on a daily basis? (e.g., practicing meditation, journaling, taking short breaks during the day)

Break these actions down into small, manageable steps, and track your progress over time.

Step 4: Reflect on the Connection Between Body and Mind

As part of understanding the importance of physical health, it's crucial to explore the connection between your body and mind. Spend 10-15 minutes practicing **mindful movement:**

1. Choose a gentle physical activity, such as stretching, yoga, or a slow walk.
2. Focus on how your body feels with each movement. Notice any areas of tension or relaxation.
3. Pay attention to your breathing, coordinating your breath with your movements.
4. After the activity, write down your thoughts:

    Did the physical movement help you feel more mentally clear or relaxed?

    How did it feel to connect your mind and body through movement?

This practice helps reinforce the idea that caring for your body also benefits your mental and emotional well-being.

Step 5: Daily Health Commitment

Commit to one small, healthy action each day for the next week. It could be:

- Drinking a glass of water first thing in the morning.
- Taking a 10-minute walk after lunch.
- Replacing one unhealthy snack with a nutritious option.
- Going to bed 30 minutes earlier to improve sleep.

Track your progress each day in a journal or a habit-tracking app, and at the end of the week, reflect on how these small actions impacted your overall health and energy levels.

Step 6: Reflection and Adjustments

At the end of the week or month, reflect on your progress:

- **Were you able to meet your SMART health goals?**
- **Which habits were easy to integrate, and which were more challenging?**
- **What improvements have you noticed in your physical health and energy levels?**
- **How has focusing on your physical health affected other areas of your life, such as your mood or productivity?**

Use these reflections to adjust your wellness routine, adding new challenges or making your goals more achievable. Remember, building a healthy foundation takes time, but small, consistent changes lead to lasting improvement.

By practicing these steps regularly, you will strengthen your foundation of physical health and create a sustainable, healthy lifestyle that supports your overall well-being.

THE FOUNDATIONS OF PHYSICAL HEALTH

CHAPTER 4
WORDSEARCH

	1	2	3	4	5	6	7	8	9	10
1	S	M	E	N	E	R	G	Y	H	U
2	L	N	U	Y	Q	J	X	Y	X	W
3	P	I	I	T	G	E	D	K	R	E
4	R	F	F	M	R	R	I	T	U	L
5	O	J	A	E	A	I	E	D	H	L
6	T	I	N	T	S	T	T	X	G	B
7	E	C	I	C	L	T	I	I	L	E
8	I	O	W	L	K	Q	Y	V	O	I
9	N	I	S	S	E	N	L	L	I	N
10	D	E	S	I	C	R	E	X	E	G

DIET   ILLNESS   VITAMINS
ENERGY   LIFESTYLE   WELLBEING
EXERCISE   NUTRITION
HYDRATION   PROTEIN

THE JOURNEY TO A FULFILLING AND MEANINGFUL LIFE

ANSWER

	1	2	3	4	5	6	7	8	9	10
1	S	M	E	N	E	R	G	Y	H	U
2	L	N	U	Y	Q	J	X	Y	X	W
3	P	I	I	T	G	E	D	K	R	E
4	R	F	F	M	R	R	I	T	U	L
5	O	J	A	E	A	I	E	D	H	L
6	T	I	N	T	S	T	T	X	G	B
7	E	C	I	C	L	T	I	I	L	E
8	I	O	W	L	K	Q	Y	V	O	I
9	N	I	S	S	E	N	L	L	I	N
10	D	E	S	I	C	R	E	X	E	G

DIET 3:7
ENERGY 1:3
EXERCISE 10:9
HYDRATION 1:9

ILLNESS 9:9
LIFESTYLE 2:1
NUTRITION 1:2
PROTEIN 3:1

VITAMINS 8:8
WELLBEING 2:10

CHAPTER 5
BUILDING HEALTHY HABITS

Healthy habits are the building blocks of a fulfilling and vibrant life.

The Bible Says

Beloved, I pray that all may go well with you and that you may be in good health, as it goes well with your soul. **3 John 1:2** ESV

Saying, "If you will diligently listen to the voice of the LORD your God, and do that which is right in his eyes, and give ear to his commandments and keep all his statutes, I will put none of the diseases on you that I put on the Egyptians, for I am the LORD, your healer." **Exodus 15:26** ESV

So, whether you eat or drink, or whatever you do, do all to the glory of God. **1 Corinthians 10:31** ESV

And God said, "Behold, I have given you every plant yielding seed that is on the face of all the earth, and

every tree with seed in its fruit. You shall have them for food. **Genesis 1:29** ESV

Wine is a mocker, strong drink a brawler, and whoever is led astray by it is not wise. **Proverbs 20:1** ESV

If anyone destroys God's temple, God will destroy him. For God's temple is holy, and you are that temple. **1 Corinthians 3:17** ESV

"Those who sanctify and purify themselves to go into the gardens, following one in the midst, eating pig's flesh and the abomination and mice, shall come to an end together, declares the LORD. **Isaiah 66:17** ESV

And the pig, because it parts the hoof and is cloven-footed but does not chew the cud, is unclean to you. **Leviticus 11:7** ESV

And the LORD spoke to Moses and Aaron, saying to them, "Speak to the people of Israel, saying, These are the living things that you may eat among all the animals that are on the earth. Whatever parts the hoof and is cloven-footed and chews the cud, among the animals, you may eat. Nevertheless, among those that chew the cud or part the hoof, you shall not eat these: The camel, because it chews the cud but does not part the hoof, is unclean to you. And the rock badger, because it chews the cud but does not part the hoof, is unclean to you. ... **Leviticus 11:1-47** ESV

I appeal to you therefore, brothers, by the mercies of God, to present your bodies as a living sacrifice, holy and acceptable to God, which is your spiritual worship. **Romans 12:1** ESV

It shall be a statute forever throughout your generations, in all your dwelling places, that you eat neither fat nor blood." **Leviticus 3:17** ESV

"You are the sons of the LORD your God. You shall not cut yourselves or make any baldness on your foreheads for the dead. For you are a people holy to the LORD your God, and the LORD has chosen you to be a people for his treasured possession, out of all the peoples who are on the face of the earth. "You shall not eat any abomination. These are the animals you may eat: the ox, the sheep, the goat, the deer, the gazelle, the roebuck, the wild goat, the ibex, the antelope, and the mountain sheep. ... **Deuteronomy 14:1-29** ESV

Thorns and thistles it shall bring forth for you; and you shall eat the plants of the field. **Genesis 3:18** ESV

And he said with a loud voice, "Fear God and give him glory, because the hour of his judgment has come, and worship him who made heaven and earth, the sea and the springs of water." **Revelation 14:7** ESV

Is anyone among you sick? Let him call for the elders of the church, and let them pray over him, anointing him with oil in the name of the Lord. And the prayer of faith will save the one who is sick, and the Lord will raise him up. And if he has committed sins, he will be forgiven. **James 5:14-15** ESV

Introduction

Healthy habits are the building blocks of a fulfilling and vibrant life. While we often aspire to improve our physical and mental well-being, the challenge lies in making those improvements stick. True wellness isn't achieved overnight—it is the result of consistent, mindful actions that become habits over time. Developing healthy habits requires commitment, discipline, and most importantly, a mindset shift. It's not about quick fixes or temporary diets, but about adopting a sustainable lifestyle that promotes lasting health.

In this chapter, we'll explore the process of building healthy habits that align with your personal goals and values. From designing a sustainable wellness routine to overcoming obstacles along the way, we will delve into practical strategies for creating a balanced approach to health. You'll also learn about the intricate connection between the body and mind, and how one affects the other in the journey toward holistic well-being.

Life Story

Maria had always been a bit of a night owl. She would stay up late watching TV or scrolling through her phone, which meant waking up tired and hitting the snooze button more times than she'd like to admit. Her mornings were always rushed, with no time for breakfast or planning her day. Her unhealthy eating habits and lack of exercise were taking their toll, leaving her feeling drained by mid-afternoon. Despite her desire to change, every Monday started with the same failed promise: "This week, I'll do better."

One evening, after feeling particularly exhausted, Maria decided to make a real commitment to her health. She realized that her failure wasn't due to a lack of willpower but the absence of sustainable habits. She started by focusing on one small change: going to bed 30 minutes earlier each night. After a week, she added a morning walk to her routine. Once that became consistent, she swapped sugary snacks for fruit and started meal prepping on Sundays.

The shift wasn't easy, and there were days when she stumbled, but Maria kept reminding herself that it wasn't about perfection—it was about progress. Over the course of several months, Maria had built a routine that worked for her. She felt more energetic, her focus improved, and her self-confidence grew as she realized she could stick to the habits she had once struggled to form.

Maria's transformation shows the power of building healthy habits gradually and consistently. When we start small and stay patient with ourselves, we create routines that support long-term health and well-being. It's not about instant results, but about committing to daily practices that will lead to lasting change.

Sayings about Building Healthy Habits

Here are some sayings about habits.

Once you understand that habits can change, you have the freedom and the responsibility to remake them. — **Charles Duhigg**

There are two types of habits: ones which comfort us, and ones which would be a comfort if we stopped. — **Catherine Pulsifer**

Habits change into character. — **Ovid**

Life is habit. Or rather life is a succession of habits. — **Samuel Beckett**

Motivation is what gets you started. Habit is what keeps you going. — **Jim Rohn**

Success is the sum of small efforts repeated day in and day out. — **Robert Collier**

Successful people are simply those with successful habits. — **Brian Tracy**

'Tis easier to prevent bad habits than to break them. — **Benjamin Franklin**

Wouldn't it be great to be gifted? In fact... It turns out that choices lead to habits. Habits become talents. Talents are labeled gifts. You're not born this way, you get this way. — **Seth**

Our character is basically a composite of our habits. Because they are consistent, often unconscious patterns, they constantly, daily, express our character. — **Stephen Covey**

Good habits are worth being fanatical about. — **John Irving**

You leave old habits behind by starting out with the thought, 'I release the need for this in my life.' — **Wayne Dyer**

The best way to stop a bad habit is to never begin it. — **J.C. Penney**

Successful people aren't born that way. They become successful by establishing the habit of doing things unsuccessful people don't like to do. — **William Makepeace Thackeray**

The secret to permanently breaking any bad habit is to love something greater than the habit. — **Bryant McGill**

Good habits, once established, are just as hard to break as are bad habits. — **Robert Puller**

If you are going to achieve excellence in big things, you develop the habit in little matters. Excellence is not an exception, it is a prevailing attitude. — **Colin Powell**

Today, many will choose to free themselves from the personal imprisonment of their bad habits. Why not you? — **Steve Maraboli**

Forget inspiration. Habit is more dependable. Habit will sustain you whether you're inspired or not. — **Ocatavia Butler**

Watch your thoughts, they become your words; watch your words, they become your actions; watch your actions, they become your habits; watch your habits, they become your character; watch your character, it becomes your destiny. — **Lao Tzu**

In a nutshell, your health, wealth, happiness, fitness, and success depend on your habits. — **Joanna Jast**

I can predict the long-term outcome of your success if you show me your daily habits. — **John Maxwell**

I never could have done what I have done without the habits of punctuality, order, and diligence, without the determination to concentrate myself on one subject at a time. — **Charles Dickens**

Creating a Sustainable Wellness Routine

The key to achieving lasting health lies in creating a wellness routine that is both effective and sustainable. Many people start with grand ambitions—extreme diets, intense workout regimens, or dramatic lifestyle changes—only to find that they can't maintain these practices in the long term. The goal of a wellness routine should be to enhance your overall quality of life, not to create additional stress or pressure.

To build a routine that lasts, begin with small, manageable changes. Start by identifying your specific health goals, whether they are related to fitness, nutrition, or mental well-being. Once you have a clear vision of what you want to achieve, break these goals down into smaller, actionable steps. For example, if your goal is to exercise more, start with three short workouts a week rather than committing to daily sessions. As you progress, you can gradually increase the intensity and frequency.

Consistency is key. Establish a schedule that fits into your life, taking into account your work, family, and personal commitments. Incorporate habits that are enjoyable, so that wellness becomes a source of joy rather than a chore. Find activities that energize you—whether it's yoga, running, or dancing—and prioritize self-care practices like relaxation, meditation, or spending time in nature.

Above all, be patient with yourself. Building a sustainable wellness routine is a journey, not a sprint. Celebrate small victories, and understand that setbacks are a natural part of the process. Over time, your routine will become second nature, and you'll find that the habits you once struggled with are now integral parts of your daily life.

Overcoming Obstacles to Physical Health

Despite the best of intentions, obstacles often arise on the path to better health. These obstacles may come in the form of time constraints, lack of motivation, stress, or even unexpected health issues. Learning how to navigate these challenges is essential to staying on course.

One of the most common obstacles is a lack of time. In our busy world, it can be difficult to find time for exercise, meal preparation, or relaxation. However, the key is prioritization. View your health as an investment. Just as you wouldn't neglect work or family responsibilities, don't neglect your well-being. Look for ways to integrate healthy practices into your routine—perhaps by preparing meals in advance, scheduling exercise sessions in the morning, or using short breaks throughout the day for mindfulness or stretching.

Another major obstacle is motivation. We all experience moments when we feel discouraged or simply lack the energy to pursue our health goals. During these times, it's important to reconnect with your "why." Why did you set these health goals in the first place? Remind yourself of the long-term benefits, such as increased energy, improved mood, and a stronger immune system. Surround yourself with a supportive community of friends, family, or health professionals who can help keep you accountable.

Finally, don't underestimate the power of mindset. A positive, growth-oriented mindset is crucial in overcoming obstacles. Rather than viewing setbacks as failures, see them as learning opportunities. Each challenge you face is a chance to strengthen your resilience and recommit to your health.

The Connection Between Body and Mind

Physical health and mental well-being are deeply intertwined. While we often think of them as separate, the truth is that the body and mind work in harmony. When one is out of balance, the other is inevitably affected.

Regular physical activity, for example, has a profound impact on mental health. Exercise releases endorphins, which improve mood and reduce feelings of anxiety and depression. It also promotes better sleep, sharper cognitive function, and higher energy levels, all of which contribute to emotional well-being.

Similarly, mental health plays a crucial role in physical health. Chronic stress, anxiety, and negative emotions can lead to physical symptoms such as fatigue, headaches, digestive issues, and even weakened immunity. Conversely, cultivating a positive mindset through practices like mindfulness, gratitude, and emotional regulation can improve overall health and longevity.

To foster both physical and mental well-being, it's essential to take a holistic approach. Engage in activities that nurture both the body and mind, such as yoga, tai chi, or mindful walking. Practice meditation and reflection as part of your daily routine to calm the mind and reduce stress. And most importantly, listen to your body—honour its signals, take breaks when needed, and approach wellness with kindness and balance.

Conclusion

Building healthy habits is not a destination but a lifelong journey toward greater well-being. It requires intentionality, self-compassion, and a willingness to make gradual, meaningful changes. By creating a sustainable wellness routine, overcoming obstacles with resilience, and acknowledging the deep connection between the body and mind, you can lay the groundwork for a life of vitality and balance.

Incorporating these healthy habits into your life will bring not only physical benefits but also mental clarity and emotional peace. It's a practice of nurturing your body and mind, allowing you to live a more fulfilled, vibrant, and harmonious life. The foundation of your well-being is in your hands—one small, consistent action at a time.

Exercise

Creating and Strengthening Healthy Habits

Perform the following exercise to solidify your understanding of habit formation and start integrating healthier behaviours into your daily routine. This exercise will help you identify, create, and maintain habits that promote well-being.

Step 1: Identify Your Current Habits

Take some time to reflect on your current daily routine. In a notebook or journal, write down the following:

- **Morning Routine:** What are the first things you do when you wake up?
- **Daytime Routine:** How do you spend your time during work, meals, and breaks?
- **Evening Routine:** What habits do you follow before going to bed?

Identify which of these habits are healthy and beneficial, and which might be unproductive or harmful. Ask yourself:

- **What habits are contributing positively to my physical and mental health?**
- **What habits are holding me back from reaching my health or wellness goals?**

Step 2: Choose One Habit to Build

Now that you've identified your current habits, choose **one healthy habit** you'd like to build into your daily routine. Make sure it's something simple, achievable, and aligned with your wellness goals.

Examples of healthy habits include:

- Drinking a glass of water before every meal.
- Walking for 15 minutes every morning.
- Practicing gratitude journaling before bed.
- Taking five minutes to meditate or practice deep breathing during your lunch break.

Step 3: Break the Habit Down Into Small Steps

To make your new habit sustainable, break it down into smaller, manageable steps. For example, if your goal is to exercise more regularly, start with something simple like walking for 10 minutes each day. Over time, you can increase the duration and intensity.

Answer the following questions to help break down your habit:

- **When will you perform this habit?** (e.g., after waking up, during lunch, after work)
- **Where will you perform this habit?** (e.g., at home, at the park, in the office)
- **How often will you perform this habit?** (e.g., daily, three times a week)

Write down the details of your new habit to clarify your plan.

Step 4: Create a Trigger and Reward System

To ensure your habit becomes a regular part of your life, pair it with a **trigger** (a cue that reminds you to do the habit) and a **reward** (a positive reinforcement to encourage consistency).

1. **Choose a trigger:** Find an existing habit or part of your routine to serve as a cue for your new habit. For example:

   After brushing your teeth, you take five minutes to meditate.

   After finishing lunch, you go for a 10-minute walk.

2. **Set a reward:** Rewards help solidify new habits by providing positive reinforcement. It could be something small and enjoyable, like:

   Treating yourself to a healthy snack after completing your walk.

   Taking five minutes to relax and listen to music after journaling.

Write down your chosen trigger and reward for the new habit.

Step 5: Track Your Progress

Track your progress with a **habit tracker** for the next 30 days. You can use a journal, a calendar, or a habit-tracking app to mark off each day you successfully complete your habit. Reflect on how the new habit is making you feel and whether it's getting easier to maintain over time.

Answer the following questions as you track your habit:

- **How consistent have I been with this habit?**
- **What challenges or obstacles have I encountered?**
- **How has this habit affected my physical, mental, or emotional well-being?**

Step 6: Overcoming Obstacles

Forming new habits can be challenging, so it's important to anticipate potential obstacles and plan ways to overcome them. Think about any difficulties you might face and how you can stay on track. Common challenges include:

- **Time constraints:** Can you schedule your habit for a more convenient time or reduce the time commitment to make it easier to fit into your day?
- **Lack of motivation:** How can you remind yourself of the long-term benefits of your habit? Can you find an accountability partner to check in with you?
- **Unexpected disruptions:** How will you bounce back if you miss a day or face interruptions?

Write down your strategies for overcoming obstacles and staying committed to your new habit.

Step 7: Reflect and Adjust

At the end of 30 days, review your progress and reflect on the impact of your new habit. In your journal, answer the following questions:

- **Did I successfully integrate this habit into my routine?**
- **How has this habit positively influenced my health and well-being?**
- **What changes or adjustments can I make to improve my consistency?**
- **Is there another healthy habit I can introduce next?**

If you've been consistent, congratulate yourself and think about how you can either build on this habit or introduce a new one. If you struggled, consider whether the habit needs to be adjusted or simplified. Building healthy habits is a process, and it's important to be patient and kind to yourself along the way.

Step 8: Maintain Your Habits for Long-Term Success

Finally, commit to maintaining your new habit by:

- Keeping your triggers and rewards in place.
- Celebrating small wins.
- Staying flexible and adjusting the habit as your needs evolve.

By consciously creating and nurturing healthy habits, you'll not only improve your physical and mental well-being, but you'll also gain greater control over your life and move closer to achieving your long-term goals.

BUILDING HEALTHY HABITS

CHAPTER 5
WORDSEARCH

	1	2	3	4	5	6	7	8	9	10	11	12	13
1	W	Z	H	M	H	S	U	S	L	J	U	J	V
2	A	O	E	A	O	L	H	O	U	Z	J	E	C
3	I	H	A	W	P	T	N	F	C	N	N	U	H
4	A	R	L	L	D	G	I	I	R	I	O	H	G
5	Y	R	T	T	I	Q	T	V	T	A	R	D	G
6	H	L	H	V	T	S	A	U	A	B	D	G	R
7	K	J	I	I	I	X	O	L	A	T	N	E	M
8	J	T	E	L	D	R	U	B	Q	M	I	N	K
9	Y	Q	O	E	Y	I	G	Y	U	N	J	O	N
10	G	H	S	S	E	N	L	L	E	W	G	E	N
11	T	O	Y	E	D	Z	A	M	O	X	U	T	R
12	P	H	Y	S	I	C	A	L	M	P	M	I	H
13	E	B	O	D	Y	S	T	I	B	A	H	V	I

BODY	LONGIVITY	ROUTINE
HABITS	MENTAL	WELLNESS
HEALTH	MOTIVATION	
HOLISTIC	PHYSICAL	

THE JOURNEY TO A FULFILLING AND MEANINGFUL LIFE

ANSWER

	1	2	3	4	5	6	7	8	9	10	11	12	13
1	W	Z	H	M	H	S	U	S	L	J	U	J	V
2	A	O	E	A	O	L	H	O	U	Z	J	E	C
3	I	H	A	W	P	T	N	F	C	N	N	U	H
4	A	R	L	L	D	G	I	I	R	I	O	H	G
5	Y	R	T	T	I	Q	T	V	T	A	R	D	G
6	H	L	H	V	T	S	A	U	A	B	D	G	R
7	K	J	I	I	I	X	O	L	A	T	N	E	M
8	J	T	E	L	D	R	U	B	Q	M	I	N	K
9	Y	Q	O	E	Y	I	G	Y	U	N	J	O	N
10	G	H	S	S	E	N	L	L	E	W	G	E	N
11	T	O	Y	E	D	Z	A	M	O	X	U	T	R
12	P	H	Y	S	I	C	A	L	M	P	M	I	H
13	E	B	O	D	Y	S	T	I	B	A	H	V	I

BODY 13:2 LONGIVITY 1:9 ROUTINE 8:6
HABITS 13:11 MENTAL 7:13 WELLNESS 10:10
HEALTH 1:3 MOTIVATION 1:4
HOLISTIC 10:2 PHYSICAL 12:1

CHAPTER 6
STRESS MANAGEMENT AND RELAXATION

Relaxation prevents stress and other emotional and physical disorders which impede your ability to enjoy a meaningful life.

The Bible Says

"My soul is overwhelmed with sorrow to the point of death," he said to them. "Stay here and keep watch." Going a little farther, he fell to the ground and prayed that if possible the hour might pass from him. "Abba, Father," he said, "everything is possible for you. Take this cup from me. Yet not what I will, but what you will."
Mark 14:34–36 (NIV)

Then Jesus said, "Come to me, all of you who are weary and carry heavy burdens, and I will give you rest. Take my yoke upon you. Let me teach you, because I am humble and gentle at heart, and you will find rest for your souls. For my yoke is easy to bear, and the burden I give you is light." **Matthew 11:28–30** (NLT)

"Therefore I tell you, do not be anxious about your life, what you will eat or what you will drink, nor about your body, what you will put on. Is not life more than food, and the body more than clothing? Look at the birds of the air: they neither sow nor reap nor gather into barns, and yet your heavenly Father feeds them. Are you not of more value than they?" **Matthew 6:25–26** (ESV)

"And which of you by being anxious can add a single hour to his span of life? ... Therefore do not be anxious, saying, 'What shall we eat?' or 'What shall we drink?' or 'What shall we wear?' ... Your heavenly Father knows that you need them all. But seek first the kingdom of God and his righteousness, and all these things will be added to you." **Matthew 6:27-33** (ESV)

"Therefore do not be anxious about tomorrow, for tomorrow will be anxious for itself. Sufficient for the day is its own trouble." **Matthew 6:34** (ESV)

Don't worry about anything; instead, pray about everything. Tell God what you need, and thank him for all he has done. **Philippians 4:6** (NLT)

I prayed to the LORD, and he answered me. He freed me from all my fears. **Psalm 34:4** (NLT)

"The LORD will fight for you; you need only to be still." **Exodus 14:14** (NIV)

"Be still, and know that I am God! **Psalm 46:10** (NLT)

Give your burdens to the LORD, and he will take care of you. He will not permit the godly to slip and fall. **Psalm 55:22** (NLT)

I wait quietly before God, for my victory comes from him. **Psalm 62:1** (NLT)

For God alone, O my soul, wait in silence, for my hope is from him. He only is my rock and my salvation, my fortress; I shall not be shaken. On God rests my salvation and my glory; my mighty rock, my refuge is God. Trust in him at all times, O people; pour out your heart before him; God is a refuge for us. **Psalm 62:5–8** (ESV)

Fix your thoughts on what is true, and honorable, and right, and pure, and lovely, and admirable. Think about things that are excellent and worthy of praise. Keep putting into practice all you learned and received from me—everything you heard from me and saw me doing. Then the God of peace will be with you. **Philippians 4:8–9** (NLT)

My child, pay attention to what I say. Listen carefully to my words. Don't lose sight of them. Let them penetrate deep into your heart, for they bring life to those who find them, and healing to their whole body. **Proverbs 4:20–22** (NLT)

But he said to me, "My grace is sufficient for you, for my power is made perfect in weakness." Therefore I will boast all the more gladly about my weaknesses, so that Christ's power may rest on me. That is why, for Christ's sake, I delight in weaknesses, in insults, in hardships, in persecutions, in difficulties. For when I am weak, then I am strong. **2 Corinthians 12:9–10** (NIV)

Cast all your anxiety on him because he cares for you. **1 Peter 5:7** (NIV)

Consider it pure joy, my brothers and sisters, whenever you face trials of many kinds, because you know that the testing of your faith produces perseverance. Let perseverance finish its work so that you may be mature and complete, not lacking anything. **James 1:2–4** (NIV)

Even when I walk through the darkest valley, I will not be afraid, for you are close beside me. Your rod and your staff protect and comfort me. **Psalm 23:4** (NLT)

"I am leaving you with a gift—peace of mind and heart. And the peace I give is a gift the world cannot give. So don't be troubled or afraid." **John 14:27** (NLT)

"I have told you all this so that you may have peace in me. Here on earth you will have many trials and sorrows. But take heart, because I have overcome the world." **John 16:33** (NLT)

Introduction

In our fast-paced world, stress has become an almost inevitable part of life. Whether it stems from work, relationships, finances, or simply the pressure to keep up with the demands of daily life, stress can take a significant toll on our physical, emotional, and mental well-being. While some stress is a natural response to challenges, chronic stress can hinder our ability to live a meaningful and fulfilling life.

This chapter explores practical strategies for managing stress and cultivating relaxation. By learning to effectively manage stress, you can create space for greater peace, joy, and balance in your life. This journey is not just about reducing stress—it's about enhancing your overall well-being and embracing a life of greater serenity.

Life Story

Alfred was a high achiever, known for his work ethic and dedication. As a project manager at a fast-paced tech company, he was used to juggling multiple tasks, meeting tight deadlines, and putting in long hours. At first, Alfred (Freddie, as we called him) thrived on the adrenaline of it all, but over time, the constant pressure began to weigh on him. He noticed himself becoming irritable, sleeping poorly, and feeling constantly on edge. The demands of work were starting to spill over into his personal life, affecting his relationships and health.

One day, after a particularly stressful meeting, Freddie felt his chest tighten and his breathing quicken. It was a panic attack—something he had never experienced before. Shaken by the incident, he realized that he could no longer ignore the impact stress was having on his life. Freddie knew he had to make a change.

He began by exploring different ways to manage stress. A friend recommended meditation, so Freddie downloaded an app and started practicing for ten minutes each morning. It was difficult at first, but soon he found it easier to calm his racing thoughts. He also began taking short breaks during the workday to stretch and breathe deeply. In the evenings, he started reading or listening to music instead of working late into the night.

Gradually, these small changes made a huge difference. Freddie found himself feeling more relaxed and better able to handle challenges. He was sleeping more soundly, and his panic attacks disappeared. Most importantly, he regained a sense of balance in his life.

Alfred's story is a reminder that stress management is essential for our well-being. By incorporating relaxation techniques and setting boundaries, we can regain control over our lives and protect our mental and physical health. Stress will always be part of life, but how we respond to it makes all the difference.

Sayings about Stress Management

Reflect on these sayings about stress.

"The darkest nights produce the brightest stars." – **John Green**

"Dear Stress, I would like a divorce. Please understand it is not you, it is me." – **Thomas E. Rojo Aubrey**

"Calmness has the power to leave dirty water as clean water on top of dirt." – **Mokokoma Mokhonoana**

"The greatest weapon against stress is our ability to choose one thought over another." – **William James**

"Tension is who you think you should be. Relaxation is who you are." – **Chinese Proverb**

"In today's rush we all think too much, seek too much, want too much and forget about the joy of just being." – **Eckhart Tolle**

"A diamond is a piece of coal that did very well under stress" – **Henry Kissinger**

"Don't let your mind bully your body into believing it must carry the burden of its worries." – **Astrid Alauda**

"I've chosen to treat my life more like a party than something to stress about." – **Martin Short**

"Laughter helps bring balance to a stressful situation." – **Kala Stevenson**

"Rule number one is, don't sweat the small stuff. Rule number two is, it's all small stuff."– **Robert Eliot**

"Stressed spelled backward is desserts." – **Loretta LaRoche**

"We must have a pie. Stress cannot exist in the presence of a pie." David Mamet

"Where there is a lack of rest, there is an abundance of stress." – **Lysa TerKeurst**

"For fast-acting relief, try slowing down. " – **Lily Tomlin**

"These mountains that you are carrying, you were only supposed to climb." – **Najwa Zebian**

"The time to relax is when you don't have time for it." – Sydney J. Harris

"If each day is a gift, I'd like to know where I can return Mondays." — **John Wagner**

"Sometimes the most important thing in a whole day is the rest we take between two deep breaths." – **Etty Hillesum**

"When you find yourself stressed, ask yourself one question: Will this matter in 5 years from now? If yes, then do something about the situation. If no, then let it go." –**Catherine Pulsifer**

Source: https://evolveinc.io/mental-health/stress/20-inspirational-quotes-to-overcome-stress/

Understanding the Sources of Stress

The first step in managing stress is understanding its root causes. Stress can arise from both external factors, such as work deadlines, and internal factors, such as negative thought patterns or unrealistic expectations. By identifying the specific sources of your stress, you can begin to address them more effectively.

Ask yourself:

- What triggers my stress?
- Are these triggers within my control, or are they external factors?
- How do my thoughts and attitudes contribute to my stress levels?

By gaining clarity on the origins of your stress, you can start to take proactive steps to mitigate its impact.

Practical Techniques for Managing Stress

Managing stress requires a multifaceted approach, combining physical, mental, and emotional strategies. Here are some practical techniques that can help you manage stress more effectively:

Mindfulness Meditation

Practicing mindfulness allows you to stay present and aware of your thoughts and feelings without judgment. This awareness can help you manage stress by preventing you from becoming overwhelmed by negative emotions.

Deep Breathing Exercises

Deep breathing is a simple yet powerful way to calm your nervous system. Try inhaling slowly through your nose for a count of four, holding your breath for a count of four, and exhaling through your mouth for a count of four. Repeat this process several times to reduce stress and promote relaxation.

Time Management

Poor time management is a common source of stress. By prioritizing tasks, setting realistic goals, and avoiding procrastination, you can reduce the pressure and create a more balanced schedule.

Physical Exercise

Regular physical activity helps to release endorphins, the body's natural stress relievers. Whether it's a brisk walk, a yoga session, or a workout at the gym, exercise can significantly reduce stress levels.

Healthy Boundaries

Learning to say no and setting healthy boundaries is essential for managing stress. Respect your limits and communicate them clearly to others.

The Importance of Relaxation

While managing stress is crucial, it is equally important to cultivate relaxation. Relaxation is not just about taking a break—it's about actively creating moments of peace and tranquility in your life. These moments of relaxation allow your body and mind to recover from the stresses of life, restoring your energy and focus.

Consider incorporating the following relaxation practices into your daily routine:

Progressive Muscle Relaxation: This technique involves tensing and then slowly relaxing each muscle group in your body, starting from your toes and working your way up to your head. This process helps to release physical tension and promotes a deep sense of relaxation.

Visualization: Close your eyes and imagine a peaceful scene—a quiet beach, a serene forest, or a calm mountain lake. Engage all your senses in this visualization, and allow yourself to become fully immersed in the tranquility of the scene.

Creative Expression: Activities such as painting, writing, or playing music can be powerful forms of relaxation. They allow you to express your emotions and engage your mind in a way that fosters relaxation and reduces stress.

Nature Walks: Spending time in nature has a calming effect on the mind and body. A walk in the park, a hike in the woods, or simply sitting by a body of water can help you reconnect with the natural world and find inner peace.

Restorative Sleep: Quality sleep is essential for relaxation and stress management. Establish a regular sleep routine, create a calming bedtime environment, and ensure you get enough rest each night.

Integrating Stress Management into Daily Life

Stress management and relaxation should not be seen as occasional activities but as integral parts of your daily life. Here are some ways to make these practices a consistent part of your routine:

Daily Rituals: Start and end your day with simple rituals that promote relaxation, such as morning meditation or an evening gratitude practice.

Scheduled Breaks: Incorporate regular breaks into your day to stretch, breathe, and relax, even if just for a few minutes.

Mindful Living: Practice mindfulness throughout your day by staying present in each moment, whether you're eating, working, or interacting with others.

Self-Care: Make self-care a priority by scheduling time for activities that nourish your body, mind, and soul.

Conclusion

Stress is an inevitable part of life, but it doesn't have to dominate your existence. By understanding the sources of your stress, adopting effective management techniques, and integrating relaxation into your daily life, you can cultivate a sense of calm and balance that enhances your overall well-being.

Remember, the path to a meaningful life is not one free of challenges but one where you learn to navigate those challenges with grace, resilience, and inner peace. As you continue on your journey, let stress management and relaxation be the tools that guide you toward a life filled with purpose, joy, and serenity.

Exercise

Practicing Stress Management and Relaxation Techniques

Do this exercise to apply practical techniques that help you manage stress and cultivate a sense of calm in your daily life. This exercise will guide you through identifying stressors, incorporating relaxation techniques, and creating a personal stress-management plan.

Step 1: Identify Your Stressors

Begin by reflecting on what triggers stress in your life. In a journal or notebook, write down the common sources of stress you encounter, including:

- **Work-related stress:** deadlines, workload, office conflicts.
- **Family or personal life stress:** relationships, household responsibilities, financial concerns.
- **Internal stress:** self-criticism, perfectionism, or worrying about the future.

Once you've identified these stressors, rate each one on a scale of 1 to 10 based on how much stress it causes. This will help you prioritize the areas where stress management is most needed.

Step 2: Track Your Stress Levels

For the next week, take a few minutes each day to write down:

- **What situations or events triggered stress** that day.

- **How your body reacted:** Did you feel tension in your shoulders? Did your heart rate increase? Did you experience headaches or fatigue?
- **What emotions you felt:** Did you feel anxious, overwhelmed, frustrated, or helpless?

By tracking your stress, you can become more aware of patterns in your behaviour and emotions. This awareness is the first step in managing stress more effectively.

Step 3: Practice Relaxation Techniques

To better manage stress, experiment with different relaxation techniques. Choose one or more of the following methods and commit to practicing them for at least 10 minutes each day:

1. **Deep Breathing:**

    Sit or lie down in a comfortable position.

    Close your eyes and take a slow, deep breath in through your nose, counting to four.

    Hold your breath for a count of four, then exhale slowly through your mouth, counting to four again.

    Repeat for five to ten minutes, focusing on the sensation of your breath filling and leaving your body.

2. **Progressive Muscle Relaxation (PMR):**

    Start by tensing the muscles in your toes and feet for five seconds, then slowly release.

Move up through your legs, abdomen, arms, and face, tensing and relaxing each muscle group.

Pay attention to the difference between tension and relaxation in your muscles.

3. **Guided Imagery:**

    Close your eyes and imagine yourself in a peaceful, relaxing place—such as a beach, forest, or mountaintop.

    Engage all your senses: What do you see, hear, smell, and feel in this serene environment?

Stay in this peaceful visualization for five to ten minutes, allowing your mind to rest and recharge.

4. **Mindful Meditation:**

    Find a quiet space and sit comfortably with your eyes closed.

    Focus your attention on your breath, letting go of any distracting thoughts.

    When your mind wanders, gently bring your focus back to your breathing.

Practice mindfulness for at least ten minutes daily to build a sense of inner calm.

After trying these techniques, note which one(s) helped you feel more relaxed and less stressed.

Step 4: Develop Your Personal Stress-Management Plan

Using the insights from Steps 1–3, create a personal plan to manage stress more effectively. Answer the following questions to guide you:

- **What are the top three stressors in your life** that you want to focus on managing?
- **Which relaxation techniques** were the most effective for you? When will you incorporate them into your day?
- **What lifestyle changes** can you make to reduce stress in the long term? (e.g., improving time management, setting boundaries at work, or asking for help with household tasks).

Write down your personalized plan in your journal. Include specific actions you will take, such as:

- **Daily relaxation practices:** Commit to at least one relaxation technique each day, even if it's just for 10 minutes.
- **Adjustments to daily routine:** Identify areas where you can reduce stress, such as delegating tasks or taking short breaks throughout the day.
- **Coping strategies for high-stress situations:** Plan how you'll handle stressful events in a healthy way (e.g., practicing deep breathing before a meeting or walking outside when feeling overwhelmed).

Step 5: Reflect and Re-evaluate

After practicing your stress-management plan for one month, reflect on its effectiveness by answering the following questions:

- **Has my overall stress level decreased?**
- **Which relaxation techniques have worked best for me?**

- **What obstacles have I encountered in managing stress, and how can I address them?**
- **Do I need to adjust my plan to better suit my needs?**

If needed, modify your stress-management plan to better fit your lifestyle. Stress management is a continuous process, and it's important to be flexible and adapt as your life and stressors change.

By consistently practicing stress management and relaxation techniques, you can enhance your overall well-being, reduce feelings of overwhelm, and bring greater calm and balance into your life.

STRESS MANAGEMENT AND RELAXATION

CHAPTER 6
WORDSEARCH

	1	2	3	4	5	6	7	8	9	10	11	12	13	14	15	16
1	R	A	S	K	P	H	N	I	L	Z	G	N	N	F	X	J
2	A	G	N	V	L	J	L	O	E	Y	O	O	M	N	S	P
3	G	O	S	H	S	Q	D	Q	I	U	I	A	G	Y	X	Y
4	Z	Y	T	C	M	A	X	G	R	T	X	J	C	A	T	W
5	F	A	R	T	S	Q	Z	I	A	F	A	I	P	I	Z	E
6	Z	B	E	N	K	N	S	Z	R	R	V	X	L	F	Q	R
7	Q	S	S	P	H	H	I	E	A	K	S	I	A	M	M	W
8	Z	H	S	Q	M	L	O	H	O	V	U	B	E	L	U	E
9	P	L	V	E	A	N	G	E	P	Q	V	D	N	G	E	W
10	Y	A	N	U	N	Q	H	N	N	R	Z	R	S	B	J	R
11	V	T	S	W	U	E	P	A	I	R	O	S	Z	T	M	Y
12	O	I	H	T	V	A	R	G	C	L	Y	D	L	W	N	N
13	V	B	H	J	C	T	T	A	P	Z	A	Z	N	E	Y	J
14	L	B	M	X	N	C	P	O	W	U	J	H	Z	E	E	E
15	L	E	R	D	J	N	G	X	O	A	R	C	N	R	I	P
16	Q	Z	B	W	D	I	I	O	X	E	N	Z	A	I	K	K

AWARENESS   RELAXATION   VISUALIZATION
ENDORPHINS   SLEEP   YOGA
INHALING   STRESS
NOURISHMENT   TRANQUILITY

THE JOURNEY TO A FULFILLING AND MEANINGFUL LIFE

ANSWER

	1	2	3	4	5	6	7	8	9	10	11	12	13	14	15	16
1	R	A	S	K	P	H	N	I	L	Z	G	N	N	F	X	J
2	A	G	N	V	L	J	L	O	E	Y	O	O	M	N	S	P
3	G	O	S	H	S	Q	D	Q	I	U	I	A	G	Y	X	Y
4	Z	Y	T	C	M	A	X	G	R	T	X	J	C	A	T	W
5	F	A	R	T	S	Q	Z	I	A	F	A	I	P	I	Z	E
6	Z	B	E	N	K	N	S	Z	R	R	V	X	L	F	Q	R
7	Q	S	S	P	H	H	I	E	A	K	S	I	A	M	M	W
8	Z	H	S	Q	M	L	O	H	O	V	U	B	E	L	U	E
9	P	L	V	E	A	N	G	E	P	Q	V	D	N	G	E	W
10	Y	A	N	U	N	Q	H	N	N	R	Z	R	S	B	J	R
11	V	T	S	W	U	E	P	A	I	R	O	S	Z	T	M	Y
12	O	I	H	T	V	A	R	G	C	L	Y	D	L	W	N	N
13	V	B	H	J	C	T	T	A	P	Z	A	Z	N	E	Y	J
14	L	B	M	X	N	C	P	O	W	U	J	H	Z	E	E	E
15	L	E	R	D	J	N	G	X	O	A	R	C	N	R	I	P
16	Q	Z	B	W	D	I	I	O	X	E	N	Z	A	I	K	K

AWARENESS 15:10 RELAXATION 10:16 VISUALIZATION 13:1

ENDORPHINS 14:14 SLEEP 11:12 YOGA 4:2
INHALING 16:14 STRESS 3:3
NOURISHMENT 1:12 TRANQUILITY 13:6

PART III
STRENGTHENING RELATIONSHIPS

CHAPTER 7
BUILDING STRONG RELATIONSHIPS

We are gregarious beings. Relationships are crucial to our well-being.

The Bible Says

Then the Lord God said, "It is not good that the man should be alone; I will make him a helper fit for him." **Genesis 2:18**

A friend loves at all times, and a brother is born for adversity. **Proverbs 17:17**

Do not be unequally yoked with unbelievers. For what partnership has righteousness with lawlessness? Or what fellowship has light with darkness? **2 Corinthians 6:14**

Above all, keep loving one another earnestly, since love covers a multitude of sins. **1 Peter 4:8**

Therefore a man shall leave his father and his mother and hold fast to his wife, and they shall become one flesh. **Genesis 2:24**

And though a man might prevail against one who is alone, two will withstand him—a threefold cord is not quickly broken. **Ecclesiastes 4:12**

An excellent wife who can find? She is far more precious than jewels. **Proverbs 31:10**

House and wealth are inherited from fathers, but a prudent wife is from the Lord. **Proverbs 19:14**

Love is patient and kind; love does not envy or boast; it is not arrogant or rude. It does not insist on its own way; it is not irritable or resentful; it does not rejoice at wrongdoing, but rejoices with the truth. Love bears all things, believes all things, hopes all things, endures all things. **1 Corinthians 13:4-7**

Greater love has no one than this, that someone lay down his life for his friends. **John 15:13**

Wives, submit to your husbands, as is fitting in the Lord. Husbands, love your wives, and do not be harsh with them. **Colossians 3:18-19**

Iron sharpens iron, and one man sharpens another. **Proverbs 27:17**

Therefore encourage one another and build one another up, just as you are doing. **1 Thessalonians 5:11**

A new commandment I give to you, that you love one another: just as I have loved you, you also are to love one another. **John 13:34**

With all humility and gentleness, with patience, bearing with one another in love. Make every effort to keep the unity of the Spirit through the bond of peace. **Ephesians 4:2**

For if they fall, one will lift up his fellow. But woe to him who is alone when he falls and has not another to lift him up! **Ecclesiastes 4:10**

Whoever walks with the wise becomes wise, but the companion of fools will suffer harm. **Proverbs 13:20**

For this very reason, make every effort to supplement your faith with virtue, and virtue with knowledge, and knowledge with self-control, and self-control with steadfastness, and steadfastness with godliness, and godliness with brotherly affection, and brotherly affection with love. **2 Peter 1:5-7**

Likewise, husbands, live with your wives in an understanding way, showing honor to the woman as the weaker vessel, since they are heirs with you of the grace of life, so that your prayers may not be hindered. **1 Peter 3:7**

Introduction

Relationships form the core of our personal and professional lives, shaping our experiences and influencing our well-being. Whether with family, friends, colleagues, or partners, the strength and quality of our connections play a significant role in our happiness, fulfillment, and success. Yet, building strong, meaningful relationships requires effort, understanding, and intentionality.

At the heart of any thriving relationship lies mutual respect, trust, and effective communication. These elements, combined with empathy and emotional intelligence, create the foundation for deep, lasting connections. In a world where digital communication and busy schedules often lead to surface-level interactions, cultivating strong relationships requires us to be present, engaged, and compassionate.

This chapter will explore the key principles of building and maintaining healthy relationships. We'll discuss the importance of active listening, vulnerability, and setting boundaries, as well as the impact of trust and emotional support. Whether in personal relationships or professional settings, these skills can help you forge bonds that are both resilient and enriching.

Strong relationships not only enhance our sense of belonging but also serve as pillars of support in times of need. By investing in meaningful connections, we create a network of people who encourage growth, provide comfort, and enrich our lives in countless ways. As you read on, you'll discover practical strategies to strengthen the relationships that matter most, leading to a more connected and fulfilling life.

This chapter offers practical advice and insights to help readers build and maintain strong, loving, and resilient relationships, an integral part of living a meaningful life.

Life Story

Sarah and Emily had been best friends since childhood. They had shared countless memories—sleepovers, school projects, family vacations—but as they grew older, life started pulling them in different directions. Sarah moved across the country for a new job, and Emily started her own family. The physical distance, combined with busy schedules, meant that their once-close relationship began to fade. Months would go by without a meaningful conversation, and their friendship, once effortless, began to feel strained.

One day, Sarah received a heartfelt letter from Emily, explaining how much she missed their bond. Emily acknowledged the drift but expressed a desire to rebuild their connection, despite the distance. Sarah, who had been feeling the same way, was touched by the sincerity of the message and realized how important their friendship still was to her.

Determined to nurture their relationship, Sarah and Emily committed to regular check-ins, whether through video calls, letters, or voice messages. They also planned yearly meet-ups, no matter how busy their lives were. Over time, they found that their friendship, while different from when they were younger, was still strong and meaningful. They grew closer through their intentional effort to stay connected and support each other, even from afar.

Sarah and Emily's story is a testament to the importance of actively building and maintaining strong relationships. Whether with friends, family, or colleagues, relationships require time, effort, and open communication. By prioritizing the people who matter most, we create deeper, more meaningful connections that enrich our lives. Strong relationships are built on the foundation of trust, empathy, and shared experiences, and with intentionality, they can last a lifetime.

Sayings about Building Strong Relationships

The following quotes will help you to form strong relationships.

"Teamwork is connected independence".--**David Cottrell**

"Even the Lone Ranger didn't do it alone."--**Harvey MacKay**

"Personal relationships are the fertile soil from which all advancement, all success, all achievement in real life grows."--**Ben Stein**

"When nobody around you seems to measure up, it's time to check your yardstick."--**Bill Lemley**

"You will become like the five people you associate with the most. This can be either a blessing or a curse."--**Billy Cox**

"It is surprising how much you can accomplish if you don't care who gets the credit."--**Abraham Lincoln**

"One of the secrets of a long and fruitful life is to forgive everybody everything every night before going to bed."--**Bernard Baruch**

"Our rewards in life will always be in exact proportion to the amount of consideration we show toward others."--**Earl Nightingale**

"The golden rule is of no use whatsoever unless you realize that it is your move."--**Frank Crane**

"Nice guys may appear to finish last, but usually they are running in a different race."--**Ken Blanchard**

"There is no exercise better for the heart than reaching down and lifting people up."--**John Andres Holmes**

"I believe that you can get everything in life you want if you will just help enough other people get what they want."--**Zig Ziglar**

Source: https://www.inc.com/lee-colan/12-quotes-to-help-you-build-more-powerful-relationships.html

The Importance of Healthy Communication

The relationships we build with others are at the heart of every meaningful life. Whether with family, friends, or romantic partners, these connections bring richness, joy, and support to our journey. However, the strength and depth of these relationships are largely determined by the quality of our communication. Healthy communication is the cornerstone of any strong relationship—it fosters understanding, builds trust, and creates a foundation for love and compassion to thrive.

Communication is not just about the words we speak; it's about how we listen, how we respond, and how we connect with others on an emotional level. It involves empathy, patience, and the willingness to be vulnerable. In this chapter, we will explore the essential role that healthy communication plays in building strong relationships and how you can nurture love and compassion through your interactions with others.

Nurturing Love and Compassion

Love and compassion are the lifeblood of any meaningful relationship. They are the forces that bind us together, allow us to see the best in others, and inspire us to be our best selves. However, nurturing these qualities requires intention and effort.

Active Listening

One of the most powerful ways to nurture love and compassion is through active listening. When we truly listen to other people—without interrupting, judging, or planning our response—we show them that they are valued and heard. Active listening involves being fully present in the moment, paying attention to both the words and the emotions being expressed, and responding with empathy and understanding.

Expressing Gratitude

Regularly expressing gratitude is a simple yet profound way to strengthen your relationships. Acknowledging the positive qualities of those around you and expressing appreciation for their presence in your life fosters a deep sense of connection and mutual respect. Whether it's a small gesture or a heartfelt conversation, letting others know that you appreciate them can have a lasting impact on the relationship.

Being Vulnerable

Vulnerability is the key to true intimacy. When we allow ourselves to be open and honest about our feelings, fears, and desires, we create a space for genuine connection. This requires courage, as it means letting go of the need to appear perfect or in control. However, it is through vulnerability that we build trust and deepen our relationships.

Practicing Patience and Understanding

Every relationship will face challenges, and it is during these times that patience and understanding become crucial. Recognize that everyone has his or her own struggles, insecurities, and moments of weakness. By approaching others with compassion and a willingness to forgive, you create an environment where love can flourish, even in difficult times.

Shared Experiences

Building strong relationships also involves creating shared experiences that bring joy, laughter, and memories. Whether it's through travel, hobbies, or simply spending quality time together, these moments help to solidify the bond between individuals and remind us of the joy that relationships can bring.

Resolving Conflicts with Grace

No relationship is immune to conflict. Disagreements and misunderstandings are natural parts of any close connection. However, the way we handle conflict can either strengthen or weaken our relationships. Resolving conflicts with grace involves approaching disagreements with a mindset of respect, empathy, and a desire for resolution rather than victory.

Keeping Calm and Centered

When conflicts arise, it's important to stay calm and centered. Reacting in anger or frustration can escalate the situation and lead to hurtful words or actions. Take a moment to breathe, collect your thoughts, and approach the conversation with a clear and calm mind.

Focusing on the Issue, Not the Person

It's easy to slip into blame and criticism during conflicts, but this only creates division. Instead, focus on the specific issue at hand and avoid making personal attacks. Use "I" statements to express how you feel and what you need, rather than accusing or blaming the other person.

Seeking to Understand Before Being Understood

Often, conflicts arise because we feel misunderstood or unheard. By seeking to understand the other person's perspective first, you demonstrate empathy and create a foundation for mutual respect. Ask questions, listen carefully, and acknowledge his or her feelings before expressing your own.

Finding Common Ground

In many conflicts, there is a common ground where both parties' needs can be met. Look for areas of agreement and work together to find a solution that respects both perspectives. This approach not only resolves the immediate issue but also strengthens the relationship by showing that you value collaboration over competition.

Letting Go of the Need to Be Right

Sometimes, the desire to "win" an argument can override the importance of the relationship itself. Letting go of the need to be right can be liberating and can open the door to resolution. Remember, the goal of conflict resolution is not to win but to understand, heal, and move forward together.

Conclusion

Building strong relationships is an essential part of leading a meaningful life. These connections provide us with love, support, and a sense of belonging. By prioritizing healthy communication, nurturing love and compassion, and resolving conflicts with grace, we can cultivate relationships that are deep, resilient, and fulfilling.

As you continue on your journey, remember that relationships are not static—they require ongoing care, attention, and effort. But the rewards are immeasurable. Strong relationships bring joy to our lives, help us cope with challenges, and remind us that we are never alone. Invest in your relationships, cherish the people in your life, and let love and compassion guide your interactions. In doing so, you will find that the path to a meaningful life is not one you walk alone, but one you share with those you hold dear.

Exercise

Strengthening Your Relationships

This exercise will help you reflect on and improve the key relationships in your life. By focusing on communication, empathy, and mutual understanding, you can cultivate deeper and more fulfilling connections.

Step 1: Evaluate Your Key Relationships

Take time to reflect on the relationships that are most important to you—whether with family, friends, colleagues, or a romantic partner. In your journal or notebook, answer the following questions:

- **Who are the people closest to me?** List 3–5 key relationships.
- **What do I value most about these relationships?** Consider qualities like trust, support, laughter, or shared experiences.
- **Are there any areas where I feel the relationship could improve?** Be honest about any issues or communication barriers.

Step 2: Practice Active Listening

Active listening is one of the most important skills for building strong relationships. This week, commit to practicing active listening with the people on your list. When you are having a conversation:

1. **Focus on the speaker:** Put away distractions like your phone or television, and make eye contact.
2. **Listen without interrupting:** Allow the person to speak without planning your response. Try to understand his or her point of view.

3. **Reflect what you've heard:** After they've finished speaking, summarize what they've said in your own words to show you've understood.

After practicing active listening, ask yourself:

- **How did the conversation feel different?**
- **Did the other person feel more understood?**

Make note of how active listening affected the quality of your interactions.

Step 3: Strengthen Empathy

Empathy is the ability to understand and share the feelings of another. This week, focus on building empathy in your relationships. For each key relationship, try the following:

- **Put yourself in the other person's shoes:** Consider his or her experiences, emotions, and challenges.
- **Ask open-ended questions:** Encourage the other person to share more about his/her thoughts and feelings. Use questions like, "How do you feel about this?" or "What has this experience been like for you?"
- **Respond with compassion:** Even if you disagree or don't fully understand, respond with kindness and support.

After practicing empathy, reflect on these questions:

- **How has empathy deepened my understanding of this person?**
- **Have I noticed any positive changes in the relationship?**

Step 4: Strengthen Your Communication Skills

Healthy communication is the foundation of strong relationships. Work on improving how you express yourself in your interactions. Practice these communication strategies:

- **Be clear and honest:** Express your thoughts and feelings openly, but with kindness and respect.
- **Use "I" statements:** Instead of saying, "You never listen," say, "I feel unheard when we talk." This reduces defensiveness and promotes understanding.
- **Address conflicts constructively:** When conflicts arise, focus on solutions rather than blame. Ask, "How can we work through this together?"

Over the next week, practice these strategies in your conversations and take note of any shifts in how you communicate.

Step 5: Express Gratitude and Appreciation

Strong relationships thrive on gratitude and appreciation. This week, make a point to express your appreciation for the people in your life. For each of the key relationships on your list:

1. **Write down at least one thing you appreciate about the person:** It could be something he or she has done recently or a quality you admire in him or her.
2. **Share it with them:** Whether through a heartfelt note, text, or face-to-face conversation, let them know how much you appreciate their presence in your life.

Reflect on these questions after you've expressed your appreciation:
- **How did the other person respond?**
- **How did it make me feel to express gratitude?**

Step 6: Set Relationship Goals

To continue building strong relationships, set specific goals for improving and nurturing your connections. For each key relationship, write down one goal. For example:
- "I will have a weekly check-in with my sibling to stay connected."
- "I will practice active listening during conversations with my partner."
- "I will make an effort to resolve conflicts with compassion and understanding."

Make sure these goals are realistic and actionable, and commit to revisiting them regularly.

Step 7: Reflect and Re-evaluate

After completing this exercise, take time to reflect on the process by answering the following questions:
- **How have my relationships improved over the past week?**
- **What did I learn about myself and the way I interact with others?**
- **Which practices were the most effective in strengthening my relationships?**
- **How can I continue to nurture these connections moving forward?**

By consistently applying the principles of active listening, empathy, healthy communication, and gratitude, you'll create stronger, more meaningful relationships that enrich your life and the lives of those around you.

CHAPTER 7
WORDSEARCH

	1	2	3	4	5	6	7	8	9	10	11	12	13	14	15	16
1	C	J	E	V	O	L	L	W	D	S	J	J	J	K	I	N
2	W	O	M	S	U	M	U	G	R	B	J	P	B	X	O	S
3	P	T	M	U	E	N	P	E	R	B	S	R	N	I	Y	C
4	I	P	I	P	O	Y	N	F	F	A	L	G	T	Z	O	Q
5	H	A	I	R	A	T	M	L	U	L	T	A	C	N	X	Y
6	S	H	T	H	R	S	B	S	V	V	C	I	N	B	Y	W
7	D	R	T	A	S	O	S	A	G	I	M	E	T	E	O	J
8	N	Q	P	G	N	N	B	I	N	R	C	P	C	U	D	X
9	E	I	K	D	T	X	O	U	O	T	D	N	S	I	D	Q
10	I	Y	S	C	R	C	M	I	I	N	E	O	F	N	R	E
11	R	K	S	Z	V	M	E	O	T	I	C	D	S	T	B	R
12	F	L	G	B	O	W	N	P	T	A	B	X	E	I	F	Z
13	R	Q	Y	C	B	S	M	A	S	E	L	U	E	M	Q	A
14	F	P	J	H	L	C	P	X	Q	E	C	E	R	A	I	V
15	Q	E	W	Y	L	I	M	A	F	W	R	K	R	C	E	C
16	Y	J	G	T	V	T	C	K	L	T	K	K	S	Y	I	T

BONDS   FRIENDSHIP   PATIENCE
COMMUNICATION   GRATITUDE   RELATIONSHIP
COMPASSION   INTIMACY   RESPECT
CONNECTIONS   LOVE
FAMILY   PARTNERS

THE JOURNEY TO A FULFILLING AND MEANINGFUL LIFE

ANSWER

	1	2	3	4	5	6	7	8	9	10	11	12	13	14	15	16
1	C	J	E	V	O	L	L	W	D	S	J	J	J	K	I	N
2	W	O	M	S	U	M	U	G	R	B	J	P	B	X	O	S
3	P	T	M	U	E	N	P	E	R	B	S	R	N	I	Y	C
4	I	P	I	P	O	Y	N	F	F	A	L	G	T	Z	O	Q
5	H	A	I	R	A	T	M	L	U	L	T	A	C	N	X	Y
6	S	H	T	H	R	S	B	S	V	V	C	I	N	B	Y	W
7	D	R	T	A	S	O	S	A	G	I	M	E	T	E	O	J
8	N	Q	P	G	N	N	B	I	N	R	C	P	C	U	D	X
9	E	I	K	D	T	X	O	U	O	T	D	N	S	I	D	Q
10	I	Y	S	C	R	C	M	I	I	N	E	O	F	N	R	E
11	R	K	S	Z	V	M	E	O	T	I	C	D	S	T	B	R
12	F	L	G	B	O	W	N	P	T	A	B	X	E	I	F	Z
13	R	Q	Y	C	B	S	M	A	S	E	L	U	E	M	Q	A
14	F	P	J	H	L	C	P	X	Q	E	C	E	R	A	I	V
15	Q	E	W	Y	L	I	M	A	F	W	R	K	R	C	E	C
16	Y	J	G	T	V	T	C	K	L	T	K	K	S	Y	I	T

BONDS 6:7
COMMUNICATION 13:4
COMPASSION 1:1
CONNECTIONS 3:16
FAMILY 15:9

FRIENDSHIP 12:1
GRATITUDE 2:8
INTIMACY 9:14
LOVE 1:6
PARTNERS 8:3

PATIENCE 14:7
RELATIONSHIP 15:13
RESPECT 15:11

CHAPTER 8
CULTIVATING COMMUNITY AND CONNECTION

Human beings are inherently social creatures. Our need for connection is deeply embedded in our nature, influencing our well-being, happiness, and sense of purpose.

The Bible Says

And let us consider how we may spur one another on toward love and good deeds, not giving up meeting together, as some are in the habit of doing, but encouraging one another—and all the more as you see the Day approaching. **Hebrews 10:24–25 (NIV)**

And now these three remain: faith, hope and love. But the greatest of these is love. **1 Corinthians 13:13 (NIV)**

I appeal to you, brothers and sisters, in the name of our Lord Jesus Christ, that all of you agree with one another in what you say and that there be no divisions among you, but that you be perfectly united in mind and thought. **1 Corinthians 1:10 (NIV)**

All the believers were one in heart and mind. No one claimed that any of their possessions was their own, but they shared everything they had. **Acts 4:32 (NIV)**

For just as each of us has one body with many members, and these members do not all have the same function, so in Christ we, though many, form one body, and each member belongs to all the others. **Romans 12:4–5 (NIV)**

Bear with each other and forgive one another if any of you has a grievance against someone. Forgive as the Lord forgave you. And over all these virtues put on love, which binds them all together in perfect unity. **Colossians 3:13–14 (NIV)**

How good and pleasant it is when God's people live together in unity! **Psalm 133:1 (NIV)**

Every day they continued to meet together in the temple courts. They broke bread in their homes and ate together with glad and sincere hearts, praising God and enjoying the favor of all the people. And the Lord added to their number daily those who were being saved. **Acts 2:46-47 (NIV)**

Perfume and incense bring joy to the heart, and the pleasantness of a friend springs from their heartfelt advice. **Proverbs 27:9 (NIV)**

Every day they continued to meet together in the temple courts. They broke bread in their homes and ate together with glad and sincere hearts, praising God and enjoying the favor of all the people. And the Lord added to their number daily those who were being saved. **Acts 2:46–47 (NIV)**

For where two or three gather in my name, there am I with them. **Matthew 18:20 (NIV)**

For we were all baptized by one Spirit so as to form one body—whether Jews or Gentiles, slave or free—and we were all given the one Spirit to drink. **1 Corinthians 12:13 (NIV)**

Carry each other's burdens, and in this way you will fulfill the law of Christ. **Galatians 6:2 (NIV)**

But if we walk in the light, as he is in the light, we have fellowship with one another, and the blood of Jesus, his Son, purifies us from all sin. **1 John 1:7 (NIV)**

Finally, all of you, be like-minded, be sympathetic, love one another, be compassionate and humble. **1 Peter 3:8 (NIV)**

Dear friends, since God so loved us, we also ought to love one another. **1 John 4:11 (NIV)**

Live in harmony with one another. Do not be proud, but be willing to associate with people of low position. Do not be conceited. **Romans 12:16 (NIV)**

My command is this: Love each other as I have loved you. Greater love has no one than this: to lay down one's life for one's friends. **John 15:12–13 (NIV)**

A friend loves at all times, and a brother is born for a time of adversity. **Proverbs 17:17 (NIV)**

Above all, love each other deeply, because love covers over a multitude of sins. Offer hospitality to one another without grumbling. **1 Peter 4:8–9 (NIV)**

Introduction

Human beings are inherently social creatures. Our need for connection is deeply embedded in our nature, influencing our well-being, happiness, and sense of purpose. While personal relationships are vital, the broader sense of community and connection with others plays an equally important role in leading a meaningful life. Cultivating a strong community and forging connections with others not only enriches our lives but also allows us to contribute to something larger than ourselves.

In this chapter, we will explore the significance of community and connection, the power of social support networks, the importance of building and maintaining friendships, and how contributing positively to society can enhance our sense of purpose and fulfillment. The chapter provides a comprehensive guide to building a sense of community and fostering connections that contribute to a meaningful and fulfilling life.

Life Story

When Daniel moved to a new city for his dream job, he was excited about the opportunity, but he didn't anticipate how lonely he would feel. He had left behind his close-knit circle of friends and family, and the initial excitement of his new role quickly gave way to a sense of isolation. He spent most evenings alone in his apartment, longing for the camaraderie he had back home.

One day, Daniel decided he needed to make a change. He signed up for a local volunteer group that worked with underprivileged youth. Through his involvement, he met people from all walks of life who shared his passion for giving back. What started as a way to pass the time turned into something much more meaningful—he found himself forming new friendships and becoming an active part of the community.

Over the following months, Daniel expanded his network by joining a running club and attending neighbourhood events. Slowly but surely, his sense of loneliness disappeared. He felt a deeper connection to the people around him, and his life became richer through these new relationships and shared experiences. He had built a community that supported him, just as he had supported others.

Daniel's story highlights the importance of cultivating community and connections, especially during times of transition or isolation. Human beings thrive on meaningful connections, and by stepping out of our comfort zones and engaging with others, we not only enrich our own lives but also contribute to the strength of the communities of which we are a part.

Sayings about Cultivating Community and Connection

Reflect on these sayings about community and connections.

"One of the marvelous things about community is that it enables us to welcome and help people in a way we couldn't as individuals." – **Jean Vanier**

"It's so important to have a genuine human regard for the people who work for you. To be a person of integrity, fight for people when they aren't in the room, and do what you say you're going to do." – **Ara Tucker**

"There is no power for change greater than a community discovering what it cares about." – **Margaret J. Wheatley**

"I alone cannot change the world, but I can cast a stone across the waters to create many ripples." – **Mother Teresa**

"In every community, there is work to be done. In every nation, there are wounds to heal. In every heart, there is the power to do it. – **Marianne Williamson**

"We cannot live only for ourselves. A thousand fibers connect us with our fellow men." – **Herman Melville**

"The greatness of a community is most accurately measured by the compassionate actions of its members." – **Coretta Scott King**

"Educate a boy, and you educate an individual. Educate a girl, and you educate a community." – **Adelaide Hoodless**

"Alone, we can do so little; together, we can do so much" – **Helen Keller**

"If you want to go quickly, go alone. If you want to go far, go together." – **African Proverb**

*"I am of the opinion that my life belongs to the whole community and as long as I live, it is my privilege to do for it whatever I can. I want to be thoroughly used up

when I die, for the harder I work the more I live." – **George Bernard Shaw**

Source: https://www.ellevatenetwork.com/articles/8538-quotes-about-the-power-of-community

The Power of Social Support Networks

Social support networks are the web of relationships that provide us with emotional, practical, and even financial assistance throughout our lives. These networks, which include family, friends, colleagues, and community members, are crucial for our well-being. They offer comfort in times of need, celebrate our successes, and provide a sense of belonging.

Emotional Support

During difficult times, having a network of people who can listen, empathize, and offer comfort is invaluable. Emotional support helps us navigate life's challenges, reduces feelings of isolation, and provides the reassurance that we are not alone in our struggles.

Practical Support

Whether it's lending a helping hand during a move, offering advice on a challenging decision, or simply being there when we need it, practical support from others makes life's burdens easier to bear. These acts of kindness strengthen our connections and remind us of the power of community.

Reciprocity

A healthy social support network is built on reciprocity. It's not just about receiving support but also about giving it. By being there for others, we reinforce our connections and contribute to the well-being of those around us. This mutual exchange fosters trust and deepens relationships.

Resilience

Social support networks contribute to our resilience, helping us bounce back from adversity. Knowing that we have a network of people who care about us provides a buffer against stress and enables us to cope more effectively with life's challenges.

Building and Maintaining Friendships

Friendships are among the most meaningful relationships we can cultivate. They provide us with companionship, joy, and a sense of belonging. However, building and maintaining friendships requires effort, intention, and a commitment to nurturing these connections over time.

Finding Common Ground

Friendships often begin with shared interests, experiences, or values. Whether it's through hobbies, work, or community activities, finding common ground is the first step in building a friendship. These shared experiences create a foundation for deeper connections to grow.

Quality Over Quantity

It's not the number of friends we have but the quality of those friendships that matters. Deep, meaningful friendships are built on trust, mutual respect, and a genuine interest in each other's well-being. Focus on cultivating a few strong friendships rather than spreading yourself too thin.

Consistency and Communication

Maintaining friendships requires consistent effort. Regular communication, whether through phone calls, messages, or in-person visits, keeps the connection alive. Even small gestures, like checking in or sending a thoughtful note, show that you value the friendship.

Being There in Good Times and Bad

True friendships are tested during both good times and bad. Celebrate your friends' successes and support them in their struggles. Being there for each other, no matter the circumstances, strengthens the bond and creates lasting connections.

Growth and Change

Friendships evolve over time, and it's important to allow space for growth and change. Be open to new experiences together, and embrace the ways in which your friendship may develop. Flexibility and understanding are key to maintaining long-lasting friendships.

Contributing Positively to Society

Cultivating community and connection extends beyond our immediate relationships—it also involves contributing positively to society. Engaging in acts of service, volunteering, and participating in community activities not only benefits others but also enriches our own lives by fostering a sense of purpose and belonging.

Volunteering

Volunteering your time and skills to help others is one of the most direct ways to contribute to society. Whether it's mentoring youth, supporting local charities, or participating in community clean-up efforts, volunteering allows you to make a tangible difference in the lives of others.

Advocacy and Activism

Standing up for causes you believe in and advocating for social change can have a profound impact on your community and beyond. Whether it's through organizing events, participating in protests, or simply raising awareness, your efforts can contribute to creating a more just and compassionate society.

Random Acts of Kindness

Small, everyday acts of kindness—like helping a neighbour, paying for someone's coffee, or offering a compliment—can have a ripple effect in your community. These gestures, though seemingly small, create a culture of kindness and connection.

Supporting Local Businesses and Initiatives

Contributing to your local economy by supporting small businesses, farmers' markets, and community events helps to build a vibrant and connected community. Your patronage not only sustains local businesses but also fosters a sense of community pride and solidarity.

Sharing Your Talents

Everyone has unique talents and skills that can benefit others. Whether it's teaching a class, sharing your knowledge, or creating art that inspires, sharing your talents with your community can create connections and leave a positive impact.

Conclusion

Cultivating community and connection is a vital aspect of leading a meaningful life. The relationships we build, the support we give and receive, and the contributions we make to society all play a significant role in shaping our sense of purpose and fulfillment. By nurturing strong social support networks, building and maintaining friendships, and actively contributing to the well-being of our community, we not only enhance our own lives but also create a ripple effect that benefits those around us.

As you continue on your journey, remember that the connections you cultivate with others are among the most valuable treasures in life. Embrace the power of community, cherish your friendships, and seek ways to contribute positively to the world around you. In doing so, you will find that the path to a meaningful life is not one you walk alone, but one that is enriched by the bonds of connection and the joy of shared purpose.

Exercise

Strengthening Community and Connection

This exercise will help you reflect on your role within your community and take practical steps to build meaningful connections with others. By engaging with those around you and contributing to a shared sense of belonging, you can strengthen your ties and enhance the quality of your relationships.

Step 1: Reflect on Your Current Communities

Take a few minutes to consider the different communities you are part of, whether it's your family, friends, workplace, local neighborhood, or spiritual group. Write down answers to the following questions:

- **Which communities am I currently a part of?**
- **How active am I in each of these communities?**
- **What do I value most about being part of these groups?**
- **Are there any communities I would like to engage with more deeply?**

Step 2: Identify Your Role in the Community

Every individual plays a unique role in the community. Consider how you contribute to your communities and how you might want to contribute more meaningfully. Answer these questions:

- **How do I currently contribute to the well-being of my community?** For example, do you offer support, leadership, resources, or a listening ear?

- **Is there anything more I could do to strengthen my role?**
- **What personal strengths can I offer to my community?** Consider skills like empathy, problem-solving, or communication.
- **Are there any unmet needs in my community where I could make a difference?**

Step 3: Take Action to Deepen Connections

This week, take specific actions to deepen your sense of connection with others. Try one or more of the following:

1. **Reconnect with someone:** Reach out to a friend or family member you haven't spoken to in a while. Make an effort to rebuild the connection by catching up or inviting him/her to an activity.

2. **Join a new community:** If there's a group or cause you've been interested in but haven't yet engaged with, take the first step. This could be volunteering, joining a club, or participating in an online forum.

3. **Host a gathering:** Invite a few people from different parts of your life—whether family, friends, or colleagues—for a small gathering, either in person or virtually, to foster connection and belonging.

4. **Engage in active listening:** In your next interaction, focus entirely on the person you're speaking to. Ask open-ended questions, listen without judgment, and show genuine interest in his/her experiences.

After taking these steps, reflect on the following:

- **How did these actions impact my sense of connection to others?**

- **What did I learn about myself through this process?**
- **How did these efforts benefit those around me?**

Step 4: Contribute to a Cause

One of the most meaningful ways to cultivate community is through service. Think about a cause or initiative that matters to you, and take action to contribute. Consider the following:

- **What social, environmental, or cultural issues are important to me?**
- **How can I contribute to this cause?** This could be through volunteering, donating, raising awareness, or simply offering your skills and time.
- **How will this contribution strengthen my connection to the community?**

Take some time this month to actively support a cause that aligns with your values, and reflect on the impact it has on both you and your community.

Step 5: Practice Gratitude for Your Community

Building a strong community often begins with recognizing and appreciating the support you already have. This week, take a moment to express gratitude for those who have made a positive impact on your life:

1. **Write down the names of 3-5 people in your community who have supported you in some way.**
2. **For each person, write a short note of appreciation** (you can choose to send it or keep it

private). Reflect on how each person's presence has enriched your life.

3. **If possible, thank them in person or through a message** and notice how it strengthens your bond with them.

Reflect on how this practice of gratitude influences your sense of connection:

- **How did expressing gratitude deepen my relationships?**
- **What new insights did I gain about the importance of community support?**

Step 6: Set Goals for Cultivating Community

To continue building meaningful connections, set personal goals for cultivating community and connection. For example:

- "I will commit to attending one community event per month."
- "I will reach out to one person each week to strengthen our connection."
- "I will actively participate in a group that aligns with my passions and values."

Write down your goals and set reminders to review your progress regularly. This will help you stay intentional about fostering deeper connections.

Step 7: Reflect and Re-evaluate

After completing this exercise, reflect on your experiences by answering the following questions:

- **What new connections did I form or strengthen?**

- **How has my sense of community evolved?**
- **Which activities helped me feel more connected to others, and why?**
- **How can I continue to build and nurture these relationships in the future?**

By actively engaging in your communities, offering your strengths, and building meaningful connections, you'll find a greater sense of belonging and fulfillment in your life.

CULTIVATING COMMUNITY AND CONNECTION

CHAPTER 8
WORDSEARCH

	1	2	3	4	5	6	7	8	9	10	11	12	13	14	15	16
1	G	I	P	P	I	S	S	I	Z	R	B	F	E	H	E	G
2	Y	N	F	W	C	Y	X	T	S	Q	B	J	S	K	N	W
3	E	T	I	M	T	F	O	U	G	K	R	S	J	O	X	V
4	R	S	H	R	W	N	P	X	A	R	E	K	I	H	H	M
5	X	Y	O	D	A	P	D	G	F	N	P	T	F	H	S	Y
6	U	T	R	P	O	H	N	Q	D	H	C	K	F	E	Q	X
7	B	I	O	R	R	S	S	N	B	E	R	N	U	G	T	J
8	K	N	T	Q	R	U	I	G	N	W	T	L	R	U	U	K
9	K	U	I	Y	R	K	P	N	N	R	A	C	W	R	Q	C
10	Z	M	I	I	M	Z	O	W	V	V	Y	O	Y	F	D	R
11	P	M	F	M	C	C	L	R	F	F	W	Z	D	J	B	H
12	X	O	P	I	H	S	N	O	I	N	A	P	M	O	C	U
13	M	C	B	H	O	C	Y	V	G	O	I	U	X	H	V	O
14	Z	C	Z	E	N	M	W	Y	T	H	V	P	Z	Z	U	Y
15	F	N	C	T	G	H	A	P	P	I	N	E	S	S	L	L
16	G	S	O	C	I	E	T	Y	O	E	Z	P	F	Z	T	W

COMMUNITY	KINDNESS	SUPPORT
COMPANIONSHIP	PURPOSE	VALUES
CONNECTION	SHARING	
HAPPINESS	SOCIETY	

THE JOURNEY TO A FULFILLING AND MEANINGFUL LIFE

ANSWER

	1	2	3	4	5	6	7	8	9	10	11	12	13	14	15	16
1	G	I	P	P	I	S	S	I	Z	R	B	F	E	H	E	G
2	Y	N	F	W	C	Y	X	T	S	Q	B	J	S	K	N	W
3	E	T	I	M	T	F	O	U	G	K	R	S	J	O	X	V
4	R	S	H	R	W	N	P	X	A	R	E	K	I	H	H	M
5	X	Y	O	D	A	P	D	G	F	N	P	T	F	H	S	Y
6	U	T	R	P	O	H	N	Q	D	H	C	K	F	E	Q	X
7	B	I	O	R	R	S	S	N	B	E	R	N	U	G	T	J
8	K	N	T	Q	R	U	I	G	N	W	T	L	R	U	U	K
9	K	U	I	Y	R	K	P	N	N	R	A	C	W	R	Q	C
10	Z	M	I	I	M	Z	O	W	V	V	Y	O	Y	F	D	R
11	P	M	F	M	C	C	L	R	F	F	W	Z	D	J	B	H
12	X	O	P	I	H	S	N	O	I	N	A	P	M	O	C	U
13	M	C	B	H	O	C	Y	V	G	O	I	U	X	H	V	O
14	Z	C	Z	E	N	M	W	Y	T	H	V	P	Z	Z	U	Y
15	F	N	C	T	G	H	A	P	P	I	N	E	S	S	L	L
16	G	S	O	C	I	E	T	Y	O	E	Z	P	F	Z	T	W

COMMUNITY 13:2   KINDNESS 9:6   SUPPORT 2:9
COMPANIONSHIP 12:15 PURPOSE 9:7   VALUES 10:10
CONNECTION 11:6   SHARING 7:7
HAPPINESS 15:6   SOCIETY 16:2

CHAPTER 9
THE ROLE OF SERVICE AND KINDNESS

Kindness comes in many forms, and every act, whether big or small, has the power to make a difference.

The Bible Says

"If you meet your enemy's ox or his donkey going astray, you shall bring it back to him. If you see the donkey of one who hates you lying down under its burden, you shall refrain from leaving him with it; you shall rescue it with him." **Exodus 23:4-5**

"You shall not take vengeance or bear a grudge against the sons of your own people, but you shall love your neighbor as yourself: I am the Lord." **Leviticus 19:18**

"If your brother becomes poor and cannot maintain himself with you, you shall support him as though he

were a stranger and a sojourner, and he shall live with you." **Leviticus 25:25**

"He who withholds kindness from a friend forsakes the fear of the Almighty." **Job 6:14**

"Whoever despises his neighbor is a sinner, but blessed is he who is generous to the poor." **Proverbs 14:21**

"Whoever is generous to the poor lends to the Lord, and he will repay him for his deed." **Proverbs 19:17**

"Whoever pursues righteousness and kindness will find life, righteousness, and honor." **Proverbs 21:21**

"If your enemy is hungry, give him bread to eat, and if he is thirsty, give him water to drink." **Proverbs 25:21**

"Is not this the fast that I choose: to loose the bonds of wickedness, to undo the straps of the yoke, to let the oppressed go free, and to break every yoke? Is it not to share your bread with the hungry and bring the homeless poor into your house; when you see the naked, to cover him, and not to hide yourself from your own flesh?" **Isaiah 58:6-7**

He has told you, O man, what is good; and what does the Lord require of you but to do justice, and to love kindness, and to walk humbly with your God? **Micah 6:8**

"Thus says the Lord of hosts, Render true judgments, show kindness and mercy to one another." **Zechariah 7:9**

"But I say to you, Love your enemies and pray for those who persecute you." **Matthew 5:44**

"So whatever you wish that others would do to you, do also to them, for this is the Law and the Prophets." **Matthew 7:12**

"But love your enemies, and do good, and lend, expecting nothing in return, and your reward will be great." **Luke 6:35**

"Love one another with brotherly affection. Outdo one another in showing honor." **Romans 12:10**

"To the contrary, if your enemy is hungry, feed him; if he is thirsty, give him something to drink; for by so doing you will heap burning coals on his head." **Romans 12:20**

"Bear one another's burdens, and so fulfill the law of Christ." **Galatians 6:2**

"Be kind to one another, tenderhearted, forgiving one another, as God in Christ forgave you." **Ephesians 4:32**

"See that no one repays anyone evil for evil, but always seek to do good to one another and to everyone." **1 Thessalonians 5:15**

"Remind them to be submissive to rulers and authorities, to be obedient, to be ready for every good work, to speak evil of no one, to avoid quarreling, to be gentle, and to show perfect courtesy toward all people." **Titus 3:1-2**

"Do not neglect to show hospitality to strangers, for thereby some have entertained angels unawares." Kindness as a Fruit of the Spirit. **Hebrews 13:2**

Introduction

Service and kindness are powerful forces that not only transform the lives of those who receive them but also profoundly impact those who offer them. Engaging in acts of service and demonstrating kindness enriches our lives, strengthens our communities, and fosters a sense of connection and purpose. In a world that often feels divided, the simple acts of giving back and showing compassion can bridge gaps, heal wounds, and bring us closer to the true essence of a meaningful life.

In this chapter, we will explore the significance of service and kindness, the benefits of altruism, the impact of both small and large acts of kindness, and the importance of creating a legacy of compassion that resonates beyond our own lifetime. This chapter will also emphasize the transformative power of service and kindness, encouraging readers to incorporate these values into their daily lives as they pursue a meaningful existence.

Life Story

Maria had always been a busy professional, focused on her career in finance. She was successful, but something felt missing in her life. One Saturday afternoon, while walking through her neighbourhood, she saw an elderly man struggling to carry groceries up a flight of stairs. Without hesitation, she offered to help him. Grateful, the man thanked her, and Maria felt an unexpected sense of fulfillment. That small act of kindness sparked a change in her perspective.

After this encounter, Maria started volunteering at a local shelter every weekend. At first, she thought it would be a way to fill her free time, but soon it became one of the most meaningful parts of her life. Through service, she connected with people in ways her career never allowed. She formed bonds with individuals who were struggling, learning about their stories and offering her time to make their days a little easier.

What Maria discovered was that acts of kindness didn't just benefit the recipients—they transformed her. The joy and purpose she felt while helping others filled the void she had been experiencing. Service gave her a new sense of purpose and a deeper appreciation for the power of compassion.

Maria's story illustrates the profound impact that service and kindness can have on both the giver and the receiver. Small gestures of kindness, whether helping a neighbour or dedicating time to those in need, can change lives. By serving others, we find a deeper sense of fulfillment, and we remind ourselves of the shared humanity that connects us all.

Sayings about Service and Kindness

Consider these sayings about kindness.

"Sometimes it takes only one act of kindness and caring to change a person's life." – **Jackie Chan**

"Do things for people not because of who they are or what they do in return, but because of who you are." – **Harold S. Kushner**

"Carry out a random act of kindness, with no expectation of reward, safe in the knowledge that one day someone might do the same for you." – **Princess Diana**

"Because that's what kindness is. It's not doing something for someone else because they can't, but because you can." – **Andrew Iskander**

"Remember there's no such thing as a small act of kindness. Every act creates a ripple with no logical end." – **Scott Adams**

"Love and kindness are never wasted. They always make a difference. They bless the one who receives them, and they bless you, the giver." – **Barbara De Angelis**

"What wisdom can you find that is greater than kindness?" – **Jean-Jacques Rousseau**

"You can accomplish by kindness what you cannot by force." – **Pubilius Syrus**

"Kindness can become its own motive. We are made kind by being kind." – **Eric Hoffer**

"Human kindness has never weakened the stamina or softened the fiber of a free people. A nation does not have to be cruel to be tough." – **Franklin D. Roosevelt**

We can't help everyone, but everyone can help someone." – **Ronald Reagan**

"Kindness begins with the understanding that we all struggle." – **Charles Glassman**

"A single act of kindness throws out roots in all directions, and the roots spring up and make new trees." – **Amelia Earhart**

"Wherever there is a human being, there is an opportunity for a kindness." – **Lucius Annaeus Seneca**

"Unexpected kindness is the most powerful, least costly, and most underrated agent of human change." – **Bob Kerrey**

"Gratitude is the inward feeling of kindness received. Thankfulness is the natural impulse to express that feeling. Thanksgiving is the following of that impulse." – **Henry Van Dyke**

"Kindness is a passport that opens doors and fashions friends. It softens hearts and molds relationships that can last lifetimes." – **Joseph B. Wirthlin**

"A little thought and a little kindness are often worth more than a great deal of money." – **John Ruskin**

"The words of kindness are more healing to a drooping heart than balm or honey." – **Sarah Fielding**

"Constant kindness can accomplish much. As the sun makes ice melt, kindness causes misunderstanding, mistrust, and hostility to evaporate." – **Albert Schweitzer**

"Kindness is like snow- It beautifies everything it covers." – **Kahlil Gibran**

"Kindness in words creates confidence. Kindness in thinking creates profoundness. Kindness in giving creates love." – **Lao Tzu**

"Kindness is the sunshine in which virtue grows." – **Robert Green Ingersoll**

"Kindness is the language which the deaf can hear and the blind can see." – **Mark Twain**

"Kindness is more important than wisdom, and the recognition of this is the beginning of wisdom." – **Theodore Isaac Rubin**

"Kindness makes you the most beautiful person in the world, no matter what you look like." – **Anonymous**

"Kindness is always fashionable, and always welcome." – **Amelia Barr**

"Kindness and politeness are not overrated at all. They're underused." – **Tommy Lee Jones**

"I've been searching for ways to heal myself, and I've found that kindness is the best way." – **Lady Gaga**

"Three things in human life are important. The first is to be kind. The second is to be kind. And the third is to be kind." – **Henry James**

Source: https://www.ftd.com/blog/kindness-quotes

Let us remember that it may not be the season for figs, or grapes, or mangoes, but it's always the season for kindness.

Giving Back: The Benefits of Altruism

Altruism, the selfless concern for the well-being of others, lies at the heart of service and kindness. When we give back to others, whether through our time, resources, or talents, we experience a multitude of benefits that enhance our own lives and the lives of those around us.

Personal Fulfillment

Acts of altruism bring a deep sense of satisfaction and fulfillment. Knowing that we have made a positive difference in someone's life, no matter how small, fosters a feeling of purpose and contentment. This fulfillment often leads to greater happiness and a more meaningful life.

Emotional Well-being

Engaging in acts of service and kindness has been shown to reduce stress, anxiety, and depression. The act of helping others triggers the release of endorphins, often referred to as the "helper's high," which enhances our emotional well-being and overall happiness.

Strengthening Connections

Altruism helps to build and strengthen connections with others. When we give back, we create bonds of trust, empathy, and mutual respect, which are essential for strong relationships and a supportive community.

Creating a Positive Impact

The ripple effect of altruism is profound. One act of kindness can inspire others to do the same, creating a chain reaction of positivity and goodwill. By giving back, we contribute to a culture of compassion and generosity that benefits everyone.

Enhancing Personal Growth

Altruistic behaviour challenges us to look beyond our own needs and desires, fostering personal growth and maturity. It encourages us to develop qualities such as patience, empathy, and humility, which are essential for leading a meaningful life.

Acts of Kindness: Big and Small

Kindness comes in many forms, and every act, whether big or small, has the power to make a difference. From grand gestures to simple, everyday acts of kindness, each one contributes to a more compassionate and connected world.

Small Acts of Kindness

Often, it's the small, seemingly insignificant acts of kindness that have the most profound impact. A smile, a kind word, holding the door for someone, or offering a helping hand can brighten someone's day and remind him or her that he or she is not alone. These small acts create a ripple effect, encouraging others to pass on the kindness.

Random Acts of Kindness

Engaging in random acts of kindness, such as paying for someone's coffee, leaving a positive note for a stranger, or donating anonymously, can bring unexpected joy to others. These acts, done without the expectation of recognition or reward, reflect the true spirit of kindness and can uplift both the giver and the receiver.

Intentional Acts of Kindness

Intentional acts of kindness involve planning and making a conscious effort to help others. This could include volunteering at a shelter, mentoring a young person, or organizing a community event. These acts require time and effort, but the rewards are immeasurable both for those who give and those who receive.

Grand Gestures

While small acts of kindness are vital, there are times when grand gestures are called for. These might include starting a charitable organization, funding a scholarship, or dedicating a significant portion of your life to serving a cause. These grand gestures can have a lasting impact on individuals, communities, and even society as a whole.

Consistent Kindness

Kindness should not be limited to isolated incidents. Cultivating a habit of consistent kindness, where we make kindness a daily practice, can transform our lives and the lives of those around us. Consistent kindness fosters a positive environment and strengthens our relationships with others.

Creating a Legacy of Compassion

A meaningful life is often measured not by what we have accumulated but by what we have given. Creating a legacy of compassion ensures that the impact of our kindness and service endures beyond our own lifetime, influencing future generations and leaving the world a better place.

Mentorship and Guidance

One way to create a legacy of compassion is by mentoring and guiding others. By sharing our knowledge, experiences, and wisdom, we can empower others to lead lives of service and kindness. Mentorship creates a ripple effect, as those we mentor often go on to mentor others, perpetuating the cycle of compassion.

Charitable Contributions

Financial contributions to causes we care about can create a lasting impact. Whether it's supporting education, healthcare, environmental conservation, or social justice, our contributions can fund initiatives that continue to serve others long after we are gone.

Establishing Foundations or Trusts

Creating a foundation or trust dedicated to a cause you are passionate about ensures that your commitment to service and kindness continues. These entities can fund scholarships, support research, or provide grants to organizations that align with your values.

Inspiring Others Through Your Actions

Our actions often speak louder than words. By consistently demonstrating kindness and compassion in our daily lives, we inspire others to do the same. This inspiration can lead to a culture of compassion that endures long after we are no longer here.

Documenting Your Values and Beliefs

Writing about your values, beliefs, and the importance of kindness and service can also create a legacy. Whether through books, essays, or letters to loved ones, documenting your commitment to compassion can influence and guide others for generations to come.

Conclusion

Service and kindness are fundamental to leading a meaningful life. Through acts of altruism, whether small or large, we create connections, foster compassion, and contribute to a more just and caring world. The benefits of service and kindness extend beyond the immediate impact—they enrich our lives, strengthen our communities, and create a legacy that endures.

As you continue your journey, remember that every act of kindness, no matter how small, has the power to make a difference. By giving back, serving others, and creating a legacy of compassion, you contribute to a world where kindness is the norm and where every life is touched by the power of love and service.

Exercise

Practicing Service and Kindness

Performing this exercise will help you reflect on how acts of service and kindness can transform your life and the lives of others. By engaging in thoughtful actions that contribute to the well-being of others, you can strengthen your sense of purpose and connection.

Step 1: Reflect on Acts of Kindness in Your Life

Take a few minutes to reflect on moments when you've received or given kindness, and how these moments made you feel. Write down your thoughts on the following:

- **What are some significant acts of kindness I've experienced from others?** How did those actions impact me?
- **When have I offered kindness or service to someone?** How did it make me feel afterward?
- **What role does kindness play in my daily interactions with others?**

Step 2: Identify Opportunities for Service

There are countless ways to serve others, both big and small. Consider the various communities you are part of and identify opportunities where you can offer service. Reflect on these questions:

- **What needs do I see in my community, workplace, or family?**
- **How can I offer my skills, time, or resources to address those needs?**

- **What areas of service align with my passions or values?**

Write down a list of 3–5 service opportunities that you can realistically engage with over the next month. These could range from volunteering for a local charity to helping a neighbour with errands or simply offering emotional support to a friend.

Step 3: Perform a Random Act of Kindness

This week, make it a point to perform a random act of kindness for someone without expecting anything in return. Choose one of the following, or come up with your own:

1. **Compliment a stranger:** Share a kind word with someone, whether it's about his/her appearance, attitude, or actions.
2. **Buy someone a coffee or meal:** Pay for a coffee for the person behind you in line or treat a friend to a surprise meal.
3. **Write a note of appreciation:** Send a handwritten note or thoughtful message to someone who has positively impacted your life.
4. **Help someone with a task:** Whether it's offering to carry groceries, help with a chore, or give someone a ride, find a way to assist someone in his/her day-to-day activities.

After completing the act of kindness, reflect on the experience:

- **How did the other person respond?**
- **How did this act of kindness make me feel?**

- **What impact did this action have on my sense of connection to others?**

Step 4: Dedicate Time to Ongoing Service

Kindness and service are not just one-time actions; they can become a part of your daily life. Set a goal to commit to ongoing service in a way that feels meaningful to you. Some examples include:

- **Volunteer regularly:** Find a local organization or cause where you can volunteer your time each month.
- **Mentor someone:** Offer guidance, support, or expertise to someone who could benefit from your experience.
- **Participate in a community project:** Whether it's cleaning up a park or organizing a charity event, get involved in projects that serve the greater good.
- **Help a family member or friend in need:** Provide emotional or practical support to someone in your inner circle who is going through a tough time.

Reflect on how this commitment to service affects both your own life and the lives of those you help. Consider:

- **What am I learning about myself through serving others?**
- **How does regular service deepen my relationships with my community?**

Step 5: Practice Daily Kindness

Kindness is not just about large gestures—it's also about small, daily interactions that uplift those around us. This week, make it a point to incorporate daily acts of kindness into your routine. Some ideas include:

- **Smile and greet people:** A warm smile or friendly greeting can brighten someone's day.
- **Listen with empathy:** In your next conversation, practice active listening without interrupting or offering unsolicited advice.
- **Offer words of encouragement:** Compliment someone's efforts or achievements, no matter how small.
- **Be patient and compassionate:** Practice patience and show compassion, even in challenging situations or with difficult people.

At the end of the week, reflect on how these daily acts of kindness impacted both you and those around you:

- **How did showing kindness shift my mood or outlook?**
- **How did others respond to my kindness?**
- **What changes did I notice in my relationships and interactions?**

Step 6: Develop a Personal Service Plan

To make service a core part of your life, create a personal plan for how you will continue to integrate kindness and service into your daily routine. Write down:

- **A cause or community you will regularly serve:** Identify a long-term service opportunity that you feel passionate about.
- **Three specific acts of kindness** you will commit to practicing daily or weekly.

- **A goal for how you want to grow in your service:** Whether it's deepening your empathy, offering more time, or expanding your reach, set a goal for growth.

Check in with yourself each month to review your progress and adjust your plan as needed.

Step 7: Reflect on the Ripple Effect of Kindness

Finally, take a moment to reflect on the broader impact of your actions. Consider how small acts of service and kindness can create a ripple effect, influencing others to pay it forward. Answer these questions:

- **How have my acts of kindness inspired others?**
- **What impact can kindness and service have on the wider community or society?**
- **How can I encourage others to embrace kindness and service in their own lives?**

By actively engaging in service and practicing kindness, you contribute to a more compassionate world. Through this chapter's exercise, you've taken the first steps toward making service a central part of your life, and the rewards will ripple far beyond what you can imagine.

THE JOURNEY TO A FULFILLING AND MEANINGFUL LIFE

CHAPTER 9
WORDSEARCH

	1	2	3	4	5	6	7	8	9	10	11	12	13	14
1	U	T	S	U	S	O	W	B	R	R	A	J	D	F
2	S	D	N	S	P	B	D	A	Y	A	L	L	H	U
3	T	O	N	E	V	P	H	T	I	B	T	E	H	Y
4	U	S	S	O	M	I	I	M	Y	D	R	G	C	T
5	C	H	U	P	I	L	V	Y	C	N	U	A	S	I
6	L	H	V	R	I	S	L	X	T	B	I	C	E	S
7	J	L	A	M	T	H	S	I	Q	A	S	Y	R	O
8	V	D	U	R	Q	V	I	E	F	A	M	T	V	R
9	O	H	U	N	I	Q	I	H	R	L	E	B	I	E
10	A	R	J	R	A	T	L	M	P	P	U	N	C	N
11	S	M	I	L	E	G	A	I	L	T	E	F	E	E
12	D	U	K	Q	W	J	V	B	Z	A	D	D	T	G
13	I	N	J	Z	J	S	A	T	L	B	P	M	C	H
14	K	I	N	D	N	E	S	S	E	E	E	V	T	R

ALTRUISM	GENEROSITY	SERVICE
CHARITABLE	HUMILITY	SMILE
DEPRESSION	KINDNESS	TRUST
FULFILLMENT	LEGACY	

THE ROLE OF SERVICE AND KINDNESS

ANSWER

	1	2	3	4	5	6	7	8	9	10	11	12	13	14
1	U	T	S	U	S	O	W	B	R	R	A	J	D	F
2	S	D	N	S	P	B	D	A	Y	A	L	L	H	U
3	T	O	N	E	V	P	H	T	I	B	T	E	H	Y
4	U	S	S	O	M	I	I	M	Y	D	R	G	C	T
5	C	H	U	P	I	L	V	Y	C	N	U	A	S	I
6	L	H	V	R	I	S	L	X	T	B	I	C	E	S
7	J	L	A	M	T	H	S	I	Q	A	S	Y	R	O
8	V	D	U	R	Q	V	I	E	F	A	M	T	V	R
9	O	H	U	N	I	Q	I	H	R	L	E	B	I	E
10	A	R	J	R	A	T	L	M	P	P	U	N	C	N
11	S	M	I	L	E	G	A	I	L	T	E	F	E	E
12	D	U	K	Q	W	J	V	B	Z	A	D	D	T	G
13	I	N	J	Z	J	S	A	T	L	B	P	M	C	H
14	K	I	N	D	N	E	S	S	E	E	E	V	T	R

ALTRUISM 1:11   GENEROSITY 12:14   SERVICE 5:13
CHARITABLE 5:1   HUMILITY 9:2   SMILE 11:1
DEPRESSION 12:12   KINDNESS 14:1   TRUST 7:5
FULFILLMENT 11:12   LEGACY 2:12

THE JOURNEY TO A FULFILLING AND MEANINGFUL LIFE

PART IV
FINDING PURPOSE AND FULFILLMENT

CHAPTER 10
DISCOVERING YOUR LIFE'S PURPOSE

Find your life's purpose and live it.

The Bible Says

"For I know the plans I have for you," says the LORD. "They are plans for good and not for disaster, to give you a future and a hope." **Jeremiah 29:11**

"Seek the Kingdom of God above all else, and live righteously, and he will give you everything you need." **Matthew 6:33**

"For we are God's masterpiece. He has created us anew in Christ Jesus, so we can do the good things he planned for us long ago." **Ephesians 2:10**

"You can make many plans, but the LORD's purpose will prevail." **Proverbs 19:21**

"The LORD will work out his plans for my life – for your faithful love, O LORD, endures forever. Don't abandon me, for you made me." **Psalm 138:8**

"And we know that God causes everything to work together for the good of those who love God and are called according to his purpose for them." **Romans 8:28**

"We can make our plans, but the LORD determines our steps." **Proverbs 16:9**

"I cry out to God Most High, to God who will fulfill his purpose for me." **Psalm 57:2**

"Bring all who claim me as their God, for I have made them for my glory. It was I who created them." **Isaiah 43:7**

"Just as our bodies have many parts and each part has a special function, so it is with Christ's body. We are many parts of one body, and we all belong to each other. In his grace, God has given us different gifts for doing certain things well." **Romans 12:4-6a**

"For God saved us and called us to live a holy life. He did this, not because we deserved it, but because that was his plan from before the beginning of time—to show us his grace through Christ Jesus." **2 Timothy 1:9**

"Furthermore, because we are united with Christ, we have received an inheritance from God, for he chose us in advance, and he makes everything work out according to his plan." **Ephesians 1:11**

"For through him God created everything in the heavenly realms and on earth. He made the things we can see and the things we can't see—such as thrones, kingdoms,

rulers, and authorities in the unseen world. Everything was created through him and for him." **Colossians 1:16**

"For God is working in you, giving you the desire and the power to do what pleases him." **Philippians 2:13**

"Trust in the LORD with all your heart; do not depend on your own understanding. Seek his will in all you do, and he will show you which path to take." **Proverbs 3:5-6**

"You will show me the way of life, granting me the joy of your presence and the pleasures of living with you forever." **Psalm 16:11**

"But you are not like that, for you are a chosen people. You are royal priests, a holy nation, God's very own possession. As a result, you can show others the goodness of God, for he called you out of the darkness into his wonderful light." **1 Peter 2:9**

"Take delight in the LORD, and he will give you your heart's desires." **Psalm 37:4**

"God saved you by his grace when you believed. And you can't take credit for this; it is a gift from God. Salvation is not a reward for the good things we have done, so none of us can boast about it. For we are God's masterpiece. He has created us anew in Christ Jesus, so we can do the good things he planned for us long ago." **Ephesians 2:8-10**

"All Scripture is inspired by God and is useful to teach us what is true and to make us realize what is wrong in our lives. It corrects us when we are wrong and teaches us to do what is right. God uses it to prepare and equip his people to do every good work." **2 Timothy 3:16-17**

"And so, dear brothers and sisters, I plead with you to give your bodies to God because of all he has done for you. Let them be a living and holy sacrifice—the kind he will find acceptable. This is truly the way to worship him. Don't copy the behavior and customs of this world, but let God transform you into a new person by changing the way you think. Then you will learn to know God's will for you, which is good and pleasing and perfect." **Romans 12:1-2**

"So, my dear brothers and sisters, be strong and immovable. Always work enthusiastically for the Lord, for you know that nothing you do for the Lord is ever useless." **1 Corinthians 15:58**

"Work willingly at whatever you do, as though you were working for the Lord rather than for people. Remember that the Lord will give you an inheritance as your reward, and that the Master you are serving is Christ." **Colossians 3:23-24**

"In the same way, let your good deeds shine out for all to see, so that everyone will praise your heavenly Father." **Matthew 5:16**

"But you will receive power when the Holy Spirit comes upon you. And you will be my witnesses, telling people about me everywhere—in Jerusalem, throughout Judea, in Samaria, and to the ends of the earth." **Acts 1:8**

"So let's not get tired of doing what is good. At just the right time we will reap a harvest of blessing if we don't give up." **Galatians 6:9**

"God has given each of you a gift from his great variety of spiritual gifts. Use them well to serve one another." **1 Peter 4:10**

"But don't just listen to God's word. You must do what it says. Otherwise, you are only fooling yourselves." **James 1:22**

"So whether you eat or drink, or whatever you do, do it all for the glory of God." **1 Corinthians 10:31**

"Therefore, go and make disciples of all the nations, baptizing them in the name of the Father and the Son and the Holy Spirit. Teach these new disciples to obey all the commands I have given you. And be sure of this: I am with you always, even to the end of the age." **Matthew 28:19-20**

"Commit your actions to the LORD, and your plans will succeed." **Proverbs 16:3**

Introduction

The journey to discovering your life's purpose is one of the most significant and transformative experiences you can undertake. Purpose acts as a compass, guiding you through the complexities of life and helping you navigate challenges with clarity and conviction. It provides a sense of direction, anchoring you in something greater than yourself, and giving your life meaning beyond the day-to-day routines. However, finding your purpose is not a simple task; it requires deep introspection, courage to face the unknown, and a commitment to live authentically.

This chapter will delve into the profound quest for meaning, explore how aligning your life with your values is essential for living purposefully, and emphasize the importance of pursuing your passions as a pathway to discovering and fulfilling your purpose. By the end of this chapter, you will be equipped with insights and strategies to embark on or deepen your journey toward a more purposeful life.

Life Story

Ted had spent most of his adult life working as an engineer. He was good at his job, earned a comfortable salary, and had the respect of his colleagues. Yet, despite his achievements, something didn't feel right. He often woke up with a nagging sense that there was more to life than what he was doing. His job paid the bills, but it didn't ignite his passion.

One summer, Ted took a trip to a rural village on a volunteer mission to help build schools. During his time there, he worked alongside local teachers and students, learning about their struggles and dreams. The experience touched him deeply. Watching the children's faces light up as they entered a classroom gave him a sense of fulfillment he had never felt in his engineering career.

After returning home, Ted couldn't shake the feeling that his true purpose lay elsewhere. He started reflecting on what truly brought him joy and fulfillment, and eventually, he made a bold decision. Ted left his engineering career to become a teacher. It wasn't easy at first—he had to go back to school and make significant life changes—but for the first time, he felt aligned with his purpose.

In the classroom, Ted found meaning in helping young minds grow. Every day, he saw the impact he was making, not just on his students' academic skills but on their confidence and dreams for the future. He had discovered that his purpose was to inspire and uplift others through education.

Ted's journey shows that discovering your life's purpose can be a gradual, transformative process. It often requires deep self-reflection, a willingness to step out of your comfort zone, and the courage to follow your passion. When we find and live our purpose, life becomes more meaningful and fulfilling, no matter the challenges we face along the way.

Sayings about Discovering Your Life's Purpose

The following quotes will help you discover your life's purpose.

"It's not enough to have lived. We should be determined to live for something." — **Winston S. Churchill**

"People take different roads seeking fulfillment and happiness. Just because they're not on your road doesn't mean they've gotten lost." — **Dalai Lama**

"The soul which has no fixed purpose in life is lost; to be everywhere, is to be nowhere." — **Michel de Montaigne**

"If you can tune into your purpose and really align with it, setting goals so that your vision is an expression of that purpose, then life flows much more easily." — **Jack Canfield**

"The person without a purpose is like a ship without a rudder." — **Thomas Carlyle**

"The best way to lengthen out our days is to walk steadily and with a purpose." — **Charles Dickens**

"Life is never made unbearable by circumstances, but only by lack of meaning and purpose." — **Viktor Frankl**

DISCOVERING YOUR LIFE'S PURPOSE

"If you can't figure out your purpose, figure out your passion. For your passion will lead you right into your purpose." — **Bishop T.D. Jakes**

"The purpose of life is a life of purpose" — **Robert Byrne**

"The secret of success is constancy to purpose" — **Benjamin Disraeli**

"Appreciate where you are in your journey, even if it's not where you want to be. Every season serves a purpose." — **Unknown**

"Believe in your heart that you're meant to live a life full of passion, purpose, magic, and miracles." — **Roy T. Bennett**

"The purpose of life is not to be happy. It is to be useful, to be honorable, to be compassionate, to have it make some difference that you have lived and lived well." — **Ralph Waldo Emerson**

"If you have a strong purpose in life, you don't have to be pushed. Your passion will drive you there." — **Roy T. Bennett**

"Your purpose in life is to find your purpose and give your whole heart and soul to it" — **Buddha**

"I want to live my life in such a way that when I get out of bed in the morning, the devil says, "aw shit, he's up!" — **Steve Maraboli**

"Nothing is more creative... nor destructive... than a brilliant mind with a purpose." — **Dan Brown**

"Be a lamp, or a lifeboat, or a ladder. Help someone's soul heal. Walk out of your house like a shepherd." — **Rumi**

"The greatest thing in this world is not so much where we stand as in what direction we are moving." — **Johann Wolfgang von Goethe**

"The purpose of life is not to be happy—but to matter, to be productive, to be useful, to have it make some difference that you lived at all." — **Leo Rosten**

"He who has a why to live can bear almost any how." — **Nietzsche**

Source: https://www.jordantarver.com/purpose-quotes

The Quest for Meaning and Direction

The quest for meaning is a universal human experience, one that has driven philosophers, theologians, and ordinary people alike to explore the deeper aspects of existence. This search often begins with a sense of restlessness or dissatisfaction, where the routines of daily life no longer seem to fulfill or satisfy the deeper longings of the heart. You might find yourself asking questions like, "What is my purpose?" or "Is there more to life than this?" These questions can be both daunting and liberating, as they open the door to new possibilities and paths that you may not have considered before.

The quest for meaning requires a willingness to step back and examine your life from a broader perspective. It involves looking beyond the surface of your daily experiences and reflecting on the underlying themes and patterns that have shaped your journey so far. This process of introspection allows you to identify what truly matters to you, what brings you joy, and what gives your life a sense of purpose.

In your quest, it's important to acknowledge that meaning is not a one-size-fits-all concept. What gives one person a sense of purpose might not resonate with another. This journey is highly personal and unique to each individual. Moreover, your sense of purpose may evolve over time as you grow, learn, and experience new aspects of life. The key is to remain open to this evolution and to embrace the changes that come with it.

This journey also often involves facing and overcoming obstacles. These can be external, such as societal expectations or financial constraints, or internal, like fear, self-doubt, or past traumas. Recognizing and addressing these challenges is a crucial part of the process, as they can either block or propel you toward your true purpose. It's through overcoming these barriers that you build resilience and gain a deeper understanding of yourself.

Ultimately, the quest for meaning is not just about finding answers but also about asking the right questions. It's about exploring your beliefs, desires, and motivations to uncover the deeper truths that lie within you. This exploration is ongoing, and while you may not find all the answers right away, the journey itself is an integral part of discovering your life's purpose.

Aligning Your Life with Your Values

Once you have begun to explore the deeper questions of meaning, the next crucial step is to align your life with your core values. Values are the principles and beliefs that serve as the foundation for your decisions, actions, and behaviours. They are the standards by which you measure your success, happiness, and fulfillment. Living a life aligned with your values is essential for achieving a sense of purpose because it ensures that you are being true to yourself and your deepest convictions.

Identifying your core values requires careful reflection and honesty. It involves examining your past experiences, both positive and negative, and recognizing the common threads that connect them. What were the moments in your life when you felt most fulfilled? What principles guided your decisions during those times? Conversely, when have you felt disconnected or dissatisfied, and what values were being compromised in those situations? Answering these questions can help you clarify your values and understand what truly matters to you.

Aligning your life with your values is not always easy. There may be times when your values conflict with external expectations or pressures. For example, you might value family time but feel compelled to work long hours because of job demands. Or you might value honesty but find yourself in situations where telling the truth could have negative consequences. In these instances, it's important to stay grounded in your values and make decisions that are consistent with your beliefs, even if they are difficult.

One of the most powerful ways to align your life with your values is by setting clear, value-driven goals. These goals should reflect what you want to achieve in various areas of your life, such as your career, relationships, health, and personal growth. By setting goals that are aligned with your values, you ensure that your actions and efforts are directed toward what truly matters to you, rather than being driven by external pressures or societal expectations.

Additionally, aligning your life with your values involves making intentional choices about how you spend your time, energy, and resources. It means prioritizing activities and relationships that support your values and letting go of those that don't. This may require making difficult decisions, such as leaving a job that doesn't align with your values or ending a relationship that isn't supportive of your goals. However, these choices are necessary to create a life that is authentic and aligned with your purpose.

Living in alignment with your values also requires ongoing self-awareness and reflection. As you grow and evolve, your values may shift, and it's important to regularly check in with yourself to ensure that your life continues to reflect what matters most to you. This alignment is a dynamic process, and it requires a commitment to living consciously and intentionally.

Pursuing Passion and Purpose

Passion is the lifeblood of purpose. It's what ignites your spirit, energizes your actions, and fuels your determination to pursue your goals, even in the face of challenges. Discovering and nurturing your passions is a key component of living a purposeful life because it connects you with the activities, people, and causes that bring you the greatest joy and fulfillment.

To pursue passion and purpose, it's essential to first identify what you are passionate about. This may involve exploring new interests, revisiting hobbies or activities you enjoyed in the past, or simply paying attention to what excites and motivates you in your daily life. Your passions may be related to your career, creative pursuits, relationships, or personal development. The important thing is to recognize that passion is not just about what you enjoy doing but also about what you are willing to invest time, effort, and energy into because it aligns with your sense of purpose.

Once you have identified your passions, the next step is to integrate them into your life in meaningful ways. This might mean pursuing a career that aligns with your passions, dedicating time to hobbies or volunteer work that you find fulfilling, or surrounding yourself with people who share your interests and values. The goal is to create a life that is rich with opportunities to engage in activities that bring you joy and satisfaction.

However, pursuing passion and purpose is not without its challenges. There may be obstacles that stand in the way, such as financial constraints, time limitations, or fear of failure. It's important to acknowledge these challenges and develop strategies to overcome them. This might involve seeking support from others, setting realistic goals, and being willing to take risks and step outside your comfort zone.

Moreover, pursuing your passions requires perseverance and resilience. There may be times when you encounter setbacks or feel discouraged, but it's important to stay committed to your purpose and keep moving forward. Remember that the journey toward a purposeful life is not always linear; there will be ups and downs, successes and failures. The key is to stay focused on your long-term vision and continue to take steps toward your goals, even when the path is difficult.

In addition to personal fulfillment, pursuing passion and purpose can also have a positive impact on others.

When you are passionate about something, it often inspires and motivates those around you. Your enthusiasm can be contagious, and your commitment to your purpose can serve as a powerful example for others to follow. In this way, pursuing your passions not only enriches your own life but also contributes to the greater good.

Conclusion

The journey to discovering your life's purpose is a deeply personal and transformative process that involves introspection, alignment with your values, and the pursuit of your passions. It is a journey that requires courage, commitment, and a willingness to explore the depths of your soul to uncover what truly matters to you.

As you continue on this journey, remember that discovering your purpose is not a destination but an ongoing process of growth and self-discovery. Your purpose may evolve over time as you experience new challenges, learn new things, and gain new perspectives. The key is to remain open to this evolution and to continue aligning your life with your values and passions.

Living a purpose-driven life brings a deep sense of fulfillment and meaning, as it allows you to live authentically and in alignment with your true self. It empowers you to make choices that are consistent with your beliefs, pursue goals that reflect your passions, and contribute to the world in ways that are meaningful to you.

Ultimately, discovering your life's purpose is about embracing who you are and what you are called to do. It's about creating a life that is rich with meaning, joy, and fulfillment. And as you walk this path, you will find that living with purpose not only enriches your own life but also leaves a lasting impact on the lives of others.

Exercise

Uncovering and Living Your Life's Purpose

At the end of Chapter 10, *Discovering Your Life's Purpose*, this exercise will help you reflect on your passions, values, and strengths, guiding you to gain deeper clarity about your purpose. By engaging in self-exploration and practical actions, you can move closer to living a purpose-driven life.

Step 1: Reflect on Past Experiences

Your life's purpose is often shaped by key moments from your past. Reflect on your personal journey and answer the following questions:

- **What have been some of the most meaningful experiences in my life?** What did I learn from them?
- **When have I felt most fulfilled or alive?** What was I doing at the time?
- **What challenges have I overcome, and how have they shaped my sense of purpose?**

Write down a few significant moments or experiences that stand out to you, and note any recurring themes.

Step 2: Identify Your Strengths and Passions

Understanding what you're good at and what excites you can help point you toward your purpose. Take time to answer the following questions:

- **What are my natural strengths and talents?** (Think about feedback you've received from others or accomplishments you're proud of.)

- **What activities or pursuits bring me joy and fulfillment?**
- **If I could spend my time doing anything, what would it be?**

Make a list of your top strengths and passions. Then, consider how these might align with potential paths or purposes in your life.

Step 3: Clarify Your Core Values

Your purpose is often rooted in your values—what you believe is most important in life. Reflect on the following:

- **What values guide my decisions and actions?** (Examples include integrity, compassion, creativity, or personal growth.)
- **What issues or causes do I feel most passionate about?**
- **How do I want to contribute to the world, my community, or my family?**

Write down 3–5 core values that resonate with you. Think about how these values influence the way you live your life and how they might guide your sense of purpose.

Step 4: Envision Your Ideal Life

Purpose is closely tied to the life you envision for yourself. To gain clarity, take a moment to imagine your ideal future:

- **What would my life look like if I were living fully in alignment with my purpose?**
- **How would I spend my days?** Who would I spend them with? What would I be contributing to the world?

- **How would I feel in this ideal life?** (Fulfilled, peaceful, energized, etc.)

Take a few minutes to write a detailed vision of what your life would look like if you were living according to your highest purpose.

Step 5: Create a Personal Mission Statement

Based on the reflections in Steps 1–4, create a personal mission statement. This should be a concise statement that captures your sense of purpose and guides your actions moving forward. Consider using this format:

- **I am committed to [action or contribution]**, using my strengths in [specific talents or abilities] to [impact or difference you want to make in the world], aligned with my values of [list your core values].

For example:

> "I am committed to empowering others through education, using my strengths in communication and creativity to make a positive impact on future generations, aligned with my values of compassion, integrity, and growth."

Step 6: Take Action Toward Your Purpose

Having clarity about your purpose is only the first step. Now, it's time to take action. Answer the following questions to identify ways to actively pursue your purpose:

- **What actions or steps can I take to begin living in alignment with my purpose?** (Consider both small, daily actions and larger, long-term goals.)

- **What obstacles might get in the way, and how can I overcome them?**
- **Who can support me in my journey toward fulfilling my purpose?** (Think about mentors, friends, or family members who can encourage you or provide guidance.)

Make a list of 3–5 concrete steps you can take in the next month to move closer to living your purpose. These steps could be anything from starting a new project, learning a new skill, or dedicating time to a cause you care about.

Step 7: Re-evaluate and Adjust Your Path

Purpose is not a static thing—it evolves as you grow and change. Set aside time to regularly reflect on your progress and realign with your purpose as needed. At the end of each month, ask yourself:

- **Am I living in alignment with my purpose?**
- **What new insights or experiences have shaped my sense of purpose?**
- **What adjustments do I need to make to stay on the path of living a meaningful life?**

By regularly re-evaluating your path, you ensure that you stay flexible and open to new opportunities while remaining rooted in your deeper sense of purpose.

Step 8: Reflect on Your Growth

Finally, take a moment to reflect on how your sense of purpose has already impacted your life. Consider the following:

- **How has identifying my purpose changed the way I approach my daily life?**
- **What positive changes or growth have I experienced since I began this journey?**
- **How can I continue to nurture and deepen my sense of purpose moving forward?**

Purpose is an ongoing journey, not a destination. Keep exploring, reflecting, and growing as you continue along your path to a meaningful life.

CHAPTER 10
WORDSEARCH

	1	2	3	4	5	6	7	8	9	10	11	12	13	14	15	16	17
1	I	N	T	R	O	S	P	E	C	T	I	O	N	I	I	T	C
2	T	R	Y	R	C	R	E	F	L	E	C	T	I	O	N	P	S
3	R	R	L	W	T	O	M	M	R	I	P	Z	M	V	L	E	W
4	I	N	A	N	I	Q	M	R	M	A	L	G	E	T	O	R	F
5	M	W	O	N	B	Q	V	M	S	C	C	E	A	E	J	S	E
6	Y	E	L	L	S	H	Q	S	I	O	D	W	N	H	U	E	S
7	L	A	K	T	Q	F	I	S	N	T	I	Q	I	V	F	V	L
8	K	K	P	N	J	O	O	V	Q	Y	M	O	N	T	E	E	A
9	H	F	U	F	N	U	I	R	N	N	P	E	G	L	A	R	O
10	D	D	R	N	G	C	F	K	M	G	E	K	N	A	R	A	G
11	D	K	C	S	T	E	V	A	J	A	B	J	Z	T	Y	N	N
12	U	M	O	I	K	C	K	W	B	G	T	N	R	T	K	C	G
13	W	M	O	G	N	C	U	A	R	D	P	I	S	X	A	E	C
14	Y	N	S	T	A	N	D	A	R	D	S	E	V	M	Q	W	U
15	K	M	E	S	O	P	R	U	P	Z	N	Z	C	E	C	I	G
16	R	Z	B	P	Q	X	N	H	Y	O	V	J	F	Q	K	J	S
17	O	L	E	S	O	Z	Z	T	H	K	W	B	D	C	A	P	O

COMMITMENT INTROSPECTION REFLECTION
CONVICTION MEANING STANDARDS
FEAR PASSION TRANSFORMATIVE
GOALS PERSEVERANCE
HONESTY PURPOSE

DISCOVERING YOUR LIFE'S PURPOSE

ANSWER

	1	2	3	4	5	6	7	8	9	10	11	12	13	14	15	16	17
1	I	N	T	R	O	S	P	E	C	T	I	O	N	I	I	T	C
2	T	R	Y	R	C	R	E	F	L	E	C	T	I	O	N	P	S
3	R	R	L	W	T	O	M	M	R	I	P	Z	M	V	L	E	W
4	I	N	A	N	I	Q	M	R	M	A	L	G	E	T	O	R	F
5	M	W	O	N	B	Q	V	M	S	C	C	E	A	E	J	S	E
6	Y	E	L	L	S	H	Q	S	I	O	D	W	N	H	U	E	S
7	L	A	K	T	Q	F	I	S	N	T	I	Q	I	V	F	V	L
8	K	K	P	N	J	O	O	V	Q	Y	M	O	N	T	E	E	A
9	H	F	U	F	N	U	I	R	N	N	P	E	G	L	A	R	O
10	D	D	R	N	G	C	F	K	M	G	E	K	N	A	R	A	G
11	D	K	C	S	T	E	V	A	J	A	B	J	Z	T	Y	N	N
12	U	M	O	I	K	C	K	W	B	G	T	N	R	T	K	C	G
13	W	M	O	G	N	C	U	A	R	D	P	I	S	X	A	E	C
14	Y	N	S	T	A	N	D	A	R	D	S	E	V	M	Q	W	U
15	K	M	E	S	O	P	R	U	P	Z	N	Z	C	E	C	I	G
16	R	Z	B	P	Q	X	N	H	Y	O	V	J	F	Q	K	J	S
17	O	L	E	S	O	Z	Z	T	H	K	W	B	D	C	A	P	O

COMMITMENT 2:5 INTROSPECTION 1:1 REFLECTION 2:6
CONVICTION 5:11 MEANING 3:13 STANDARDS 14:3
FEAR 7:15 PASSION 3:11 TRANSFORMATIVE 2:1
GOALS 10:17 PERSEVERANCE 2:16
HONESTY 17:9 PURPOSE 15:9

CHAPTER 11
SETTING AND ACHIEVING GOALS

Goals give structure and direction to your efforts, transforming dreams and aspirations into actionable plans.

The Bible Says

"Except the Lord build the house, they labor in vain that build it: except the Lord keep the city, the watchman waketh but in vain." **Psalms 127:1**

"Trust in the Lord with all thine heart; and lean not unto thine own understanding. In all thy ways acknowledge him, and he shall direct thy paths." **Proverbs 3:5-6**

"There are many devices in a man's heart; nevertheless, the counsel of the Lord, that shall stand." **Proverbs 19:21**

"Without counsel purposes are disappointed: but in the multitude of counsellors they are established." **Proverbs 15:22**

"Where there is no vision, the people perish: but he that keepeth the law, happy is he." **Proverbs 29:18**

"Finally, brethren, whatsoever things are true, whatsoever things are honest, whatsoever things are just, whatsoever things are pure, whatsoever things are lovely, whatsoever things are of good report; if there be any virtue, and if there be any praise, think on these things." **Philippians 4:8**

"Whether therefore ye eat, or drink, or whatsoever ye do, do all to the glory of God." **1 Corinthians 10:31**

"Delight thyself also in the Lord: and he shall give thee the desires of thine heart. Commit thy way unto the Lord; trust also in him; and he shall bring it to pass." **Psalms 37:4**

"Commit thy works unto the Lord, and thy thoughts shall be established." **Proverbs 16:3**

"For I know the thoughts that I think toward you, saith the Lord, thoughts of peace, and not of evil, to give you an expected end." **Jeremiah 29:11**

"And Jesus said unto them, Because of your unbelief: for verily I say unto you, if ye have faith as a grain of mustard seed, ye shall say unto this mountain, remove hence to yonder place; and it shall remove; and nothing shall be impossible unto you." **Matthew 17:20**

"But seek ye first the kingdom of God, and his righteousness; and all these things shall be added unto

you. Take therefore no thought for the morrow: for the morrow shall take thought for the things of itself. Sufficient unto the day is the evil thereof." **Matthew 6:33-34**

"Lay not up for yourselves treasures upon earth, where moth and rust doth corrupt, and where thieves break through and steal: But lay up for yourselves treasures in heaven, where neither moth nor rust doth corrupt, and where thieves do not break through nor steal: For where your treasure is, there will your heart be also." **Matthew 6:19-21**

"Go to now, ye that say, Today or tomorrow we will go into such a city, and continue there a year, and buy and sell, and get gain: Whereas ye know not what shall be on the morrow. For what is your life? It is even a vapor, that appeared for a little time, and then vanished away. For that ye ought to say, If the Lord will, we shall live, and do this, or that" **James 4:13-15**

"Labour not for the meat which perished, but for that meat which endured unto everlasting life, which the Son of man shall give unto you: for him hath God the Father sealed. **John 6:27**

"And be not conformed to this world: but be ye transformed by the renewing of your mind, that ye may prove what is that good, and acceptable, and perfect, will of God." **Romans 12:2**

"A man's heart deviseth his way: but the Lord directeth his steps." **Proverbs 16:9**

"For which of you, intending to build a tower, sitteth not down first, and counteth the cost, whether he have sufficient to finish it?" **Luke 14:28**

"I can do all things through Christ which strengtheneth me." **Philippians 4:13**

Introduction

Setting and achieving goals is a fundamental aspect of living a purposeful and fulfilling life. Goals give structure and direction to your efforts, transforming dreams and aspirations into actionable plans. Whether you're striving to improve your personal life, advance your career, or make a difference in the world, goals serve as a roadmap that guides you toward your desired outcomes. However, the process of setting and achieving goals is not always straightforward. It requires careful planning, persistence, and the ability to overcome obstacles along the way.

This chapter will explore the science behind effective goal setting, strategies for overcoming common challenges such as procrastination and self-doubt, and the importance of celebrating milestones and successes. By the end of this chapter, you will have a deeper understanding of how to set meaningful goals and the tools to achieve them, empowering you to turn your aspirations into reality.

Life Story

Sheila had always been a dreamer. Since childhood, she envisioned herself becoming a published author, but as the years passed, her dream seemed to slip away. Life got busy—between her career as a marketing executive and raising two children, writing always took a backseat. Still, the desire to write lingered, and she knew she had to take action or the dream would remain just that—a dream.

One day, Sheila sat down and made a commitment to herself. She decided that no matter how hectic her life became, she would carve out time to write. She set a concrete goal: finish the first draft of her novel within a year. To achieve this, she broke the goal into smaller, manageable steps—writing 500 words a day, setting aside an hour each evening, and using weekends to catch up if she fell behind.

At first, it was challenging to stay disciplined. Some nights she was exhausted after work, and the words didn't come easily. But Sheila stayed focused, tracking her progress and celebrating each milestone, no matter how small. Over time, her daily writing routine became second nature, and the pages began to pile up.

After a year of persistence and dedication, Sheila finished her first draft. It was an emotional moment, one she had waited for her entire life. She realized that setting clear, achievable goals and staying committed to them had transformed her dream into a reality.

Sheila's story demonstrates the power of setting specific goals and working toward them with consistent effort. Achieving our goals doesn't happen overnight—it requires planning, discipline, and perseverance. But by breaking down big dreams into smaller steps and sticking to the plan, we can accomplish things we once thought impossible.

Sayings about Setting and Achieving Goals

"If you want to live a happy life, tie it to a goal, not to people or things." — **Albert Einstein**

"Begin with the end in mind." — **Stephen Covey**

"All who have accomplished great things have had a great aim, have fixed their gaze on a goal which was high, one which sometimes seemed impossible." — **Orison Swett Marden**

"Our goals can only be reached through a vehicle of a plan, in which we must fervently believe, and upon which we must vigorously act. There is no other route to success." — **Pablo Picasso**

"You have to set goals that are almost out of reach. If you set a goal that is attainable without much work or thought, you are stuck with something below your true talent and potential." — **Steve Garvey**

"By recording your dreams and goals on paper, you set in motion the process of becoming the person you most want to be. Put your future in good hands—your own." — **Mark Victor Hansen**

"One way to keep momentum going is to have constantly greater goals." — **Michael Korda**

"All successful people have a goal. No one can get anywhere unless he knows where he wants to go and what he wants to be or do." — **Norman Vincent Peale**

"A goal properly set is halfway reached." — **Zig Ziglar**

"If you set goals and go after them with all the determination you can muster, your gifts will take you places that will amaze you." — **Les Brown**

"It must be borne in mind that the tragedy of life doesn't lie in not reaching your goal. The tragedy lies in having no goals to reach." — **Benjamin E. Mays**

"It's harder to stay on top than it is to make the climb. Continue to seek new goals." — **Pat Summitt**

"Reach high, for stars lie hidden in you. Dream deep, for every dream precedes the goal." – **Rabindranath Tagore**

"Setting goals is the first step in turning the invisible into the visible." — **Tony Robbins**

"If you want to be happy, set a goal that commands your thoughts, liberates your energy and inspires your hopes." — **Andrew Carnegie**

"We must have a theme, a goal, a purpose in our lives. If you don't know where you're aiming, you don't have a goal. My goal is to live my life in such a way that when I die, someone can say, she cared." — **Mary Kay Ash**

"To sit on an idea or fail to act on a goal is not really goal-setting, but wishful thinking." — **Les Brown**

"If you want to succeed at a goal, you need to understand why you want it. This is critical. You have to do this process for any goal you set for yourself." — **Michael S. Dobson**

"Time frame is an essential part of goal-setting, because it helps you commit and increases your focus." — **Ted Robbins**

"The reason most people never reach their goals is that they don't define them, or ever seriously consider them as believable or achievable. Winners can tell you where they are going, what they plan to do along the way, and who will be sharing the adventure with them." — **Denis Waitley**

"For most of us, goal-setting sounds and usually is a grueling process, because we most often confuse a goal with a wish, an objective with a desire." — **Michael Lombardi**

"I believe there are two ingredients necessary to make every day a masterpiece: decisions and discipline. They are like two sides of the same coin; you could call them 'goal-setting' and 'goal-getting.' And they can't be separated because one is worthless without the other." — **John C. Maxwell**

"Focus, discipline, hard work, goal-setting and, of course, the thrill of finally achieving your goals. These are all lessons in life." — **Kristi Yamaguchi**

"To unlock and unleash your full potential, you should make a habit of daily goal-setting and achieving for the rest of your life." — **Brian Tracy**

"If you don't design your own life plan, chances are you'll fall into someone else's plan. And guess what they have planned for you? Not much." — **Jim Rohn**

"Goals are the fuel in the furnace of achievement." — **Brian Tracy**

"There are two things to aim at in life; first to get what you want, and after that to enjoy it. Only the wisest of mankind has achieved the second." — **Logan Pearsall Smith**

"The greater danger for most of us isn't that our aim is too high and miss it, but that it is too low and we reach it." — **Michelangelo**

"I do know that when I am 60, I should be attempting to achieve different personal goals than those which had priority at age 20." — **Warren Buffett**

"The trouble with not having a goal is that you can spend your life running up and down the field and never score." — **Bill Copeland**

"We aim above the mark to hit the mark." — **Ralph Waldo Emerson**

"If you're bored with life—you don't get up every morning with a burning desire to do things—you don't have enough goals." — **Lou Holtz**

"I think goals should never be easy, they should force you to work, even if they are uncomfortable at the time." — **Michael Phelps**

"Envision, create, and believe in your own universe, and the universe will form around you." — **Tony Hsieh**

"Some people want it to happen, some wish it would happen, and others make it happen." — **Michael Jordan**

"A good goal is like a strenuous exercise—it makes you stretch." — **Mary Kay Ash**

"Most impossible goals can be met simply by breaking them down into bite size chunks, writing them down, believing them and going full speed ahead as if they were routine." — **Don Lancaster**

"There are only two rules for being successful. One, figure out exactly what you want to do, and two, do it." — **Mario Cuomo**

"A goal is not always meant to be reached, it often serves simply as something to aim at." — **Bruce Lee**

"Discipline is the bridge between goals and accomplishment." — **Jim Rohn**

"It is not enough to take steps which may someday lead to a goal; each step must be itself a goal and a step likewise." — **Johann Wolfgang von Goethe**

"To reach a port, we must sail. Sail, not tie at anchor. Sail, not drift." — **Franklin Roosevelt**

"Decide whether or not the goal is worth the risks involved. If it is, stop worrying." — **Amelia Earhart**

"A goal without a timeline is just a dream." — **Robert Herjavec**

"Start where you are. Use what you have. Do what you can." — **Arthur Ashe**

"My philosophy of life is that if we make up our mind what we are going to make of our lives, then work hard toward that goal, we never lose—somehow we always win out." — **Ronald Reagan**

Source: https://evantarver.com/goal-setting-quotes/

The Science of Goal Setting

Goal setting is more than just deciding what you want to achieve; it's a scientifically-backed process that can significantly enhance your chances of success. Research has shown that individuals who set specific, challenging goals are more likely to achieve their objectives than those who set vague or easy goals. This is because well-defined goals provide clarity, focus, and motivation, which are essential for sustained effort and progress.

The SMART Framework

One of the most effective tools for goal setting is the SMART framework, which stands for **S**pecific, **M**easurable, **A**chievable, **R**elevant, and **T**ime-bound. This framework helps you create clear and actionable goals by breaking them down into key components:

Specific: A goal should be clear and specific, answering the questions of what you want to accomplish, why it's important, and how you plan to achieve it. For example, instead of setting a goal to "get fit," you might set a goal to "run three times a week to improve cardiovascular health."

Measurable: To track your progress, your goal should have measurable criteria. This could involve quantifying your goal (e.g., lose 10 pounds, save $5,000) or setting benchmarks to assess your progress along the way.

Achievable: While it's important to set challenging goals, they should also be realistic and attainable. Consider your resources, time, and capabilities to ensure that your goal is within reach.

Relevant: Your goal should align with your broader life objectives and values. It should be something that matters to you and contributes to your long-term vision.

Time-bound: Setting a deadline creates a sense of urgency and helps you stay focused. Whether it's a short-term or long-term goal, having a timeline keeps you accountable and motivated.

The Role of Motivation and Commitment

Motivation plays a crucial role in goal achievement. Understanding what drives you and tapping into that motivation can help sustain your efforts over time. Whether it's the desire for personal growth, financial stability, or contributing to a cause you care about, identifying your underlying motivations can give you the energy to persevere.

Commitment is equally important. Once you've set your goals, it's essential to commit to them fully. This involves not just a mental commitment but also a practical one, where you allocate time, resources, and effort to your goals. Creating a plan, setting priorities, and being consistent are key components of staying committed to your goals.

The Power of Visualization

Visualization is a powerful tool in the goal-setting process. By picturing yourself achieving your goals, you can create a mental image of success that boosts your confidence and motivation. Visualization can help you overcome challenges by reinforcing your belief in your ability to succeed. It also allows you to mentally rehearse the steps you need to take, making the process feel more achievable and familiar.

Incorporating visualization into your daily routine, such as spending a few minutes each morning visualizing your goals, can help keep you focused and motivated. When combined with the SMART framework and a strong commitment, visualization can significantly enhance your ability to set and achieve meaningful goals.

Overcoming Procrastination and Self-Doubt

According to the English poet, Edward Young (1683-1765), "Procrastination is the thief of time." Even with well-defined goals and a strong commitment, many people struggle with procrastination and self-doubt. These internal barriers can hinder your progress and prevent you from achieving your full potential. Understanding the root causes of these challenges and developing strategies to overcome them is essential for success.

Understanding Procrastination

Procrastination is the tendency to delay or avoid tasks, often leading to stress and decreased productivity. It can be driven by various factors, including fear of failure, perfectionism, or a lack of motivation. Understanding why you procrastinate is the first step in addressing it.

Fear of Failure: The fear of not succeeding can lead to avoidance behaviours. If you find yourself procrastinating because you're afraid of failing, it's important to reframe your mindset. Instead of seeing failure as a negative outcome, view it as a learning opportunity that can help you grow and improve.

Perfectionism: Perfectionists often procrastinate because they set unrealistically high standards for themselves. This can lead to paralysis, where the fear of not doing something perfectly prevents them from taking any action at all. To overcome this, focus on progress rather than perfection. Accept that mistakes are part of the process and that doing something imperfectly is better than doing nothing at all.

Lack of Motivation: If you're not motivated by the task at hand, it's easy to put it off. In these cases, it's helpful to connect the task to your broader goals and values. Remind yourself of why the task is important and how it contributes to your long-term objectives.

Strategies for Overcoming Procrastination

There are several strategies you can use to overcome procrastination and stay on track with your goals.

Break Tasks into Smaller Steps: Large tasks can be overwhelming, leading to procrastination. By breaking them down into smaller, manageable steps, you make the process less daunting and easier to start.

Set Short Deadlines: Long deadlines can create a false sense of security, leading to procrastination. Setting short, incremental deadlines can help you stay focused and maintain momentum.

Use the "Two-Minute Rule": If a task takes less than two minutes to complete, do it immediately. This simple rule can help you tackle small tasks quickly and prevent them from piling up.

Reward Yourself: Set up a system of rewards for completing tasks. This can provide motivation and make the process more enjoyable.

Seek Accountability: Sharing your goals with someone else can create accountability and provide support. Whether it's a friend, family member, or mentor, having someone to check in with can help you stay on track.

Overcoming Self-Doubt

Self-doubt is another common barrier to achieving goals. It can manifest as a lack of confidence, fear of judgment, or feelings of inadequacy. Overcoming self-doubt requires a combination of self-awareness, positive thinking, and action.

Challenge Negative Thoughts: Self-doubt often stems from negative thoughts and beliefs about yourself. When these thoughts arise, challenge them by asking yourself whether they are based on facts or assumptions. Replace negative thoughts with positive affirmations and reminders of your past successes.

Focus on Your Strengths: Instead of dwelling on your weaknesses, focus on your strengths and what you bring to the table. Recognize your skills, talents, and achievements, and use them as a foundation for building confidence.

Take Action: One of the most effective ways to overcome self-doubt is to take action, even if it's small. Each step you take toward your goal reinforces your belief in your ability to succeed and helps diminish self-doubt.

Embrace Failure as a Learning Tool: Fear of failure can fuel self-doubt, but it's important to remember that failure is a natural part of the learning process. Embrace failure as an opportunity to learn and grow, rather than as a reflection of your worth.

Celebrating Milestones and Successes

Celebrating milestones and successes is an often overlooked but vital aspect of goal achievement. Recognizing your progress and accomplishments not only boosts your motivation and morale but also reinforces the positive behaviours and habits that led to your success.

The Importance of Milestones

Milestones are the smaller goals or benchmarks you set on the way to achieving your larger goals. They provide opportunities to assess your progress, make adjustments, and celebrate achievements along the way. Setting and acknowledging milestones can help maintain momentum and prevent burnout by giving you something to celebrate even before the final goal is reached.

Types of Celebrations

Celebrating your milestones and successes can take many forms, depending on the significance of the achievement and your personal preferences. Some ideas include:

Personal Rewards: Treat yourself to something special, such as a day off, a favorite meal, or a small gift, as a reward for reaching a milestone.

Public Recognition: Share your success with others, whether it's through social media, a group meeting, or a personal conversation. Public recognition can enhance your sense of accomplishment and inspire others.

Reflection and Gratitude: Take time to reflect on your journey and express gratitude for the progress you've made. Journaling or meditating on your achievements can deepen your sense of fulfillment.

Sharing Your Success: Celebrate with others who have supported you along the way. Acknowledging the contributions of friends, family, or colleagues can strengthen your relationships and create a shared sense of achievement.

Reinforcing Positive Behaviours

Celebrating successes is not just about the momentary pleasure of recognition; it's also a way to reinforce the positive behaviors that led to your achievement. By associating your efforts with positive outcomes, you create a feedback loop that encourages continued progress. This reinforcement helps you build the habits and mindset needed for ongoing success.

Learning from Setbacks

While celebrating successes is crucial, it's equally important to learn from setbacks. Not every goal will be achieved on the first attempt, and obstacles are inevitable. When you encounter setbacks, view them as opportunities to gain insights and grow. Reflect on what went wrong, what could have been done differently, and how you can apply these lessons moving forward.

Setbacks can also be a time to reassess your goals. Sometimes, a setback reveals that a goal needs to be adjusted or that a new approach is necessary. Being flexible and open to change can turn setbacks into stepping stones on your path to success.

Conclusion

Setting and achieving goals is a dynamic process that requires clarity, commitment, and resilience. By understanding the science of goal setting, overcoming obstacles like procrastination and self-doubt, and celebrating your milestones and successes, you can transform your aspirations into reality.

Remember that goal setting is not just about the destination but also about the journey. Each step you take toward your goals is an opportunity to learn, grow, and become more aligned with your true purpose. Embrace the process with an open heart and mind, and trust that with persistence and determination, you can achieve great things.

As you continue on your journey, keep in mind that goals are tools for personal and professional growth. They should challenge you, inspire you, and ultimately lead you to a more meaningful and fulfilling life. Celebrate your achievements, learn from your setbacks, and never stop striving toward the life you envision for yourself.

Exercise

Setting and Achieving Your Personal Goals

This exercise is designed to help you define clear, actionable goals and create a plan to achieve them. By focusing on specific areas of your life, you'll learn how to set meaningful objectives and take steps toward realizing your dreams.

Step 1: Identify Key Areas for Growth

Start by reflecting on the different areas of your life where you want to set goals. Think about the following categories:

- **Personal growth** (e.g., learning a new skill, practicing mindfulness)
- **Health and wellness** (e.g., exercise, nutrition, self-care)
- **Career or professional development** (e.g., advancing your career, starting a new business)
- **Relationships** (e.g., strengthening connections with family, friends, or a partner)
- **Financial goals** (e.g., saving for a major purchase, reducing debt)
- **Hobbies or passions** (e.g., pursuing a creative project, traveling)

List 2–3 key areas of your life that you want to focus on for goal setting.

Step 2: Define SMART Goals

Once you've identified the areas of growth, use the SMART framework to define clear and achievable goals. SMART stands for:

- **Specific:** Clearly define what you want to accomplish.
- **Measurable:** Ensure there is a way to track your progress.
- **Achievable:** Set realistic goals that are within your reach.
- **Relevant:** Make sure the goal aligns with your overall vision for your life.
- **Time-bound:** Set a deadline to help you stay focused.

For each of the key areas you listed in Step 1, write one SMART goal. For example:

- *Personal Growth:* "I will read one book on mindfulness by the end of next month and incorporate one mindfulness practice into my daily routine."
- *Health and Wellness:* "I will exercise for 30 minutes, three times a week, for the next three months."

Step 3: Break Goals Into Actionable Steps

Big goals can sometimes feel overwhelming, so it's important to break them down into smaller, manageable steps. For each of your SMART goals, outline the specific actions you need to take:

- **What is the first step you can take today?**
- **What are the subsequent steps you need to take to make progress?**
- **What resources or support do you need to accomplish this goal?**

For example, if your goal is to exercise regularly, your steps might include finding a gym or home workout routine, scheduling your workouts in a calendar, and tracking your progress.

Step 4: Overcome Obstacles

Think about potential obstacles that might get in the way of achieving your goals. Consider the following questions:

- **What challenges or distractions might prevent me from reaching my goal?**
- **How can I prepare for or overcome these obstacles?**
- **What strategies can I use to stay motivated during setbacks?**

Write down 2–3 potential challenges for each goal, and brainstorm solutions for overcoming them. This will help you stay proactive and resilient when difficulties arise.

Step 5: Create a Timeline and Accountability Plan

Now that you have your goals and action steps, create a timeline for achieving them. Set deadlines for completing each action step, and think about how you will hold yourself accountable:

- **When do you plan to achieve this goal?**
- **How often will you check in with your progress?**
- **Is there someone who can help keep you accountable, such as a friend, mentor, or coach?**

Write down your timeline and accountability plan for each goal. You might choose to check in weekly or monthly to track your progress and make adjustments as needed.

Step 6: Visualize Success

Visualization can be a powerful tool for achieving your goals. Take a moment to close your eyes and imagine yourself successfully completing your goals:

- **How will you feel once you've achieved your goal?**
- **What will be different in your life?**
- **How will your success impact others around you?**

By visualizing success, you reinforce the positive emotions and motivation needed to keep moving forward.

Step 7: Celebrate Milestones

As you work toward your goals, it's important to recognize and celebrate your progress along the way. For each of your goals, write down a few milestones and consider how you'll reward yourself when you reach them:

- **What milestones will you celebrate?** (e.g., completing the first step, reaching the halfway mark, etc.)
- **How will you reward yourself for staying committed?** (e.g., a small treat, taking a break, celebrating with a friend)

Celebrating small wins can help you stay motivated and reinforce your commitment to achieving your bigger goal.

Step 8: Reflect on the Process

At the end of each week or month, take time to reflect on your progress:

- **What progress have I made toward my goal?**
- **What challenges have I encountered, and how have I handled them?**
- **What adjustments do I need to make moving forward?**

Write down your reflections and adjust your action plan if needed. This will help you stay flexible and responsive as you continue your goal-setting journey.

Step 9: Set New Goals

Once you've achieved one of your goals, use what you've learned to set new ones. Personal growth and goal setting are ongoing processes, so don't stop once you've reached a milestone. Take a moment to celebrate your achievements and then start thinking about what you want to accomplish next.

By using this structured approach to setting and achieving goals, you'll be well on your way to creating lasting positive change in your life.

CHAPTER 11
WORDSEARCH

	1	2	3	4	5	6	7	8	9	10	11	12	13	14	15	16	17	18
1	W	L	E	D	G	D	S	E	A	Y	A	N	I	Z	M	M	Q	A
2	Q	T	M	I	P	R	M	C	B	C	Q	L	R	E	D	F	N	C
3	G	J	S	R	D	V	C	V	D	D	H	B	N	Y	S	I	K	N
4	O	P	I	E	T	C	E	W	N	W	W	I	V	S	R	C	O	E
5	A	R	N	C	R	H	L	C	I	F	I	C	E	P	S	I	L	V
6	L	P	O	T	A	Z	E	P	U	L	Y	C	S	V	T	B	K	R
7	S	P	I	I	M	F	B	H	W	O	C	Z	V	A	A	X	Q	N
8	F	O	T	O	S	Q	R	O	S	U	O	H	N	R	M	B	M	M
9	F	B	C	N	T	W	A	Y	S	Z	U	I	U	I	Y	I	L	V
10	T	J	E	W	D	U	T	Z	P	Y	T	S	Y	T	L	I	Y	E
11	Q	E	F	G	J	N	I	W	E	S	A	M	P	E	M	T	G	S
12	G	C	R	F	R	C	O	R	A	E	Z	Q	S	T	S	I	H	C
13	H	T	E	G	A	O	N	R	M	H	K	T	H	J	Q	N	E	U
14	P	I	P	R	G	P	C	B	P	Z	O	Q	S	O	N	C	O	C
15	R	V	E	O	D	O	M	U	N	N	Y	F	U	L	U	W	G	G
16	O	E	B	D	R	D	I	Y	E	W	K	I	S	Z	S	V	M	X
17	R	S	D	P	C	U	B	S	U	P	S	Z	H	S	C	R	U	K
18	N	U	R	L	R	Z	P	V	V	F	G	A	J	G	C	L	C	N

ACHIEVABLE   MEASURABLE   SMART
CAREER   MILESTONES   SPECIFIC
CELEBRATION OBJECTIVES   SUCCESS
DIRECTION   PERFECTIONISM
GOALS   PROCRASTINATION

THE JOURNEY TO A FULFILLING AND MEANINGFUL LIFE

ANSWER

	1	2	3	4	5	6	7	8	9	10	11	12	13	14	15	16	17	18
1	W	L	E	D	G	D	S	E	A	Y	A	N	I	Z	M	M	Q	A
2	Q	T	M	I	P	R	M	C	B	C	Q	L	R	E	D	F	N	C
3	G	J	S	R	D	V	C	V	D	D	H	B	N	Y	S	I	K	N
4	O	P	I	E	T	C	E	W	N	W	W	I	V	S	R	C	O	E
5	A	R	N	C	R	H	L	C	I	F	I	C	E	P	S	I	L	V
6	L	P	O	T	A	Z	E	P	U	L	Y	C	S	V	T	B	K	R
7	S	P	I	I	M	F	B	H	W	O	C	Z	V	A	A	X	Q	N
8	F	O	T	O	S	Q	R	O	S	U	O	H	N	R	M	B	M	M
9	F	B	C	N	T	W	A	Y	S	Z	U	I	U	I	Y	I	L	V
10	T	J	E	W	D	U	T	Z	P	Y	T	S	Y	T	L	I	Y	E
11	Q	E	F	G	J	N	I	W	E	S	A	M	P	E	M	T	G	S
12	G	C	R	F	R	C	O	R	A	E	Z	Q	S	T	S	I	H	C
13	H	T	E	G	A	O	N	R	M	H	K	T	H	J	Q	N	E	U
14	P	I	P	R	G	P	C	B	P	Z	O	Q	S	O	N	C	O	C
15	R	V	E	O	D	O	M	U	N	N	Y	F	U	L	U	W	G	G
16	O	E	B	D	R	D	I	Y	E	W	K	I	S	Z	S	V	M	X
17	R	S	D	P	C	U	B	S	U	P	S	Z	H	S	C	R	U	K
18	N	U	R	L	R	Z	P	V	V	F	G	A	J	G	C	L	C	N

ACHIEVABLE 1:9

CAREER 12:6

CELEBRATION 3:7

DIRECTION 1:4

GOALS 3:1

MEASURABLE 13:9

MILESTONES 8:17

OBJECTIVES 8:2

PERFECTIONISM 14:3

PROCRASTINATION 17:4

SMART 8:5

SPECIFIC 5:15

SUCCESS 9:9

CHAPTER 12
LIVING A BALANCED AND FULFILLED LIFE

A balanced life allows us to navigate life's demands without feeling overwhelmed.

The Bible Says

For everything there is a season, and a time for every matter under heaven. **Ecclesiastes 3:1 (ESV)**

But seek first the kingdom of God and his righteousness, and all these things will be added to you. **Matthew 6:33**

Do not be conformed to this world, but be transformed by the renewal of your mind, that by testing you may discern what is the will of God, what is good and acceptable and perfect. **Romans 12:2**

Finally, brothers, whatever is true, whatever is honorable, whatever is just, whatever is pure, whatever is lovely, whatever is commendable, if there is any excellence, if there is anything worthy of praise, think about these things. **Philippians 4:8**

Not that I am speaking of being in need, for I have learned in whatever situation I am to be content. **Philippians 4:11**

And he said to them, "Come away by yourselves to a desolate place and rest a while." For many were coming and going, and they had no leisure even to eat. **Mark 6:31**

And he answered, "You shall love the Lord your God with all your heart and with all your soul and with all your strength and with all your mind, and your neighbor as yourself." **Luke 10:27**

In these days he went out to the mountain to pray, and all night he continued in prayer to God. **Luke 6:12**

And going a little farther he fell on his face and prayed, saying, "My Father, if it be possible, let this cup pass from me; nevertheless, not as I will, but as you will." **Matthew 26:39**

And whatever you do, in word or deed, do everything in the name of the Lord Jesus, giving thanks to God the Father through him. **Colossians 3:17**

Introduction

In the modern world, where time is often perceived as a luxury, the idea of living a balanced and fulfilled life can feel elusive. We are constantly bombarded with messages urging us to do more, achieve more, and be more. Whether it's climbing the career ladder, raising a family, or pursuing personal aspirations, the pressure to excel in all areas often leads to burnout and dissatisfaction.

However, balance and fulfillment are not found in perfection or relentless striving; rather, they are cultivated by aligning our daily actions with our values, setting realistic goals, and finding joy in the present. A balanced life allows us to navigate life's demands without feeling overwhelmed, while fulfillment stems from knowing that we are living authentically, honoring our deepest needs, and contributing meaningfully to the world around us.

This chapter delves into the strategies for achieving balance in key areas of life—work, family, and personal growth—while also exploring the profound fulfillment that comes from finding joy in simplicity and embracing a mindset of contentment. By the end, you'll discover that balance and fulfillment are less about external achievements and more about how we choose to engage with the world around us and within us.

Life Story

When Darius graduated from university, he was driven by ambition. He landed a high-paying job in finance, quickly rising through the ranks. His life seemed perfect on the surface—he owned a luxury apartment, traveled for work, and had an active social life. But behind the success, Darius felt increasingly burned out. He worked long hours, often neglecting his health, relationships, and personal passions. The constant grind left him feeling empty and disconnected.

One evening, while catching up with an old friend, Darius was struck by the contrast in their lives. His friend, Maura, was a teacher earning far less than he did, but she radiated joy. She talked about her hobbies, her family, and her weekends spent hiking and volunteering. Maura seemed deeply content, while Darius, despite all his outward achievements, felt a gnawing sense of dissatisfaction.

That conversation planted a seed in Darius' mind. Over the next few months, he reflected on what truly mattered to him. He realized that a successful career alone wasn't enough to bring fulfillment. He craved balance—a life where work, health, relationships, and personal growth all had space to thrive.

Determined to make a change, Darius started by setting boundaries at work. He left the office on time, made time for regular exercise, and rekindled his love for photography, a hobby he had long abandoned. He also focused on nurturing his relationships, spending more quality time with family and friends. Over time, Darius found that living a more balanced life brought him a deeper sense of purpose and happiness.

Darius' story illustrates that true fulfillment comes not from chasing external success but from finding balance in all areas of life. When we make time for our passions, prioritize our well-being, and nurture meaningful connections, we can lead lives that are both balanced and deeply rewarding.

Sayings about Living a Balanced and Fulfilled Life

"Life is about balance. Be kind, but don't let people abuse you. Trust, but don't be deceived. Be content, but never stop improving yourself."— **Zig Ziglar**

"Life is a balance of holding on and letting go." — **Rumi**

"Throughout the infinite, the forces are in a perfect balance, and hence the energy of a single thought may determine the motion of a universe." — **Nikola Tesla**

"In the end, it's all a question of balance." — **Rohinton Mistry**

"A balance of giving and receiving is essential to keeping your energy, mood and motivation at a consistently high level." — **Doreen Virtue**

"To put everything in balance is good, to put everything in harmony is better." — **Victor Hugo**

"Work is a rubber ball. If you drop it, it will bounce back. The other four balls – family, health, friends, integrity – are made of glass. If you drop one of these, it will be irrevocably scuffed, nicked, perhaps even shattered." — **Gary W. Keller**

"If you restore balance in your own self, you will be contributing immensely to the healing of the world." — **Deepak Chopra**

"Don't confuse having a career with having a life." — **Hillary Clinton**

"Love is the undisturbed balance that binds this universe together." — **Mahavatar Babaji**

"The key to finding a happy balance in modern life is simplicity." — **Sogyal Rinpoche**

"Retire to the center of your being, which is calmness." — **Paramahansa Yogananda**

"There's no such thing as work-life balance. There are work-life choices, and you make them, and they have consequences." — **Jack Welch**

"Balance every thought with its opposition. Because the marriage of them is the destruction of illusion." — **Aleister Crowley**

"We have to balance the lineality of the known universe with the nonlineality of the unknown universe." — **Carlos Castaneda**

"The balance of power is the scale of peace." — **Thomas Paine**

"Find a balance between head and heart." — **Colleen Hoover**

"If you strive only to avoid the darkness or to cling to the light, you cannot live in balance. Try striving to be conscious of all that you are." — **Gary Zukav**

"The aim is to balance the terror of being alive with the wonder of being alive." — **Carlos Castaneda**

"Nature is about balance. All the world comes in pairs – Yin and Yang, right and wrong, men and women; what's pleasure without pain?" — **Angelina Jolie**

"Happiness isn't real unless it is shared." — **Christopher McCandless**

"There is no balance, all or nothing." — **David Choe**

"The most important career decision you'll make is who your life partner is." — **Sheryl Sandberg**

"Balance and good fortune can only come to a person who is balanced and feels fortunate." — **Stuart Wilde**

"Never slouch as doing so compresses the lungs, overcrowds other vital organs, rounds the back, and throws you off balance." — **Joseph Pilates**

"There is no such thing as work-life balance. Everything worth fighting for unbalances your life." — **Alain de Botton**

"To lose balance sometimes for love is part of living a balanced life." — **Elizabeth Gilbert**

"Don't confuse symmetry with balance." — **Tom Robbins**

"Mathematics expresses values that reflect the cosmos, including orderliness, balance, harmony, logic, and abstract beauty." — **Deepak Chopra**

"Economy without ecology means managing the human nature relationship without knowing the delicate balance between humankind and the natural world." — **Satish Kumar**

"A beginning is the time for taking the most delicate care that the balances are correct." — **Frank Herbert**

"Work, love and play are the great balance wheels of man's being." — **Orison Swett Marden**

"Shabbat is a day of rest, of mental scrutiny and of balance. Without it the workdays are insipid." — **Hayim Nahman Bialik**

"When conscious activity is wholly concentrated on some one definite purpose, the ultimate result, for most people, is lack of balance accompanied by some form of nervous disorder." — **Bertrand Russell**

"Find your balance and stand with it. Find your song and sing it out. Find your cadence and let it appear like a dance. Find the questions that only you know how to ask and The answers that you are content to not know." — **Mary Anne Radmacher**

"A good reputation for yourself and your company is an invaluable asset not reflected in the balance sheets." — **Li Ka-shing**

"Life is like riding a bicycle. To keep your balance, you must keep moving." — **Albert Einstein**

"Holiness is the balance between my nature and the law of God as expressed in Jesus Christ." — **Oswald Chambers**

"Being an impatient person, I wanted to do what my grandmother said: "Do as much as you can as fast as you can; be as productive as possible." But you must be patient. So I have struggled to balance patience with being an impatient person, and trying to find a happy medium." — **Farrah Gray**

"Science-fiction balances you on the cliff. Fantasy shoves you off." — **Ray Bradbury**

"We're on the verge of a financial collapse unless we balance the budget, and that means some really, really tough decisions." — **Gary Johnson**

Source: https://quotefancy.com/balance-quotes

Balancing Work, Family, and Personal Growth

Achieving balance in life requires ongoing adjustment, reflection, and the courage to make intentional choices. The three main pillars of modern life—work, family, and personal growth—are often viewed as competing forces, each demanding time, energy, and attention. Yet, finding equilibrium between these spheres is crucial for long-term well-being.

Work

In many ways, work defines who we are. It provides not only financial stability but also a sense of purpose and contribution to society. However, an overemphasis on work can come at a cost, straining personal relationships and personal well-being. The key to a healthy work-life balance lies in setting clear boundaries. This means not only managing time effectively but also learning when to say no to projects or tasks that do not align with your broader goals. Create a daily or weekly schedule that respects your non-work hours, allowing for genuine downtime. Be mindful of the work culture you're a part of, and if possible, advocate for a balanced approach within your workplace.

Family

Family, whether chosen or biological, forms the emotional foundation of our lives. However, balancing family responsibilities with other obligations can be tricky, especially when demands overlap. The key here is intentional time. Too often, we mistake proximity for presence. It's not enough to be physically near your family; genuine connection comes from undivided attention. Set aside quality time, even if brief, where family interactions are prioritized—this could be dinner together, weekend outings, or simply being present during important moments. When family bonds are nurtured, the sense of support and security they provide strengthens all other areas of life.

Personal Growth

Amid the demands of work and family, personal growth is often the first area to be sacrificed. Yet neglecting this part of your life can lead to a sense of stagnation. Personal growth can take many forms, including learning new skills, developing hobbies, or nurturing spiritual practices. Investing in yourself—whether by taking a class, reading a book, or engaging in mindful reflection—is not selfish. It's essential to your overall well-being. Allocating time for personal development can energize and inspire you, enabling you to bring your best self to your work and family relationships.

Balancing these areas of life may never feel perfect. Life circumstances change, and priorities shift, but maintaining a flexible mindset and a commitment to aligning your time with your values will lead to greater harmony.

Finding Joy in Simple Pleasures

Amid the busyness of modern life, it is easy to overlook the beauty in the ordinary moments that surround us. We often believe that happiness comes from grand achievements or significant milestones—getting a promotion, buying a home, or going on a dream vacation. While these moments are undoubtedly meaningful, a truly fulfilled life is built on the joy found in daily, simple pleasures.

The Beauty of Mindfulness

Mindfulness is the practice of being fully present in the moment. It allows us to slow down and appreciate life as it unfolds, rather than always rushing toward the next task. When we practice mindfulness, we begin to notice the small but profound joys that exist in everyday life—the warmth of a cup of coffee in the morning, the sound of birds singing outside your window, or the feel of a gentle breeze on your skin. These moments, though small, can uplift and sustain us when we take the time to fully experience them.

The Power of Gratitude

Gratitude is a powerful force for cultivating joy in simplicity. By focusing on what we have, rather than what we lack, we shift our mindset from scarcity to abundance. Practicing gratitude can be as simple as keeping a journal where you write down a few things you're thankful for each day. Over time, this practice trains your brain to recognize and appreciate the goodness that already exists in your life. It could be the kindness of a stranger, the comfort of a warm meal, or the love of a pet. When we are grateful, even life's smallest blessings take on a greater meaning.

Finding Joy in Connection

Human beings are wired for connection, and some of the greatest joys in life come from the relationships we nurture. This doesn't have to mean grand gestures or expensive outings. It could be a heartfelt conversation with a friend, playing with your children, or sharing a meal with your partner. These simple interactions create deep fulfillment, reminding us that life's greatest treasures are often found in the connections we build with others.

In short, joy is not something we need to chase. It is something we create by being fully present, practicing gratitude, and valuing the connections that give life meaning.

Creating a Life of Contentment and Fulfillment

Contentment and fulfillment are often misunderstood in a culture that prioritizes constant growth, ambition, and comparison. We are conditioned to believe that happiness lies in reaching the next goal, acquiring more, or becoming "better" than we currently are. Yet, true contentment arises not from external achievements but from within—by cultivating a mindset of peace and satisfaction with where we are right now.

The Myth of More

Many of us have bought into the myth that "more" equals better—more success, more money, more recognition. While growth and achievement are essential for personal satisfaction, they should not define our self-worth. Contentment comes from appreciating what we have while still aspiring to improve. It is the balance between striving and surrendering, knowing that who we are and what we have is enough for this moment.

The Freedom of Letting Go

One of the keys to living a life of contentment is letting go—of perfectionism, of the need for control, and of the expectations that we or others place upon us. When we cling too tightly to how things *should* be, we lose sight of the beauty of how things *are*. Letting go frees us from the burden of constantly seeking external validation, and instead, we focus on inner peace and well-being.

Living with Purpose

Fulfillment comes from living a life of purpose. Purpose doesn't have to be grand or world-changing; it can be found in the quiet ways we contribute to the well-being of others or pursue our passions. Whether it's raising a family, supporting a cause, or mastering a craft, having a clear sense of purpose gives our lives meaning and direction. Purpose grounds us, even in times of difficulty, and gives us a reason to keep moving forward with hope and determination.

Aligning Values and Actions

Ultimately, contentment and fulfillment arise when our daily actions align with our deepest values. Ask yourself: What do I truly value? Is it family, creativity, spirituality, service to others? Once we have clarity on our values, we can make conscious choices that reflect them. This alignment between values and actions creates harmony within, fostering a deep sense of fulfillment that cannot be shaken by external circumstances.

Conclusion

Living a balanced and fulfilled life is not about achieving perfection or eliminating challenges. It is about making deliberate choices that honor our values, finding joy in the small moments, and embracing contentment with where we are. Balance may look different at various stages of life, but the pursuit of it creates a sense of peace and well-being. Fulfillment, on the other hand, is the result of living authentically, pursuing our purpose, and finding meaning in our everyday existence. By striving for balance and cultivating fulfillment, we create a life that feels rich in experience and abundant in joy.

Exercise

Cultivating Balance and Fulfillment

The purpose of this exercise is to help you assess the areas of your life that need more balance and guide you in creating steps toward greater fulfillment.

Step 1: Assess Your Current Balance

Begin by reflecting on the different aspects of your life. These may include:

- **Work or Career**
- **Family and Relationships**
- **Personal Growth**
- **Health and Wellness**
- **Hobbies and Leisure**
- **Spirituality**

Draw a circle and divide it into sections, with each section representing one of these areas. This is your "Life Balance Wheel." Now, rate your satisfaction with each area on a scale of 1 to 10, where 1 means you are deeply unsatisfied and 10 means you are completely satisfied. Colour in each section to reflect your level of fulfillment in each area.

Step 2: Reflect on the Results

Look at your Life Balance Wheel and ask yourself the following questions:

- **Which areas of my life are well-balanced, and which need more attention?**
- **Am I focusing too much on one area at the expense of others?**

- **What areas are the most important to me but may not be getting enough attention?**

Write down your reflections. This awareness will help you focus on the areas that need more balance and fulfillment.

Step 3: Set Intentions for Improvement

For each area of your life where you rated your satisfaction below an 8, set an intention to improve your balance. Consider what small changes you can make to enhance each area. Write down at least one intention for each area that needs improvement.

Examples:

- **Work/Career:** "I will create boundaries by not checking work emails after 6 p.m. to make more time for family and relaxation."
- **Health/Wellness:** "I will commit to a 30-minute morning walk three times a week to improve my physical health."

Step 4: Find Joy in Simple Pleasures

To cultivate a more fulfilled life, it's important to find joy in everyday moments. Write down a list of 5–10 simple activities or experiences that bring you happiness and peace. These might include:

- Spending time in nature
- Reading a book you love
- Enjoying a meal with family
- Practicing gratitude at the end of the day

Make a commitment to incorporate at least one of these simple pleasures into your daily routine for the next week.

Step 5: Create a Life of Contentment

Living a balanced and fulfilled life often comes from cultivating contentment in the present moment. Take a few moments to reflect on what you are grateful for right now:

- **What are three things you are most grateful for in your life?**
- **How can you focus on appreciating these things more fully?**

Write down your reflections and commit to practicing gratitude daily. Contentment is nurtured by recognizing the blessings you already have.

Step 6: Identify One Change You Can Make Today

Living a balanced life requires small, mindful adjustments over time. Think about one small change you can make today to bring more balance and fulfillment into your life. It could be related to spending more time with loved ones, taking better care of your health, or carving out quiet time for yourself.

Write down this action step and commit to doing it within the next 24 hours.

Step 7: Reflect on Your Progress Weekly

At the end of each week, take a few minutes to reflect on your progress:

- **Have you made strides toward more balance in your life?**
- **Did you take time to enjoy simple pleasures?**
- **How are you feeling overall—more or less fulfilled?**

Write down your reflections in a journal or notebook. Use this practice to assess where you need to adjust and where you're thriving, so you can continue to create a life of balance and fulfillment.

By regularly checking in on your progress and making conscious adjustments, you'll gradually move closer to a more balanced and meaningful life.

THE JOURNEY TO A FULFILLING AND MEANINGFUL LIFE

CHAPTER 12
WORDSEARCH

	1	2	3	4	5	6	7	8	9	10	11	12
1	G	W	O	I	P	W	X	W	P	T	M	C
2	R	Y	K	Z	U	V	O	O	S	N	V	T
3	O	Y	R	Y	O	J	I	U	Y	A	A	A
4	W	I	G	Q	J	S	C	M	Y	N	P	M
5	T	X	F	P	V	I	S	P	Z	L	D	F
6	H	Z	G	E	M	W	E	Z	E	T	M	Y
7	F	G	B	O	C	R	I	A	T	O	Y	S
8	F	A	A	E	S	N	S	S	D	I	K	N
9	I	K	M	O	A	U	A	E	M	R	D	E
10	J	Z	N	I	R	U	E	L	O	G	O	S
11	W	A	O	E	L	R	T	W	A	G	F	O
12	L	Y	S	P	F	Y	F	Y	I	B	I	G

BALANCE   FREEDOM   PERSONAL
BEAUTY   GROWTH   PLEASURES
FAMILY   JOY   WORK

LIVING A BALANCED AND FULFILLED LIFE

ANSWER

	1	2	3	4	5	6	7	8	9	10	11	12
1	G	W	O	I	P	W	X	W	P	T	M	C
2	R	Y	K	Z	U	V	O	O	S	N	V	T
3	O	Y	R	Y	O	J	I	U	Y	A	A	A
4	W	I	G	Q	J	S	C	M	Y	N	P	M
5	T	X	F	P	V	I	S	P	Z	L	D	F
6	H	Z	G	E	M	W	E	Z	E	T	M	Y
7	F	G	B	O	C	R	I	A	T	O	Y	S
8	F	A	A	E	S	N	S	S	D	I	K	N
9	I	K	M	O	A	U	A	E	M	R	D	E
10	J	Z	N	I	R	U	E	L	O	G	O	S
11	W	A	O	E	L	R	T	W	A	G	F	O
12	L	Y	S	P	F	Y	F	Y	I	B	I	G

BALANCE 12:10   FREEDOM 12:5   PERSONAL 5:8
BEAUTY 7:3   GROWTH 1:1   PLEASURES 4:11
FAMILY 7:1   JOY 3:6   WORK 11:8

THE JOURNEY TO A FULFILLING AND MEANINGFUL LIFE

PART V
FINANCIAL WELL-BEING AND ECONOMIC EMPOWERMENT

CHAPTER 13
UNDERSTANDING PERSONAL FINANCE

Understanding personal finance is essential for achieving financial stability and peace of mind.

The Bible Says

"Whoever loves money never has enough; whoever loves wealth is never satisfied with their income. This too is meaningless." **(Ecclesiastes 5:10)**

"But remember the LORD your God, for it is he who gives you the ability to produce wealth, and so confirms his covenant, which he swore to your ancestors, as it is today." **(Deuteronomy 8:18)**

"No one can serve two masters, for either he will hate the one and love the other, or he will be devoted to the one and despise the other. You cannot serve God and money." **(Matthew 6:24)**

"Be shepherds of God's flock that is under your care, serving as overseers-not because you must, but because you are willing, as God wants you to be; not greedy for money, but eager to serve;" **(1 Peter 5:2)**

"Whoever is greedy for unjust gain troubles his own household, but he who hates bribes will live." **(Proverbs 15:27)**

"Dishonest money dwindles away, but whoever gathers money little by little makes it grow." **(Proverbs 13:11)**

"Look! The wages you failed to pay the workers who mowed your fields are crying out against you. The cries of the harvesters have reached the ears of the Lord Almighty. You have lived on earth in luxury and self-indulgence. You have fattened yourselves in the day of slaughter. You have condemned and murdered the innocent one, who was not opposing you." **(James 5:4-6)**

"The plans of the diligent lead to profit as surely as haste leads to poverty." **(Proverbs 21:5)**

"Suppose one of you wants to build a tower. Won't you first sit down and estimate the cost to see if you have enough money to complete it? **(Luke 14:28)**

"Four things on earth are small, yet they are extremely wise: Ants are creatures of little strength, yet they store up their food in the summer;" **(Proverbs 30:24-25)**

"But if anyone does not provide for his own, and especially for those of his household, he has denied the faith and is worse than an unbeliever." **(1 Timothy 5:8)**

"Be not one of those who give pledges, who put up security for debts. If you have nothing with which to pay,

why should your bed be taken from under you? **(Proverbs 14:23)**

"Now this I say, he who sows sparingly will also reap sparingly, and he who sows bountifully will also reap bountifully. Each one must do just as he has purposed in his heart, not grudgingly or under compulsion, for God loves a cheerful giver. And God is able to make all grace abound to you, so that always having all sufficiency in everything, you may have an abundance for every good deed;" **(Proverbs 14:23)**

"If anyone is poor among your fellow Israelites in any of the towns of the land the LORD your God is giving you, do not be hardhearted or tightfited toward them." **(Deuteronomy 15:7)**

"In all things I have shown you that by working hard in this way we must help the weak and remember the words of the Lord Jesus, how he himself said, 'It is more blessed to give than to receive.'" **(Act 20:25)**

"So when you give to the needy, do not announce it with trumpets, as the hypocrites do in the synagogues and on the streets, to be honored by others. Truly I tell you, they have received their reward in full. But when you give to the needy, do not let your left hand know what your right hand is doing, so that your giving may be in secret. Then your Father, who sees what is done in secret, will reward you." **(Matthew 6:2-5)**

"Then Jacob made a vow, saying, "If God will be with me and will keep me in this way that I go, and will give me bread to eat and clothing to wear, so that I come again to my father's house in peace, then the Lord shall be my God, and this stone, which I have set up for a pillar, shall

be God's house. And of all that you give me I will give a full tenth to you." **(Genesis 28:20-22)**

"Honor the LORD from your wealth and from the first of all your produce; So your barns will be filled with plenty and your vats will overflow with new wine." **(Proverbs 3:9-10)**

"And it is a good thing to receive wealth from God and the good health to enjoy it. To enjoy your work and accept your lot in life—this is indeed a gift from God." **(Ecclesiastes 5:19)**

"Instruct those who are rich in this present world not to be conceited or to fix their hope on the uncertainty of riches, but on God, who richly supplies us with all things to enjoy. Instruct them to do good, to be rich in good works, to be generous and ready to share, storing up for themselves the treasure of a good foundation for the future, so that they may take hold of that which is life indeed." **(1 Timothy 6:17-19)**

"And my God will supply all your needs according to His riches in glory in Christ Jesus." **(Philippians 4:19)**

"I am the Lord Your God, who brought you up out of the land of Egypt. Open your mouth wide, and I will fill it." **(Psalms 81:10)**

"If that is how God clothes the grass of the field, which is here today, and tomorrow is thrown into the fire, how much more will he clothe you—you of little faith!" **(Luke 12:28)**

Introduction

Personal finance plays a crucial role in shaping our lives, yet it is often one of the most misunderstood and neglected aspects of adulthood. Many people enter the workforce or start a family without a solid grasp of financial management, which can lead to stress, poor decision-making, and long-term financial instability. Understanding personal finance is not just about accumulating wealth—it's about achieving financial security, making informed decisions, and creating a stable foundation for the future.

In this chapter, we will explore the fundamentals of personal finance, starting with the basics of budgeting and saving, followed by strategies for managing debt and building credit. We'll also delve into planning for major life expenses, such as buying a home, funding education, or preparing for retirement. By gaining a comprehensive understanding of these areas, you will be better equipped to navigate the financial challenges and opportunities that life presents. Ultimately, mastering personal finance is key to living with greater peace of mind and achieving both short- and long-term goals.

Life Story

When Maria got her first full-time job after college, she felt on top of the world. She was finally earning her own money, had rented her first apartment, and was excited to live independently. However, after a few months, Maria began to feel overwhelmed by her finances. She found herself living paycheck to paycheck, relying on credit cards more than she wanted to admit, and unsure of how to manage her growing expenses.

Despite earning a decent salary, Maria realized she had no savings and often made impulse purchases. She didn't understand how interest worked on her credit card debt, and the idea of budgeting seemed daunting. One day, after a particularly stressful month of bills piling up, Maria decided to take control of her financial situation.

She started by educating herself on the basics of personal finance—reading books, attending financial literacy workshops, and even meeting with a financial advisor. Slowly, Maria began to understand the importance of budgeting, saving, and living within her means. She created a simple budget that prioritized essentials and savings, and she started paying off her credit card debt little by little.

With discipline and a clearer understanding of how money works, Maria eventually built up an emergency fund and even began investing for the future. Her stress levels dropped, and she felt empowered knowing she had a plan in place for her financial well-being.

Maria's story shows the importance of understanding personal finance. Financial literacy is a key component of living a stable and secure life, and it can make the difference between constant financial stress and true peace of mind. By taking the time to learn about managing money, anyone can gain control over his or her financial future.

Sayings about Personal Finance

"Opportunities come infrequently. When it rains gold, put out the bucket, not the thimble." – **Warren Buffett**

"Beware of little expenses. A small leak will sink a great ship." – **Benjamin Franklin**

"A budget tells us what we can't afford, but it doesn't keep us from buying it." – **William Feather**

"Make sure you have financial intelligence... I don't care if you have money or you don't have money... you need to go and study finance no matter what." – ***Daymond John***

"Tough times never last, but tough people do." – **Robert H. Schuller**

"The way to get started is to quit talking and begin doing." – **Walt Disney**

"Personal finance is only 20% head knowledge. It's 80% behavior!" – **Dave Ramsey**

"A big part of financial freedom is having your heart and mind free from worry about the what-ifs of life." – **Suze Orman**

"Money, like emotions, is something you must control to keep your life on the right track." -**Natasha Munson**

"A man who does not plan long ahead will find trouble right at his door." – **Confucius**

"Don't tell me what you value, show me your budget, and I'll tell you what you value." – **Joe Biden**

"It's simple arithmetic: Your income can grow only to the extent that you do." — **T. Harv Eker**

"Money isn't everything, but it's right up there with oxygen." – **Zig Ziglar**

"You can have excuses or you can have success; you can't have both." — **Jen Sincero**

"In fact, what determines your wealth is not how much you make but how much you keep of what you make." — **David Bach**

Source: https://www.chime.com/blog/15-quotes-from-our-favorite-money-saving-experts/

The Basics of Budgeting and Saving

At the heart of personal finance is the concept of budgeting and saving. These two practices are essential for gaining control over your money and ensuring that you're living within your means. While budgeting may seem tedious or restrictive, it is actually the cornerstone of financial freedom. A well-crafted budget allows you to see exactly where your money is going, prioritize your spending, and allocate funds toward future goals.

Creating a Budget

The first step in building a budget is tracking your income and expenses. This means documenting all sources of income, such as salary, bonuses, or side gigs, and comparing them to your monthly expenses. Expenses should be divided into two categories: fixed and variable. Fixed expenses include things like rent or mortgage payments, utility bills, and loan payments, while variable expenses cover items like groceries, entertainment, and dining out. By examining these figures, you can identify areas where you might be overspending and make adjustments accordingly.

The 50/30/20 Rule

A popular and straightforward method for budgeting is the 50/30/20 rule. Under this framework, 50% of your income is allocated to needs (essential expenses like housing and groceries), 30% goes toward wants (non-essential spending like entertainment or dining out), and 20% is reserved for savings and debt repayment. This rule provides a clear structure while allowing flexibility based on individual circumstances.

Saving for the Future

Saving is the key to achieving long-term financial security. It's not enough to simply budget for today's expenses; you must also plan for future needs and unexpected emergencies. The first step is building an emergency fund, ideally covering three to six months' worth of living expenses. This fund acts as a safety net, protecting you from financial hardship in the event of job loss, medical emergencies, or major repairs.

Beyond an emergency fund, it's important to set specific savings goals. These could include short-term goals, like saving for a vacation or a new car, as well as long-term goals, such as retirement or a child's education. Automating your savings by setting up recurring transfers to a separate savings account can help ensure that you consistently set aside money for the future.

Managing Debt and Building Credit

Debt is a reality for many people, whether it's in the form of student loans, credit card balances, mortgages, or car loans. While debt can be a useful financial tool when managed responsibly, it can also become a heavy burden if it gets out of control. Understanding how to manage debt and build credit wisely is essential for maintaining financial health.

Types of Debt

Not all debt is created equal. Some debts, like mortgages or student loans, are often considered "good debt" because they are investments in your future. These types of debt typically come with lower interest rates and contribute to long-term wealth-building. On the other hand, "bad debt" refers to high-interest debt, such as credit card balances or payday loans, which can quickly spiral out of control if not managed properly.

Debt Repayment Strategies

If you're dealing with significant debt, it's important to develop a strategy for paying it off. One common approach is the **debt snowball method**, where you focus on paying off your smallest debt first while making minimum payments on other debts. Once the smallest debt is paid off, you move on to the next smallest, creating momentum and motivation as you eliminate each balance. Another approach is the **debt avalanche method**, where you prioritize paying off the debt with the highest interest rate first. This method saves you the most money over time but may take longer to see progress.

The Importance of Credit

Your credit score is a key indicator of your financial health and can impact everything from your ability to secure a loan to the interest rate you're offered. Building and maintaining a good credit score should be a priority. The primary factors influencing your credit score include your payment history, credit utilization (how much of your available credit you're using), the length of your credit history, the types of credit you have, and recent credit inquiries.

To build good credit, always pay your bills on time, avoid maxing out your credit cards, and aim to keep your credit utilization below 30%. It's also wise to diversify your credit mix by having a combination of credit cards, installment loans, or mortgages, as long as you can manage them responsibly.

Avoiding Debt Traps

To avoid falling into debt traps, it's essential to live within your means and avoid taking on unnecessary debt. It can be tempting to use credit cards for convenience or rewards, but carrying a balance can quickly become costly due to high interest rates. If possible, pay off your credit card balance in full each month. Additionally, be cautious of taking out loans that you cannot realistically afford to repay, and always read the fine print to understand the terms and conditions.

Planning for Major Life Expenses

Major life expenses can often feel overwhelming, but with careful planning, they don't have to derail your financial stability. Whether you're buying a home, funding a college education, or preparing for retirement, understanding the financial implications of these milestones is key to making informed decisions.

Buying a Home

Purchasing a home is one of the largest financial commitments most people will make in their lifetime. It requires not only a substantial down payment but also ongoing costs such as mortgage payments, property taxes, and maintenance expenses. Before buying a home, it's essential to assess your financial readiness by considering your credit score, the size of your down payment, and your debt-to-income ratio. A general rule of thumb is that your monthly housing costs (including mortgage, taxes, and insurance) should not exceed 30% of your monthly income. Additionally, don't forget to budget for unexpected costs, such as repairs or renovations, which are a normal part of homeownership.

Funding Education

Education is a significant expense, whether it's your own higher education or saving for your children's future. For many, taking out student loans is necessary to cover tuition and related costs. However, it's important to research all available options, such as scholarships, grants, and work-study programs, before taking on debt. If you have children, setting up a 529 savings plan or other tax-advantaged educational savings accounts can help you prepare for their future without the burden of significant student loans.

Retirement Planning

Retirement may seem far off, but the earlier you start planning, the more secure your financial future will be. Building a retirement fund requires long-term commitment and strategic planning. One of the most effective tools for retirement savings is an employer-sponsored 401(k) plan, especially if your employer offers matching contributions. If you're self-employed or don't have access to a 401(k), consider opening an individual retirement account (IRA). Aiming to save 10-15% of your income for retirement is a good starting point, though this may vary based on your goals and financial situation.

As you approach retirement age, it's also important to consider other sources of income, such as Social Security benefits, pensions, or part-time work. Additionally, evaluating your expected living expenses in retirement will help you determine whether your savings will be sufficient to maintain your lifestyle.

Conclusion

Understanding personal finance is essential for achieving financial stability and peace of mind. By mastering the basics of budgeting and saving, managing debt wisely, building strong credit, and planning for major life expenses, you set yourself up for a lifetime of financial security. Personal finance is not about perfection—it's about making informed decisions, setting realistic goals, and being proactive in managing your money.

Whether you are just starting your financial journey or are looking to improve your current situation, the principles covered in this chapter provide a foundation for long-term financial health. Remember, personal finance is a lifelong learning process, and the more you educate yourself and take control of your finances, the greater your ability to create a stable and fulfilling future.

Exercise

Building a Strong Financial Foundation

This exercise is designed to help you assess your current financial situation, set realistic goals, and build healthier financial habits.

Step 1: Assess Your Current Financial Health

Start by taking a snapshot of your current financial situation. Answer the following questions:

- **Income:** How much do you earn each month (after taxes)?
- **Expenses:** What are your fixed expenses (rent, mortgage, utilities, insurance, etc.)? What are your variable expenses (groceries, entertainment, transportation, etc.)?
- **Savings:** How much do you save each month? What percentage of your income goes to savings?
- **Debt:** What debts do you currently owe (credit cards, loans, mortgages)? What is the total amount, and what are the interest rates?

Write down these numbers in a notebook or on a financial tracking sheet. Understanding your financial health is the first step toward making informed financial decisions.

Step 2: Set Financial Goals

Now that you have a clearer understanding of your finances, it's time to set some specific financial goals. Think of both short-term and long-term goals:

- **Short-term goals:** These could include paying off a certain amount of debt, saving for a vacation, or building an emergency fund.
- **Long-term goals:** These might include saving for retirement, purchasing a home, or funding a child's education.

Write down 1-2 short-term and 1-2 long-term financial goals. Be as specific as possible, including how much money you'll need to achieve them and by what date.

Step 3: Create a Budget

One of the most important aspects of financial health is budgeting. Based on the financial information you gathered in Step 1, create a budget that aligns with your goals:

- **Income:** Start with your total monthly income.
- **Expenses:** Categorize your fixed and variable expenses. How much can you realistically allocate to each category?
- **Savings and Debt Repayment:** How much can you save each month? How much can you allocate toward paying off debt?

Use this budget to guide your spending and saving for the next month. Be sure to adjust it as necessary to stay aligned with your financial goals.

Step 4: Develop Healthy Financial Habits

Good financial health depends on developing consistent habits. Reflect on your current habits and ask yourself:

- **Do I stick to my budget?**
- **Do I spend impulsively on things I don't need?**

- **Do I regularly contribute to savings?**

Identify one or two habits that need improvement and commit to working on them over the next month. For example, if you tend to overspend on non-essential items, try limiting your spending in that category. If saving is challenging, consider setting up an automatic transfer to a savings account.

Step 5: Track Your Progress

For the next month, track all of your income and expenses. Use an app or a financial journal to record:

- Every source of income
- All expenses, including small purchases
- Debt payments and savings contributions

At the end of the month, review your progress:

- **Were you able to stick to your budget?**
- **Did you make progress toward your financial goals?**
- **Did you develop any healthier financial habits?**

Adjust your budget or habits based on what you learned, and continue tracking your progress to improve your financial situation over time.

Step 6: Improve Your Financial Literacy

To build long-term financial health, it's important to keep learning about personal finance. Commit to improving your financial literacy by doing one of the following:

- **Read a book** on personal finance, such as *Wealth Creation and Preservation* by Elijah M. James or *The Total Money Makeover* by Dave Ramsey.
- **Listen to a financial podcast** like *The Dave Ramsey Show*.
- **Take an online course** on personal finance basics, investing, or budgeting.

Write down one action you'll take to improve your financial knowledge over the next month, and schedule time to make it happen.

Step 7: Reflect on Your Financial Mindset

Your mindset plays a critical role in how you handle money. Take a moment to reflect on how you view money:

- **Do you see money as a tool for achieving your goals, or as a source of stress?**
- **Do you believe you have control over your financial future, or do you feel limited by your current situation?**

Write a brief reflection about your current financial mindset. If you recognize negative beliefs, identify one way you can shift your thinking to a more positive and empowering view of money.

Step 8: Make a Commitment to Your Financial Future

Finally, think about how you want your financial future to look. Imagine yourself achieving your financial goals and living without financial stress. What steps can you take today to move closer to that vision?

Write down a commitment to your financial future. This could be as simple as, "I commit to sticking to my budget for the next three months" or "I commit to paying off $500 of my debt by the end of this year." Make this commitment visible—place it somewhere where you'll see it every day as a reminder of your goals.

By working through this exercise, you'll develop a deeper understanding of your financial situation, set clear goals, and build healthy financial habits that will guide you toward long-term financial security.

THE JOURNEY TO A FULFILLING AND MEANINGFUL LIFE

CHAPTER 13
WORDSEARCH

	1	2	3	4	5	6	7	8	9	10	11	12
1	F	B	Q	G	T	E	C	N	A	N	I	F
2	I	K	Z	L	N	O	F	T	O	M	C	H
3	I	N	I	U	E	I	A	V	A	H	E	S
4	S	S	S	L	M	X	T	P	V	X	A	E
5	G	N	F	U	E	O	B	E	P	R	C	V
6	N	O	S	S	R	K	R	E	G	R	A	C
7	I	I	A	C	I	A	N	T	O	D	R	F
8	N	S	V	V	T	S	N	F	G	E	U	X
9	N	N	I	Q	E	I	K	C	D	A	S	B
10	A	E	N	S	R	R	A	I	E	R	G	S
11	L	P	G	A	O	V	T	L	B	U	I	E
12	P	V	S	W	U	T	R	E	T	Z	R	L

BUDGETING	INSURANCE	SAVINGS
CREDIT	MORTGAGE	TAXES
DEBT	PENSIONS	WORKFORCE
EXPENSES	PLANNING	
FINANCE	RETIREMENT	

UNDERSTANDING PERSONAL FINANCE

ANSWER

	1	2	3	4	5	6	7	8	9	10	11	12
1	F	B	Q	G	T	E	C	N	A	N	I	F
2	I	K	Z	L	N	O	F	T	O	M	C	H
3	I	N	I	U	E	I	A	V	A	H	E	S
4	S	S	S	L	M	X	T	P	V	X	A	E
5	G	N	F	U	E	O	B	E	P	R	C	V
6	N	O	S	S	R	K	R	E	G	R	A	C
7	I	I	A	C	I	A	N	T	O	D	R	F
8	N	S	V	V	T	S	N	F	G	E	U	X
9	N	N	I	Q	E	I	K	C	D	A	S	B
10	A	E	N	S	R	R	A	I	E	R	G	S
11	L	P	G	A	O	V	T	L	B	U	I	E
12	P	V	S	W	U	T	R	E	T	Z	R	L

BUDGETING 9:12 INSURANCE 2:1 SAVINGS 6:3
CREDIT 6:12   MORTGAGE 4:5   TAXES 2:8
DEBT 9:9   PENSIONS 11:2 WORKFORCE 12:4
EXPENSES 3:11 PLANNING 12:1
FINANCE 1:12   RETIREMENT 10:5

CHAPTER 14
INVESTING FOR THE FUTURE

Investing offers the potential for significant growth over time by putting your money to work in assets that appreciate in value, generate income, or both.

The Bible Says

"Wealth gained hastily will dwindle, but whoever gathers little by little will increase it." – **Proverbs 13:11**

"The plans of the diligent lead surely to abundance, but everyone who is hasty comes only to poverty." – **Proverbs 21:5**

"Better is a little with righteousness than great revenues with injustice." – **Proverbs 16:8**

"A faithful man will abound with blessings, but whoever hastens to be rich will not go unpunished." – **Proverbs 28:20**

"Whoever trusts in his riches will fall, but the righteous will flourish like a green leaf." – **Proverbs 11:28**

"Whoever loves pleasure will be a poor man; he who loves wine and oil will not be rich." – **Proverbs 21:17**

Divide your portion to seven, or even to eight, for you do not know what misfortune may occur on the earth. **Ecclesiastes 11:2**

A good man leaves an inheritance to his children's children,
And the wealth of the sinner is stored up for the righteous. **Proverbs 13:22**

Then you ought to have put my money in the bank, and on my arrival I would have received my money back with interest. **Matthew 25:27**

One who is gracious to a poor man lends to the Lord,
And He will repay him for his good deed. **Proverbs 19:17**

The one who had received the five talents came up and brought five more talents, saying, 'Master, you entrusted five talents to me. See, I have gained five more talents.' **Matthew 25:20**

He who increases his wealth by interest and usury
Gathers it for him who is gracious to the poor. **Proverbs 28:8**

Source: https://bible.knowing-jesus.com/topics/Investing

Introduction

Investing is one of the most powerful tools available for building wealth and achieving long-term financial security. Unlike saving, which typically involves setting aside money in low-risk, low-return accounts, investing offers the potential for significant growth over time by putting your money to work in assets that appreciate in value, generate income, or both. While investing can seem intimidating to beginners, understanding the fundamentals can help you make informed decisions, manage risk, and set yourself on the path toward financial independence.

In this chapter, we will explore the basics of investing, including common types of investments, the importance of diversification, and strategies for planning for retirement. The goal is to provide a comprehensive overview that can help you make smarter financial decisions, grow your wealth over the long term, and achieve both short- and long-term financial goals. By the end of this chapter, you should have a clearer understanding of how to approach investing in a way that aligns with your financial aspirations.

Life Story

When Harry turned 30, he felt proud of what he had accomplished so far. He had a steady job as a software engineer, owned a small home, and had started a family with his wife, Sarah. While they lived comfortably, Harry often wondered about the future—especially when it came to finances. He had heard about investing but had always thought it was something only wealthy people did or something too risky for an average person like he was.

One day, while talking to a co-worker, Harry learned that the power of investing wasn't in how much money you started with, but in how early you began. His co-worker shared how compounding interest helped grow even modest investments into significant amounts over time. This conversation sparked Harry's curiosity, and he decided to look into investing more seriously.

He began by educating himself, reading up on basic investment strategies and consulting a financial advisor. The idea of putting his hard-earned money into stocks and bonds was intimidating at first, but he learned the value of diversification—spreading his investments across different asset classes to reduce risk. Harry started small, setting up an automatic contribution to a retirement account and gradually investing in low-cost index funds.

As time passed, Harry saw his investments grow, and he realized that this wasn't just about building wealth—it was about securing a future for himself, his family, and the life they envisioned. With every passing year, he became more confident, knowing that his early efforts would pay off in the long term, providing him with financial independence and peace of mind.

Harry's journey highlights the importance of starting to invest early and the power of patience in growing wealth. Investing isn't just for the wealthy; it's a tool that, when used wisely, can help anyone build a solid financial foundation for the future. By learning about investing and taking action, Harry transformed his financial outlook and set his family on a path toward long-term security.

Sayings about Investing

These quotes are designed to help you think seriously about investing.

"An investment in knowledge pays the best interest." — **Benjamin Franklin**

"Bottoms in the investment world don't end with four-year lows; they end with 10- or 15-year lows." — **Jim Rogers**

"I will tell you how to become rich. Close the doors. Be fearful when others are greedy. Be greedy when others are fearful." — **Warren Buffett**

"With a good perspective on history, we can have a better understanding of the past and present, and thus a clear vision of the future." — **Carlos Slim Helu**

"It's not whether you're right or wrong that's important, but how much money you make when you're right and how much you lose when you're wrong." — **George Soros**

"Given a 10% chance of a 100 times payoff, you should take that bet every time." — **Jeff Bezos**

"Don't look for the needle in the haystack. Just buy the haystack!" — **John Bogle**

"I don't look to jump over seven-foot bars; I look around for one-foot bars that I can step over." — **Warren Buffett**

"The stock market is filled with individuals who know the price of everything, but the value of nothing." — **Phillip Fisher**

"In investing, what is comfortable is rarely profitable." — **Robert Arnott**

"How many millionaires do you know who have become wealthy by investing in savings accounts? I rest my case." — **Robert G. Allen**

"If there is one common theme to the vast range of the world's financial crises, it is that excessive debt accumulation, whether by the government, banks, corporations, or consumers, often poses greater systemic risks than it seems during a boom." — **Carmen Reinhart**

"We don't prognosticate macroeconomic factors, we're looking at our companies from a bottom-up perspective on their long-run prospects of returning." — **Mellody Hobson**

"Courage taught me no matter how bad a crisis gets ... any sound investment will eventually pay off." — **Carlos Slim Helu**

"The individual investor should act consistently as an investor and not as a speculator." — **Ben Graham**

"The biggest risk of all is not taking one." — **Mellody Hobson**

"Returns matter a lot. It's our capital." — **Abigail Johnson**

"It's not how much money you make, but how much money you keep, how hard it works for you, and how many generations you keep it for." — **Robert Kiyosaki**

"Know what you own, and know why you own it." — **Peter Lynch**

"Financial peace isn't the acquisition of stuff. It's learning to live on less than you make, so you can give money back and have money to invest. You can't win until you do this." — **Dave Ramsey**

"Investing should be more like watching paint dry or watching grass grow. If you want excitement, take $800 and go to Las Vegas." — **Paul Samuelson**

"The four most dangerous words in investing are, it's different this time." — **Sir John Templeton**

"Wide diversification is only required when investors do not understand what they are doing." — **Warren Buffett**

"You get recessions, you have stock market declines. If you don't understand that's going to happen, then you're not ready, you won't do well in the markets." — **Peter Lynch**

"The most contrarian thing of all is not to oppose the crowd but to think for yourself." — **Peter Thiel**

Source: https://www.investopedia.com/financial-edge/0511/the-top-17-investing-quotes-of-all-time.aspx

The Fundamentals of Investing

At its core, investing involves allocating money to assets with the expectation of generating a return over time. These returns can come in the form of capital appreciation (the increase in the value of an asset) or income (such as dividends or interest). While all investments carry some degree of risk, the potential rewards often outweigh the risks when approached with a solid understanding of the market and a long-term perspective.

Common Types of Investments

Stocks: When you purchase a stock, you are buying a share of ownership in a company. Stocks are often considered a high-risk, high-reward investment because their value can fluctuate significantly over short periods. However, historically, stocks have provided higher long-term returns compared to other asset classes. Stocks are particularly attractive for investors with a long-term horizon, as they can benefit from compounding growth over decades.

Bonds: Bonds are essentially loans you provide to a government or corporation in exchange for regular interest payments and the return of your principal investment when the bond matures. Bonds are considered lower-risk investments compared to stocks, making them a popular choice for those seeking stability in their portfolios. However, they generally offer lower returns than stocks.

Mutual Funds and ETFs: These are pooled investment vehicles that allow you to invest in a diversified portfolio of stocks, bonds, or other assets. Mutual funds are actively managed by professional fund managers, while exchange-traded funds (ETFs) track specific market indexes and are passively managed. Both options provide an easy way for investors to diversify without picking individual stocks or bonds.

Real Estate: Real estate investing involves purchasing property with the intent to generate income (through rental properties) or profit from appreciation when the property is sold. While real estate can be a stable and lucrative investment, it requires significant capital upfront and ongoing management.

Commodities: Commodities, such as gold, oil, and agricultural products, can be used as a hedge against inflation or economic downturns. However, they are often more volatile and speculative compared to other investments.

Cryptocurrencies: A newer asset class, cryptocurrencies like Bitcoin and Ethereum are highly speculative and volatile. While they have gained popularity as alternative investments, they carry significant risks and should be approached with caution.

The Risk-Return Trade-off

One of the fundamental concepts in investing is the relationship between risk and return. Generally, the higher the potential return on an investment, the greater the risk involved. Stocks, for example, have the potential for high returns but can also experience significant short-term losses. Conversely, bonds offer more stability but typically have lower returns. Understanding your own risk tolerance—how much risk you are willing and able to take on—is crucial when determining which investments are appropriate for your portfolio.

The Importance of Time Horizon

Another key factor in investing is your time horizon, or the length of time you plan to hold an investment before you need to access the funds. Those with a longer time horizon, such as younger investors saving for retirement, can afford to take on more risk because they have time to ride out market fluctuations. On the other hand, individuals nearing retirement may prefer more conservative investments to preserve their capital and ensure liquidity.

Diversifying Your Investment Portfolio

One of the most effective strategies for managing risk in investing is diversification. Diversification involves spreading your investments across different asset classes (such as stocks, bonds, and real estate) and sectors (such as technology, healthcare, and energy) to reduce the impact of a poor-performing investment on your overall portfolio. In essence, diversification allows you to avoid putting all your eggs in one basket.

Why Diversification Matters

The goal of diversification is to reduce the volatility of your portfolio. While no investment is risk-free, a well-diversified portfolio can help protect you from significant losses. When one asset class or sector experiences a downturn, others may perform well, balancing out the overall performance of your investments. For example, if the stock market is down, bonds or real estate may continue to provide steady returns, mitigating the impact of the stock market decline.

Types of Diversification

Across Asset Classes: Allocating your investments among different asset classes—such as stocks, bonds, real estate, and commodities—helps ensure that you are not overly exposed to the risk of one specific type of investment.

Within Asset Classes: Diversification can also occur within an asset class. For instance, in a stock portfolio, you might invest in companies from various industries, such as technology, healthcare, and consumer goods. This reduces the risk that a downturn in one industry will severely impact your portfolio.

Geographic Diversification: Investing in companies or assets from different regions of the world can help protect your portfolio from localized economic issues. International investments provide exposure to the growth potential of emerging markets and can reduce the risk associated with relying solely on the performance of your home country's economy.

Using Mutual Funds and ETFs for Diversification

For many investors, mutual funds and ETFs provide a simple and efficient way to achieve diversification. Rather than trying to pick individual stocks or bonds, these funds pool your money with other investors and invest in a broad range of assets. This allows you to gain exposure to a diversified portfolio with a relatively small investment. Additionally, these funds are managed by professionals, so you benefit from their expertise without having to constantly monitor and adjust your investments.

Rebalancing Your Portfolio

Over time, the value of your investments will fluctuate, causing your portfolio to become unbalanced. For example, if stocks perform particularly well, they may grow to represent a larger portion of your portfolio than you originally intended. Rebalancing involves periodically adjusting your portfolio to restore your desired asset allocation. This may involve selling some investments that have increased in value and purchasing others that have underperformed, ensuring that you maintain a balanced and diversified portfolio.

Retirement Planning and Financial Independence

Investing plays a critical role in retirement planning and achieving financial independence. While saving is an essential component of retirement preparation, investing allows your money to grow over time and provides the opportunity to build a substantial nest egg that can support you in your later years. The earlier you start investing, the more you can benefit from compounding returns, which is the process by which your investment gains generate additional gains over time.

Retirement Accounts

One of the most effective ways to invest for retirement is through tax-advantaged retirement accounts. These accounts offer benefits such as tax deductions, tax-free growth, or tax-free withdrawals, depending on the type of account.

401(k) Plans: Employer-sponsored 401(k) plans allow you to contribute a portion of your pre-tax income, which reduces your taxable income for the year. Many employers also offer matching contributions, which is essentially free money that boosts your retirement savings. The funds in your 401(k) grow tax-deferred, meaning you don't pay taxes on the gains until you withdraw the money in retirement.

IRAs (Individual Retirement Accounts): IRAs are another popular retirement savings vehicle, offering both traditional and Roth options. In a traditional IRA, contributions are tax-deductible, and the funds grow tax-deferred. In a Roth IRA, contributions are made with after-tax dollars, but withdrawals in retirement are tax-free. Both options have contribution limits and income restrictions, so it's important to understand which one is right for you.

The Power of Compound Interest

The key to building wealth for retirement is taking advantage of compound interest. Compound interest occurs when your investment earnings generate additional earnings over time. The longer your money is invested, the more it can grow exponentially. This is why starting early is so important—time is one of the most powerful tools in investing for retirement.

Achieving Financial Independence

Financial independence is the point at which you have accumulated enough wealth to support your lifestyle without needing to work for income. For many, this is the ultimate goal of investing. Achieving financial independence requires disciplined saving and investing, careful budgeting, and a long-term focus. It often involves saving a significant portion of your income, investing in a diversified portfolio, and controlling spending to ensure that your investments grow over time.

To reach financial independence, it's essential to determine how much you need to live comfortably without relying on a paycheck. This involves calculating your annual living expenses and estimating how much you'll need to withdraw from your investments each year in retirement. A common rule of thumb is the 4% rule, which suggests that you can withdraw 4% of your portfolio each year in retirement without running out of money. However, individual circumstances may require adjustments to this rule.

Conclusion

Investing is a powerful tool for building wealth, achieving financial independence, and securing a comfortable retirement. While it may seem complex or risky, understanding the fundamentals of investing, the importance of diversification, and the strategies for planning your financial future can help you navigate the world of investments with confidence. By starting early, setting clear goals, and maintaining a diversified portfolio,

Exercise

Crafting Your Investment Strategy for the Future

The purpose of this exercise is to guide you through the essential steps of creating a personalized investment plan and taking the first steps toward building wealth for the long term.

Step 1: Assess Your Investment Knowledge

Before diving into investments, take stock of your current understanding. Reflect on the following questions:

- **Have you invested before?** If so, what type of investments have you made (stocks, bonds, mutual funds, real estate, etc.)?
- **What is your level of knowledge?** Are you familiar with investment concepts like risk, diversification, and returns?
- **How do you feel about investing?** Are you confident, curious, or perhaps a bit anxious?

Write a brief summary of your current investment experience and knowledge. If you're new to investing, this will serve as your starting point for learning more.

Step 2: Define Your Investment Goals

Investing is most effective when tied to clear goals. Think about what you hope to achieve with your investments. Examples might include:

- **Saving for retirement:** How much money will you need for a comfortable retirement?
- **Building wealth:** Are you focused on growing your wealth over time?

- **Saving for specific goals:** Are you investing for a home, education, or other long-term financial needs?

Write down 1-2 long-term financial goals that will guide your investment decisions. Be specific about the time frame (e.g., 10 years, 20 years) and the amount of money you aim to accumulate.

Step 3: Understand Your Risk Tolerance

Investing involves balancing risk and reward. Reflect on your comfort level with risk by considering the following:

- **How do you react to financial loss?** Would losing a portion of your investment cause significant stress, or are you comfortable with some ups and downs in the market?
- **What is your time horizon?** The longer your time horizon, the more risk you can usually tolerate, as you'll have more time to recover from any losses.
- **What is your investment style?** Are you conservative (prefer low-risk investments like bonds), moderate (balance of stocks and bonds), or aggressive (high-risk, high-reward investments like stocks)?

Write a short reflection on your risk tolerance. This will help guide the type of investments that align with your comfort level.

Step 4: Start Learning About Investment Options

Educate yourself on the different types of investments available. Begin by researching the following:

- **Stocks:** Ownership in a company that offers higher potential returns but comes with more volatility.
- **Bonds:** Loans to governments or corporations, typically lower risk but with lower returns.
- **Mutual funds and ETFs:** Pooled investment funds that offer diversification by investing in a range of assets.
- **Real estate:** Investing in property for rental income or appreciation.
- **Retirement accounts:** Research options like IRAs or 401(k)s, which offer tax advantages.

Write down one or two types of investments you are interested in learning more about. Use reputable financial websites, books, or podcasts to deepen your understanding of these options.

Step 5: Develop a Diversified Portfolio

One of the most important principles in investing is diversification—spreading your investments across different asset classes to manage risk.

- **Create a sample portfolio:** Based on your risk tolerance and goals, sketch out a diversified portfolio. For example, if you're risk-averse, your portfolio might include 70% bonds and 30% stocks. If you're more risk-tolerant, you might allocate 80% to stocks and 20% to bonds.
- **Include different asset classes:** Think about mixing stocks, bonds, real estate, and other investments. This will help you spread risk and increase the chances of steady returns over time.

Write down your sample investment portfolio. This is your starting point—over time, you can adjust your allocations as your financial situation and goals change.

Step 6: Automate Your Investments

A key to long-term success in investing is consistency. One of the easiest ways to ensure you're investing regularly is to automate the process:

- **Set up automatic contributions:** Whether it's through your employer-sponsored retirement plan or a personal brokerage account, set up automatic monthly transfers. Even small amounts add up over time.
- **Choose investment accounts:** If you're saving for retirement, look into tax-advantaged accounts like IRAs or 401(k)s. If you're saving for other goals, a regular brokerage account may be more appropriate.

Commit to automating a portion of your income for investing. Write down how much you plan to contribute each month and where these contributions will go.

Step 7: Monitor and Adjust Your Investments

Investing isn't a set-it-and-forget-it process. Regularly review your portfolio to ensure it aligns with your goals:

- **Check your portfolio's performance:** Is it meeting your expectations? Are any investments underperforming?
- **Rebalance your portfolio:** Over time, the value of different investments will change. Rebalancing ensures that your portfolio maintains the right mix of assets based on your risk tolerance.

- **Update your goals:** If your financial goals change (e.g., you decide to retire earlier), adjust your investments accordingly.

Write down a commitment to review your investments regularly (e.g., every six months). This will help you stay on track and ensure your portfolio continues to align with your goals.

Step 8: Stay Informed and Continue Learning

The world of investing is constantly changing, and staying informed is key to long-term success.

- **Read investment news:** Stay up to date with market trends and changes in the economy that could affect your portfolio.
- **Learn about new investment strategies:** As you gain more experience, explore different strategies such as dollar-cost averaging, value investing, or real estate investing.

Commit to reading one investment-related article, book, or taking an online course within the next month. Write down your plan for continuing your education in investing.

Step 9: Reflect on Your Investment Mindset

Investing is as much about mindset as it is about strategy. Reflect on your attitudes toward money and risk:

- **Do you see investing as a path to financial freedom?**
- **Are you comfortable with the uncertainty that comes with investing?**

- **How do you handle market downturns?**

Write a brief reflection on your current investment mindset. If you notice any limiting beliefs, think about how you can shift to a more positive and confident mindset toward investing.

Step 10: Take Action

The most important step is to start. Investing can be intimidating, but the earlier you begin, the more time your money has to grow.

- **Open an investment account:** If you don't already have one, open an account with a reputable brokerage.
- **Make your first investment:** Choose an investment based on your research and portfolio goals, and take that first step toward building your future.

Write down the first action you'll take in your investment journey. Whether it's opening an account, buying a stock, or increasing your retirement contributions, commit to taking that step within the next week.

By completing this exercise, you'll be on your way to developing a sound investment strategy that aligns with your financial goals and sets you up for long-term success.

CHAPTER 14
WORDSEARCH

	1	2	3	4	5	6	7	8	9	10	11	12	13	14	15	16	17	18	19
1	K	I	Q	C	Q	O	I	L	O	F	T	R	O	P	Y	C	T	T	O
2	H	A	A	V	G	N	I	T	S	E	V	N	I	A	B	X	W	N	B
3	L	F	C	C	J	R	I	A	E	V	U	O	P	R	E	Q	P	E	X
4	W	J	D	Q	R	K	O	A	R	O	A	E	S	V	O	M	Q	M	E
5	R	I	I	C	O	Y	H	F	S	I	T	S	D	N	O	B	N	T	N
6	Y	F	V	P	S	D	P	J	N	S	S	N	W	H	I	D	C	S	Q
7	G	R	E	V	X	U	Q	T	Q	Z	E	K	I	T	W	V	M	E	I
8	N	J	R	D	L	D	B	H	O	W	R	T	U	D	Q	H	R	V	B
9	I	C	S	A	V	I	N	G	S	C	J	Q	S	A	Y	T	V	N	S
10	D	S	I	I	A	W	P	D	R	J	U	R	E	B	L	A	K	I	K
11	N	P	F	V	C	A	P	I	T	A	L	R	E	Y	C	S	S	A	C
12	U	Y	I	L	C	S	V	X	L	J	M	U	R	T	R	A	M	F	O
13	O	G	C	D	D	A	E	I	K	E	D	T	J	E	U	H	Q	X	T
14	P	I	A	M	Z	O	F	C	L	O	L	D	E	G	N	R	O	F	S
15	M	N	T	Q	M	L	Y	E	U	D	G	T	J	J	O	C	N	A	Z
16	O	N	I	J	T	B	I	M	E	R	J	M	A	C	L	F	I	D	K
17	C	T	O	E	S	C	A	C	L	V	I	D	D	N	E	E	H	E	V
18	P	N	N	Y	E	X	B	O	L	Y	C	T	W	E	A	L	T	H	S
19	G	I	C	Y	K	W	S	W	W	Z	Z	P	Y	C	B	Z	S	D	I

ASSETS
BONDS
CAPITAL
COMPOUNDING
CRYPTOCURRENCIES
DIVERSIFICATION
INVESTING
INVESTMENT
PORTFOLIO
RETURN
RISK
SAVINGS
SECURITY
STOCKS
WEALTH

INVESTING FOR THE FUTURE

ANSWER

	1	2	3	4	5	6	7	8	9	10	11	12	13	14	15	16	17	18	19
1	K	I	Q	C	Q	O	I	L	O	F	T	R	O	P	Y	C	T	T	O
2	H	A	A	V	G	N	I	T	S	E	V	N	I	A	B	X	W	N	B
3	L	F	C	C	J	R	I	A	E	V	U	O	P	R	E	Q	P	E	X
4	W	J	D	Q	R	K	O	A	R	O	A	E	S	V	O	M	Q	M	E
5	R	I	I	C	O	Y	H	F	S	I	T	S	D	N	O	B	N	T	N
6	Y	F	V	P	S	D	P	J	N	S	S	N	W	H	I	D	C	S	Q
7	G	R	E	V	X	U	Q	T	Q	Z	E	K	I	T	W	V	M	E	I
8	N	J	R	D	L	D	B	H	O	W	R	T	U	D	Q	H	R	V	B
9	I	C	S	A	V	I	N	G	S	C	J	Q	S	A	Y	T	V	N	S
10	D	S	I	I	A	W	P	D	R	J	U	R	E	B	L	A	K	I	K
11	N	P	F	V	C	A	P	I	T	A	L	R	E	Y	C	S	S	A	C
12	U	Y	I	L	C	S	V	X	L	J	M	U	R	T	R	A	M	F	O
13	O	G	C	D	D	A	E	I	K	E	D	T	J	E	U	H	Q	X	T
14	P	I	A	M	Z	O	F	C	L	O	L	D	E	G	N	R	O	F	S
15	M	N	T	Q	M	L	Y	E	U	D	G	T	J	J	O	C	N	A	Z
16	O	N	I	J	T	B	I	M	E	R	J	M	A	C	L	F	I	D	K
17	C	T	O	E	S	C	A	C	L	V	I	D	D	N	E	E	H	E	V
18	P	N	N	Y	E	X	B	O	L	Y	C	T	W	E	A	L	T	H	S
19	G	I	C	Y	K	W	S	W	W	Z	Z	P	Y	C	B	Z	S	D	I

ASSETS 4:8
DIVERSIFICATION 4:3
RISK 4:9
BONDS 5:16
INVESTING 2:13
SAVINGS 9:3
CAPITAL 11:5
INVESTMENT 10:18
SECURITY 12:6
COMPOUNDING 17:1
PORTFOLIO 1:14
STOCKS 14:19
CRYPTOCURRENCIES 3:4
RETURN 10:12
WEALTH 18:13

CHAPTER 15
ECONOMIC LITERACY AND DECISION-MAKING

Economic literacy is the foundation for making informed decisions in a world where the economy shapes nearly every aspect of our lives.

The Bible Says

I will instruct you and teach you in the way you should go; I will counsel you with my eye upon you. **Psalm 32:8**

Practice what you learned from me. What you have learned and received and heard and seen in me—practice these things, and the God of peace will be with you. **Philippians 4:9**

Therefore encourage one another and build one another up, just as you are doing. **1 Thessalonians 5:11**

My son, do not despise the Lord's discipline or be weary of his reproof, for the Lord reproves him whom he loves, as a father the son in whom he delights. **Proverbs 3:11-12**

Lead me in your truth and teach me, for you are the God of my salvation; for you I wait all the day long. **Psalm 25:5**

Teach me to do your will, for you are my God! Let your good Spirit lead me on level ground! **Psalm 143:10**

Whoever loves discipline loves knowledge, but he who hates reproof is stupid. **Proverbs 12:1**

But the Helper, the Holy Spirit, whom the Father will send in my name, he will teach you all things and bring to your remembrance all that I have said to you. **John 14:26**

Do not forsake her, and she will keep you; love her, and she will guard you. The beginning of wisdom is this: Get wisdom, and whatever you get, get insight. **Proverbs 4:6-7**

For to the one who pleases him God has given wisdom and knowledge and joy, but to the sinner he has given the business of gathering and collecting, only to give to one who pleases God. This also is vanity and a striving after wind. **Ecclesiastes 2:26**

If any of you lacks wisdom, let him ask God, who gives generously to all without reproach, and it will be given him. **James 1:5**

Introduction

Economic literacy is the foundation for making informed decisions in a world where the economy shapes nearly every aspect of our lives. From determining how to spend money to understanding national policies that impact our day-to-day existence, having a grasp of basic economic principles empowers individuals to navigate complex financial landscapes with confidence. Without a solid understanding of economic fundamentals, it becomes difficult to assess risks, weigh opportunities, and make choices that align with both personal and societal well-being.

This chapter will explore the importance of economic literacy and how it influences decision-making at both personal and broader levels. We will begin by discussing how to analyze economic data, interpret key indicators, and recognize the impact of various economic forces on individual choices. Following this, we will examine how economic knowledge can shape the quality of your financial and life decisions. Finally, we'll discuss how economic awareness plays a crucial role in planning for the future, helping you make proactive choices about career, family, and retirement.

Life Story

When Linda opened her own small bakery, she was thrilled to finally pursue her passion. However, after the initial excitement wore off, she quickly realized how much she didn't know about running a business—especially when it came to finances. She was great at baking, but when it came to pricing, managing costs, and making business decisions, she often felt overwhelmed.

One month, sales were down, and Linda had to make tough choices about inventory and staffing. Unsure of how to move forward, she spoke to a mentor who told her, "Understanding the economics of your business is just as important as knowing how to bake." Encouraged, Linda took a step back and decided to learn more about economic principles and how they applied to her bakery.

She started by learning the basics of supply and demand, how to analyze market trends, and how pricing could influence her sales. She also began tracking her expenses more closely and discovered areas where she could cut costs without sacrificing quality. Armed with this knowledge, Linda was able to adjust her pricing strategy, optimize her spending, and even identify new opportunities to expand her customer base.

Over time, Linda's bakery became more profitable, and she felt empowered by her newfound understanding of how economic literacy directly influenced the decisions she made. By learning to make data-driven decisions, she transformed her business from struggling to thriving.

Linda's story shows that economic literacy isn't just for economists—it's essential for everyday decision-making. Whether running a business or managing personal finances, understanding economic principles helps people make informed, confident decisions. For Linda, gaining that knowledge made all the difference in achieving her dream and securing her future.

Sayings about Economic Literacy

You should find the following sayings interesting and useful as they help you to experience a meaningful life.

"Money is only a tool. It will take you wherever you wish, but it will not replace you as the driver." — **Ayn Rand**

"Financial peace isn't the acquisition of stuff. It's learning to live on less than you make, so you can give money back and have money to invest. You can't win until you do this." — **Dave Ramsey**

"Money, like emotions, is something you must control to keep your life on the right track." — **Natasha Munson**

"The real measure of your wealth is how much you'd be worth if you lost all your money." — **Bernard Meltzer**

"You can only become truly accomplished at something you love. Don't make money your goal. Instead, pursue the things you love doing, and then do them so well that people can't take their eyes off you." — **Maya Angelou**

"It takes as much energy to wish as it does to plan." — **Eleanor Roosevelt**

"The person who doesn't know where his next dollar is coming from usually doesn't know where his last dollar went." — **Unknown**

"There is a gigantic difference between earning a great deal of money and being rich." — **Marlene Dietrich**

"It's better to look ahead and prepare than to look back and regret." — **Jackie Joyner-Kersee**

"No one has ever become poor by giving." — **Anne Frank**

"If you don't value your time, neither will others. Stop giving away your time and talents. Value what you know & start charging for it." — **Kim Garst**

"What we really want to do is what we are really meant to do. When we do what we are meant to do, money comes to us, doors open for us, we feel useful, and the work we do feels like play to us." — **Julia Cameron**

"A wise person should have money in their head, but not in their heart." — **Jonathan Swift**

"A woman's best protection is a little money of her own."
— **Clare Boothe Luce**

"If you want to be financially free, you need to become a different person than you are today and let go of whatever has held you back in the past." — **Robert Kiyosaki**

"Forget about the fast lane. If you really want to fly, harness your power to your passion. Honor your calling. Everybody has one. Trust your heart, and success will come to you." — **Oprah Winfrey**

"When we give cheerfully and accept gratefully, everyone is blessed." — **Maya Angelou**

"Money is multiplied in practical value depending on the number of W's you control in your life: what you do, when you do it, where you do it, and with whom you do it." — **Tim Ferriss**

"A budget is more than just a series of numbers on a page; it is an embodiment of our values." — **Barack Obama**

"I don't focus on what I'm up against. I focus on my goals and I try to ignore the rest."— **Venus Williams**

Source: https://www.watchherthrive.co/blog/21-wise-money-quotes-affirmations

Analyzing Economic Data

Economic data is a critical tool for understanding how economies function and for making informed decisions, whether you're a business owner, investor, or individual planning your finances. But before you can leverage this data, you need to know how to analyze and interpret it.

Key Economic Indicators

Economic indicators are statistics that provide insight into the health and direction of the economy. Here are some of the most commonly watched indicators:

Gross Domestic Product (GDP): GDP measures the total value of goods and services produced in a country over a specific period, usually a quarter or a year. It's a key indicator of economic health, as rising GDP signals economic growth, while a falling GDP may indicate a recession. By tracking GDP trends, individuals and businesses can make informed decisions about investment and spending.

Inflation: Inflation measures the rate at which the general price level of goods and services is rising. A moderate inflation rate (2–3%) is considered healthy because it reflects a growing economy. However, high inflation erodes purchasing power, making everyday goods more expensive. Understanding inflation trends helps individuals make better decisions about saving, spending, and investing.

Unemployment Rate: The unemployment rate reflects the percentage of the labour force that is unemployed but actively seeking work. A low unemployment rate is generally seen as a sign of a strong economy, while a rising rate can indicate economic downturns. When unemployment is high, consumers may be more cautious with their spending, while businesses may cut back on hiring and investments.

Interest Rates: Central banks, such as the Federal Reserve in the United States, the Bank of England, and the Bank of Canada, set interest rates to control inflation and stimulate or slow down the economy. Higher interest rates make borrowing more expensive, which can reduce consumer spending and business investment, while lower rates encourage borrowing and spending. Monitoring interest rate trends can guide decisions on loans, mortgages, and savings.

Consumer Confidence Index (CCI): The CCI measures how optimistic or pessimistic consumers are about the economy. When confidence is high, people are more likely to spend money, which drives economic growth. Low consumer confidence can signal that consumers are worried about the economy and are tightening their belts.

Interpreting Data for Personal Decisions

Once you understand these indicators, the next step is knowing how to apply them to your personal or professional life. For example, rising interest rates may signal that it's time to lock in a fixed-rate mortgage before rates climb higher. On the other hand, if inflation is high, you may need to adjust your budget to account for rising costs of living. Similarly, during periods of economic growth (as indicated by rising GDP and a low unemployment rate), businesses might find it an ideal time to expand.

Analyzing economic data isn't just for financial experts; it's a skill that anyone can develop. By paying attention to key economic reports and understanding what they mean, you can make informed choices that help you protect and grow your wealth.

Making Informed Economic Decisions

Economic literacy directly influences the quality of your financial decisions. Whether you're deciding how much to save, whether to buy a home, or when to invest in stocks, a good understanding of economic principles can be invaluable.

Personal Budgeting:

One of the most important applications of economic knowledge in everyday life is personal budgeting. A budget is essentially a financial plan that helps you allocate your income toward expenses, savings, and investments. To create a successful budget, you need to be aware of factors like inflation, wage growth, and the cost of living in your area. An understanding of these variables allows you to adjust your spending and saving habits as needed.

Income and Spending: Your income is the foundation of your budget. By tracking changes in the economy, such as salary trends in your industry or shifts in minimum wage laws, you can anticipate changes to your earning potential. On the spending side, inflation or deflation can impact the prices of goods and services, affecting how much you need to allocate for essentials like food, housing, and healthcare.

Savings and Investment: Knowing when and where to save or invest is a crucial decision influenced by economic conditions. For example, during periods of low interest rates, it may make more sense to invest in equities or real estate rather than keeping large amounts of cash in a savings account. Conversely, when markets are volatile, a more conservative approach to saving may be prudent.

Risk Management

All economic decisions involve some degree of risk, whether it's the risk of losing a job, experiencing an unexpected expense, or investing in a volatile market. Understanding economic cycles can help you assess risk more effectively.

Emergency Funds: Building an emergency fund is a fundamental aspect of financial planning, and economic knowledge plays a role in determining the right size for this fund. In times of economic uncertainty or high unemployment, a larger emergency fund is advisable. When the economy is stable, individuals may feel comfortable reducing the size of their cash reserves and investing more aggressively.

Insurance: Economic conditions can also impact insurance needs. During times of economic contraction, individuals may face higher risks of unemployment or health issues, making it essential to review and possibly increase insurance coverage. In a booming economy, one might focus on other types of financial protection, such as disability or life insurance, to safeguard wealth.

The Role of Economic Awareness in Life Planning

Economic literacy doesn't just help with day-to-day financial decisions; it also plays a crucial role in long-term life planning. Your career, homeownership, education, and retirement all depend on understanding how economic forces will affect your future.

Career Planning

Choosing a career or deciding when to switch jobs is a major life decision that should be informed by economic trends. For example, understanding which industries are growing and which are in decline can help guide your career choices. In an economy increasingly shaped by technology, investing in skills related to automation, data analysis, or software development may offer better long-term prospects than industries that are shrinking due to outsourcing or technological disruption.

Market Demand

By analyzing trends in labour markets, you can identify which skills are in demand, helping you align your education and career goals with areas that offer the best opportunities for growth and stability.

Geographic Considerations

Economic literacy also helps in making decisions about where to live and work. If certain regions or cities are experiencing economic booms owing to industries like tech or finance, moving to these areas could provide more job opportunities and better wages.

Homeownership

Purchasing a home is one of the largest financial commitments a person can make, and economic conditions play a significant role in determining when and where it makes sense to buy. Factors like interest rates, housing market trends, and regional economic growth can influence whether buying a home is a smart investment or a risky gamble.

Interest Rates: When interest rates are low, mortgages become more affordable, making homeownership more attractive. However, rising rates can increase the cost of borrowing, which might make renting a better option in the short term.

Housing Markets: Understanding housing market trends is also critical. In areas where home prices are appreciating due to strong local economies, buying a home can be a good investment. Conversely, in regions where prices are stagnant or declining, it may be wiser to wait or consider renting.

Retirement Planning: Planning for retirement involves making decisions that will affect your financial security in your later years, and economic literacy is essential for ensuring you have enough saved and invested to support your lifestyle. Inflation, interest rates, and market performance all impact how much you need to save for retirement and how you should allocate your investments.

Pension and Social Security

Economic trends can affect the stability of pension funds and social security systems. By staying informed about changes to retirement policies, individuals can make better decisions about how much to rely on these sources of income versus personal savings and investments.

Investment Strategies

As you near retirement, your investment strategy should shift toward preserving capital and ensuring a stable income. Economic awareness can help you understand how to balance risk and reward in your investment portfolio, particularly when planning for a retirement that could last 20 or 30 years.

Conclusion

Economic literacy is an essential skill for making informed decisions, managing risk, and planning for the future. By understanding how to analyze economic data, individuals can better navigate the complex financial landscape and make decisions that align with both their short-term needs and long-term goals. Whether it's choosing a career, purchasing a home, or planning for retirement, economic awareness empowers individuals to make sound financial decisions that lead to greater security and success. Investing time in understanding basic economic principles and trends will not only improve your personal finances but also help you navigate life's many uncertainties with confidence and foresight.

Exercise

Strengthening Your Economic Literacy for Better Decision-making

This exercise is designed to help you apply basic economic principles to real-life decisions. By improving your economic literacy, you'll be better equipped to make informed financial choices and navigate complex economic environments.

Step 1: Assess Your Current Economic Understanding

Start by evaluating your current knowledge of economics. Reflect on the following:

- **What is your current understanding of basic economic concepts?** (e.g., supply and demand, inflation, interest rates, opportunity cost).
- **How often do you consider economic factors when making decisions?** (e.g., when budgeting, purchasing, or investing).
- **Do you follow news about the economy?** If so, how does it influence your choices?

Write down a short reflection on your current level of economic literacy. Identify any gaps in your knowledge or areas where you'd like to improve.

Step 2: Analyze a Recent Financial Decision

Think about a recent financial decision you've made, whether it's large or small (e.g., buying a new car, investing in a savings account, or choosing a service provider). Now analyze that decision using the following economic principles:

- **Opportunity Cost:** What did you give up in exchange for this decision? (e.g., could the money have been better spent elsewhere or saved for future use?)
- **Cost-Benefit Analysis:** What were the benefits and costs of your decision? Did the benefits outweigh the costs in the short and long term?
- **Supply and Demand:** Did market conditions, such as high demand or low supply, impact your decision? How did it affect the price or availability of the item or service?

Write a brief analysis of how economic principles influenced (or could have influenced) your decision.

Step 3: Practice Economic Forecasting

Using your knowledge of economic indicators, try to forecast how current economic trends might impact your future financial decisions. For example:

- **Inflation:** How might rising prices affect your purchasing power or budget in the next 6 months?
- **Interest Rates:** If you have loans or are considering taking out a loan, how will changing interest rates affect your borrowing costs?
- **Job Market:** If you're in the workforce, how do employment trends or technological advancements in your industry affect your job security or future opportunities?

Write down a forecast for one or more economic trends and how they may influence your personal or financial decisions in the coming year.

Step 4: Set an Economic Education Goal

Improving your economic literacy is an ongoing process. Choose an area of economics that you'd like to learn more about (e.g., taxation, global trade, personal finance management, or investment strategies). Set a goal to:

- **Read a book** such as *Economics for Everyday Life* by Elijah M. James.
- **Take a course** on financial literacy or economics, either online or in person.
- **Follow economic news** more closely by subscribing to a newsletter or listening to a podcast.

Write down your economic education goal and the first step you will take to achieve it. Be specific (e.g., "I will read *Economics for Everyday Life* by the end of the month" or "I will complete an online course on personal finance next week").

Step 5: Apply Economic Literacy to Your Future Decisions

Choose a future financial or life decision where you can apply your growing economic knowledge. This could be:

- **Planning a budget:** Use your understanding of opportunity costs and market conditions to set a realistic budget for an upcoming purchase or financial goal.
- **Evaluating investments:** Apply economic principles to decide where and how to invest your money.
- **Negotiating a contract:** Use supply and demand dynamics to negotiate a better deal for a service or product.

Write down the decision you plan to make and how you will incorporate economic thinking into your process.

Step 6: Track and Reflect on Your Progress

Over the next few months, track how applying economic literacy influences your decision-making. Reflect on the following:

- **Did your decisions become more informed and deliberate?**
- **Were there any decisions where considering economic principles led to better outcomes?**
- **What new economic concepts did you learn, and how did they help?**

Write a reflection on how your improved economic literacy has impacted your financial and life decisions. This will help reinforce the importance of continuously enhancing your understanding of economic factors in everyday life.

By completing this exercise, you'll take active steps toward becoming more economically literate and making well-informed decisions that support your long-term financial and personal goals.

ECONOMIC LITERACY AND DECISION-MAKING

CHAPTER 15
WORDSEARCH

	1	2	3	4	5	6	7	8	9	10	11	12	13	14	15	16
1	Y	Y	U	U	G	Q	T	F	P	D	G	T	T	C	Y	F
2	C	Z	P	P	H	Z	G	L	O	I	O	Q	N	T	R	Y
3	S	K	L	P	Z	N	A	Q	K	T	Q	F	E	U	H	M
4	Q	E	R	M	S	R	S	J	W	C	G	I	M	D	X	A
5	A	T	I	N	O	I	T	A	L	F	N	I	Y	N	Z	R
6	T	X	Z	T	U	Z	I	H	H	Y	D	E	O	F	Z	K
7	C	I	C	K	I	M	S	O	F	Z	F	I	L	C	Q	E
8	E	G	Q	O	C	N	I	Q	Y	I	S	B	P	G	F	T
9	T	C	F	X	N	F	U	M	M	I	N	Y	M	M	H	S
10	Y	S	O	O	B	S	B	T	C	D	M	A	E	M	Q	B
11	I	X	E	N	P	B	U	E	R	I	E	K	N	L	O	P
12	T	Q	Q	R	O	K	D	M	L	O	E	D	U	C	Y	A
13	K	P	F	T	E	M	V	I	E	O	P	Z	H	E	E	E
14	A	M	V	R	M	T	I	L	F	R	Y	P	N	Q	U	S
15	V	S	Z	E	F	X	N	C	F	Q	K	O	O	M	W	E
16	R	S	J	T	D	Y	U	I	S	V	M	H	E	E	C	A

CONSUMER	INFLATION	OPPORTUNITIES
DECISION	INTEREST	UNEMPLOYMENT
ECONOMICS	MARKETS	
FINANCES	MONEY	

THE JOURNEY TO A FULFILLING AND MEANINGFUL LIFE

ANSWER

	1	2	3	4	5	6	7	8	9	10	11	12	13	14	15	16
1	Y	Y	U	U	G	Q	T	F	P	D	G	T	T	C	Y	F
2	C	Z	P	P	H	Z	G	L	O	I	O	Q	N	T	R	Y
3	S	K	L	P	Z	N	A	Q	K	T	Q	F	E	U	H	M
4	Q	E	R	M	S	R	S	J	W	C	G	I	M	D	X	A
5	A	T	I	N	O	I	T	A	L	F	N	I	Y	N	Z	R
6	T	X	Z	T	U	Z	I	H	H	Y	D	E	O	F	Z	K
7	C	I	C	K	I	M	S	O	F	Z	F	I	L	C	Q	E
8	E	G	Q	O	C	N	I	Q	Y	I	S	B	P	G	F	T
9	T	C	F	X	N	F	U	M	M	I	N	Y	M	M	H	S
10	Y	S	O	O	B	S	B	T	C	D	M	A	E	M	Q	B
11	I	X	E	N	P	B	U	E	R	I	E	K	N	L	O	P
12	T	Q	Q	R	O	K	D	M	L	O	E	D	U	C	Y	A
13	K	P	F	T	E	M	V	I	E	O	P	Z	H	E	E	E
14	A	M	V	R	M	T	I	L	F	R	Y	P	N	Q	U	S
15	V	S	Z	E	F	X	N	C	F	Q	K	O	O	M	W	E
16	R	S	J	T	D	Y	U	I	S	V	M	H	E	E	C	A

CONSUMER 7:3   INFLATION 5:12   OPPORTUNITIES 15:13

DECISION 12:7   INTEREST 16:8   UNEMPLOYMENT 12:13

ECONOMICS 8:1   MARKETS 3:16

FINANCES 7:9   MONEY 16:11

PART VI
SPIRITUAL GROWTH AND INNER PEACE

CHAPTER 16
EXPLORING SPIRITUALITY

Spirituality is an integral part of the human experience, shaping the way we understand ourselves, our purpose, and our connection to the world around us.

The Bible Says

But the fruit of the Spirit is love, joy, peace, longsuffering, gentleness, goodness, faith, **Galatians 5:22**

For to be carnally minded is death; but to be spiritually minded is life and peace. **Romans 8:6**

That the righteousness of the law might be fulfilled in us, who walk not after the flesh, but after the Spirit. **Romans 8:4**

Even the Spirit of truth; whom the world cannot receive, because it seeth him not, neither knoweth him: but ye know him; for he dwelleth with you, and shall be in you. **John 14:17**

Labour not for the meat which perisheth, but for that meat which endureth unto everlasting life, which the Son of man shall give unto you: for him hath God the Father sealed. **John 6:27**

Likewise reckon ye also yourselves to be dead indeed unto sin, but alive unto God through Jesus Christ our Lord. **Romans 6:11**

For the kingdom of God is not meat and drink; but righteousness, and peace, and joy in the Holy Ghost. **Romans 14:17**

God is a Spirit: and they that worship him must worship him in spirit and in truth. **John 4:24**

Introduction

Spirituality is an integral part of the human experience, shaping the way we understand ourselves, our purpose, and our connection to the world around us. It goes beyond religious practices or rituals, delving into the deep questions of meaning, inner peace, and the sense of belonging to something greater than ourselves. For many, spirituality offers guidance and comfort, especially during times of hardship or uncertainty. It is a source of strength that helps individuals navigate life's complexities with grace and purpose.

In this chapter, we will explore the multifaceted nature of spirituality, how it manifests in different forms, and the role it plays in enhancing our overall well-being. We will delve into the different paths to spiritual fulfillment, emphasizing that spirituality is a deeply personal journey. We will also examine the powerful connection between spirituality and happiness, revealing how nurturing our spiritual side can lead to a more content and meaningful life.

Life Story

Daniel had always been focused on his career, climbing the corporate ladder and achieving success in the eyes of the world. He worked long hours and pushed himself to excel, but despite his accomplishments, he felt an unshakable emptiness growing inside. Something was missing, though he couldn't put his finger on what it was.

One evening, after a particularly stressful day, Daniel found himself walking by a quiet park. He sat on a bench, watching the sunset, and for the first time in a long while, he felt a sense of calm. A thought crossed his mind—perhaps his restlessness wasn't about what he didn't have, but about what he hadn't explored within himself.

Curious, Daniel started reading books on spirituality and began meditating each morning before work. He sought out conversations with friends about their beliefs and attended different places of worship. He wasn't looking for a particular religion but was on a quest to understand the deeper questions of life—his purpose, his connection to the universe, and the meaning of fulfillment.

As Daniel's spiritual exploration deepened, he found that he was more at peace with himself and his choices. He started to view his career as part of a larger journey, rather than the sole measure of his worth. His relationships became more meaningful, and he developed a sense of gratitude for the present moment, rather than constantly striving for the next achievement.

Daniel's journey into spirituality didn't provide all the answers, but it opened his heart and mind to a deeper understanding of life. Through exploring spirituality, he found the sense of wholeness he had been searching for all along.

His story reminds us that exploring spirituality is a deeply personal journey—one that can help us discover purpose, inner peace, and a connection to something greater than ourselves.

Sayings about Spirituality

Here are some quotes to help you on your spiritual journey.

"Nature does not hurry, yet everything is accomplished." – **Lao Tzu**

"We are not human beings having a spiritual experience. We are spiritual beings having a human experience." – **Teilhard de Chardin**

"The purpose of our lives is to be happy." – **Dalai Lama**

"The only true journey is the one within." – **Rainer Maria Rilke**

"The best way to find yourself is to lose yourself in the service of others." – **Mahatma Gandhi**

"The only way to make sense out of change is to plunge into it, move with it, and join the dance." – **Alan Watts**

"The universe is not outside of you. Look inside yourself; everything that you want, you already are." – **Rumi**

"The journey towards enlightenment is not about arrival, but about the path we take to get there." – **Jiddu Krishnamurti**

"We are not given a good life or a bad life. We make it good or bad through our actions." – **Confucius**

"The journey of self-discovery is a never-ending process of constant growth." – **Oprah Winfrey**

"We are all just walking each other home." – **Ram Dass**

"The journey is the reward." – **Chinese Proverb**

"The journey towards enlightenment is a journey of the heart, not just the mind." – **Thich Nhat Hanh**

"The journey is not just about finding yourself, but creating yourself." – **George Bernard Shaw**

"Life is a journey, not a destination." – **Ralph Waldo Emerson**

"The journey of personal growth is not always easy, but it is always rewarding." – **Brené Brown**

"Life is a journey, enjoy the ride." – **Tony Robbins**

"The journey towards enlightenment is a journey of transformation, not just knowledge." – **Deepak Chopra**

"The journey of a lifetime starts with a single step." – **Lao Tzu**

"The journey towards enlightenment is a journey of self-discovery and self-awareness." – **Eckhart Tolle**

"The journey of life is not a journey from one place to another, but a journey from ignorance to wisdom." – **Socrates**

"The journey towards enlightenment is a journey of connection, not just separation." – **Marianne Williamson**

"The journey of life is not just about finding happiness, but creating it." **Gretchen Rubin**

"The journey towards enlightenment is a journey of love, compassion, and understanding." – **Dalai Lama**

"The journey of life is a journey of growth, and the destination is inner peace." – **Pema Chodron**

Understanding the Role of Spirituality in Life

Spirituality influences every aspect of life, from the way we perceive ourselves to how we relate to others and the universe. At its core, spirituality offers a sense of purpose and direction, grounding us in the present while also opening our minds to larger existential questions. By connecting with our spiritual side, we gain insight into our deepest values and desires, which in turn shape our actions, decisions, and relationships.

Spirituality and Personal Growth

One of the key roles of spirituality is its connection to personal growth. It prompts introspection, helping us explore the deepest layers of our identity. This often leads to a more profound understanding of our strengths, weaknesses, hopes, and fears. Through spiritual practices like meditation, prayer, or reflection, we cultivate self-awareness and learn to approach challenges with resilience and humility. In this sense, spirituality becomes a tool for inner transformation, offering us the clarity to grow into the best version of ourselves.

Navigating Life's Challenges

Life is filled with ups and downs, and spirituality provides the emotional and mental tools to face these challenges with strength and grace. Whether dealing with loss, illness, or uncertainty, a spiritual outlook offers a sense of hope and the belief that we are not alone in our struggles. Spirituality helps individuals find meaning in their suffering, viewing it as an opportunity for growth rather than a burden. This perspective can be a powerful source of comfort, helping us stay grounded during tumultuous times.

Spirituality and Relationships

Spirituality also plays a significant role in shaping our relationships with others. It encourages empathy, compassion, and kindness, promoting deeper connections with family, friends, and even strangers. By embracing the spiritual concept of interconnectedness, we recognize that our actions impact those around us. As we grow spiritually, we often feel a greater sense of responsibility toward others, leading to more fulfilling and meaningful relationships.

Different Paths to Spiritual Fulfillment

There is no single "correct" path to spiritual fulfillment. The journey is highly personal, with each individual finding meaning and connection in different ways. While some may seek spiritual growth through organized religion, others may find their spiritual path through nature, art, or personal reflection. The diversity of spiritual practices reflects the variety of human experiences and beliefs, and each path offers unique opportunities for growth and enlightenment.

Religious Traditions

For many people, spirituality is deeply rooted in religious practices and teachings. Organized religion provides a structured framework for exploring spiritual questions, offering rituals, sacred texts, and community support. Whether through prayer, worship, or participation in religious ceremonies, individuals can cultivate a deeper connection to their faith and to the divine. Religions like Christianity, Islam, Hinduism, Buddhism, and Judaism each offer unique perspectives on spirituality, emphasizing different paths to enlightenment, salvation, or self-realization.

Nature as a Spiritual Path

For others, nature serves as a powerful source of spiritual inspiration. The beauty and majesty of the natural world often evoke feelings of awe, wonder, and connection to something greater than ourselves. Many people find spiritual fulfillment by spending time in nature, whether through hiking, gardening, or simply observing the changing seasons. Nature provides a space for reflection and renewal, helping individuals feel grounded and at peace. This connection to the earth fosters a sense of stewardship and reverence for the environment, reinforcing the spiritual principle of interconnectedness.

Meditation and Mindfulness

Meditation and mindfulness practices have become increasingly popular as tools for spiritual growth. These practices involve focusing on the present moment, quieting the mind, and cultivating a state of inner peace.

Meditation allows individuals to connect with their deeper selves, gaining insight into their thoughts, emotions, and desires. Mindfulness, on the other hand, emphasizes living in the present and appreciating the beauty of each moment. Both practices encourage self-awareness, reduce stress, and promote emotional well-being, making them powerful tools for spiritual development.

Creative Expression

Art, music, and creative expression can also be profound paths to spiritual fulfillment. Many artists and musicians describe their creative process as a deeply spiritual experience, one that allows them to tap into a higher state of consciousness. Whether through painting, writing, or playing music, creative expression offers a way to explore and express deep emotions, ideas, and experiences. It provides a sense of connection to something beyond the self, whether that is a higher power, the collective human experience, or the mysteries of existence.

Acts of Service

For some, spirituality is best expressed through acts of service to others. Volunteering, helping those in need, and practicing kindness are ways to live out spiritual values in everyday life. By serving others, individuals can feel a deeper sense of purpose and connection, embodying spiritual principles like compassion, empathy, and generosity. Acts of service not only benefit others but also enhance personal spiritual growth by fostering a sense of gratitude and humility.

The Connection Between Spirituality and Happiness

There is a strong link between spirituality and happiness, as numerous studies have shown that people who engage in spiritual practices often report higher levels of life satisfaction and emotional well-being. Spirituality provides a sense of purpose, belonging, and peace that transcends the material concerns of daily life. By nurturing the spiritual side of life, individuals can achieve a deeper and more enduring form of happiness that is not dependent on external circumstances.

Inner Peace and Contentment

One of the key reasons spirituality contributes to happiness is its ability to cultivate inner peace. Spirituality encourages individuals to look within for answers, focusing on personal growth and self-acceptance rather than external validation. This inward focus fosters a sense of contentment, reducing anxiety and stress by shifting the focus away from material concerns and toward more meaningful, fulfilling experiences.

Resilience and Coping with Adversity

Spirituality also plays a crucial role in helping individuals cope with adversity. Whether facing illness, loss, or personal setbacks, spiritual beliefs offer a framework for understanding and finding meaning in suffering. This can lead to greater emotional resilience, allowing individuals to navigate difficult times with a sense of hope and purpose. By viewing challenges as opportunities for growth, spirituality fosters a sense of optimism and helps individuals maintain a positive outlook, even in the face of hardship.

A Sense of Connection and Belonging

Another way spirituality contributes to happiness is by fostering a sense of connection to others and to the world at large. Spirituality encourages empathy, compassion, and kindness, promoting deeper, more meaningful relationships. Whether through religious communities, acts of service, or a connection to nature, spirituality helps individuals feel less isolated and more connected to the larger human experience. This sense of belonging enhances emotional well-being, providing a support system during difficult times and increasing overall life satisfaction.

Purpose and Meaning

At its core, spirituality provides a sense of purpose and meaning that is essential for happiness. It encourages individuals to reflect on their values, passions, and the impact they want to have on the world. By aligning their actions with their spiritual beliefs, individuals can live more authentically and intentionally, creating a life that feels purposeful and fulfilling. This sense of meaning is one of the most important contributors to lasting happiness, as it gives individuals a reason to wake up each day with enthusiasm and gratitude.

Conclusion

Spirituality is a deeply personal journey that offers profound insights into the nature of life, purpose, and happiness. Whether expressed through religious practices, connection to nature, creative endeavors, or acts of service, spirituality provides a framework for exploring the deeper questions of existence. By nurturing our spiritual side, we can cultivate inner peace, resilience, and a sense of purpose that transcends the material concerns of daily life.

Ultimately, spirituality is not about reaching a specific destination but about embracing the journey of self-discovery and growth. It reminds us that we are part of something greater, and that by seeking meaning and connection, we can lead more fulfilled and joyful lives. Through spirituality, we find the strength to navigate life's challenges, the wisdom to appreciate the present, and the peace that comes from living in harmony with our deepest values.

Exercise

Deepening Your Spiritual Exploration

The main purpose of this exercise is to help you reflect on your personal spiritual journey and explore different ways to connect with your spiritual self.

Step 1: Reflect on Your Current Spiritual Beliefs

Take 10-15 minutes to sit quietly and reflect on the following questions:

- **What does spirituality mean to you?** Is it connected to religion, nature, meditation, or something else?
- **How have your spiritual beliefs or practices evolved over time?** Have significant life events shaped your spirituality?
- **In what areas do you feel spiritually fulfilled, and where do you feel there is room for growth?**

Write down your reflections in a journal. This will help you understand where you are on your spiritual path.

Step 2: Explore New Spiritual Practices

Choose one spiritual practice to try for the next week. This could be:

- **Meditation or prayer:** Dedicate 10-20 minutes each day to quiet reflection, focusing on mindfulness, gratitude, or connecting with a higher power.
- **Nature walks:** Spend time in nature to ground yourself and feel a connection to the world around you.

- **Reading sacred texts:** Choose passages from spiritual or religious texts that resonate with you and reflect on their meaning. You can read some of the verses in this book.
- **Acts of kindness:** Practice spirituality through service by helping someone in need or performing small acts of kindness.

After one week, write about your experience. How did it feel to engage in this practice? Did it help you feel more connected to your spirituality?

Step 3: Identify Your Spiritual Values

Take time to identify 3-5 core spiritual values that are important to you. These could include values such as compassion, forgiveness, gratitude, or humility. Consider the following:

- **Why are these values important to you?**
- **How do you live by these values in your daily life?**
- **Are there areas where you could more fully embody these values?**

Write down your spiritual values and consider one small action you can take to integrate these values more fully into your life.

Step 4: Create a Personal Spiritual Practice Plan

Now that you've reflected on your beliefs, values, and practices, create a plan to deepen your spiritual exploration. Consider the following elements:

- **Daily practices:** What can you do each day to nurture your spiritual well-being (e.g., morning meditation, prayer, or reflection)?
- **Community involvement:** How can you engage with others on your spiritual path (e.g., attending a place of worship, joining a spiritual discussion group, or volunteering)?
- **Learning and growth:** How will you continue to expand your spiritual knowledge and practice (e.g., reading spiritual books, attending retreats, or taking classes)?

Write down your spiritual practice plan, making it simple and sustainable. Start small and build up over time.

Step 5: Reflect on Your Spiritual Growth

After one month of following your plan, take some time to reflect on how your spiritual exploration has influenced your life:

- **Have you noticed any changes in your outlook, mood, or relationships?**
- **What spiritual practices have had the most impact on your sense of peace and fulfillment?**
- **Are there any adjustments you'd like to make to your spiritual practice plan?**

Write a short reflection on how your spiritual journey has evolved and what steps you'd like to take next.

By completing this exercise, you'll gain deeper insight into your spiritual self and create a personalized path for continued exploration and growth.

CHAPTER 16
WORDSEARCH

	1	2	3	4	5	6	7	8	9	10	11	12	13	14	15	16	17	18	19	20	21
1	D	F	N	J	A	N	O	I	T	C	E	R	I	D	D	S	L	P	H	W	W
2	M	L	Y	S	M	E	P	W	M	G	E	M	E	H	Y	D	G	R	M	H	F
3	E	N	L	I	G	H	T	E	N	M	E	N	T	Q	V	G	W	N	T	M	Q
4	B	B	B	P	L	W	Z	F	O	B	V	B	Y	B	L	C	Z	G	L	P	T
5	S	E	C	S	V	S	G	D	X	V	H	R	E	A	L	H	S	Y	X	I	E
6	I	Z	U	I	O	Y	U	P	O	E	W	P	I	L	H	R	T	L	R	X	L
7	U	T	T	E	B	L	T	T	D	C	W	T	P	H	O	O	Y	S	S	O	A
8	W	Y	J	Q	Z	I	Z	N	M	I	N	A	A	Q	U	N	F	P	M	Q	N
9	T	W	F	U	L	Z	F	Z	R	E	B	I	D	A	Y	E	G	B	R	J	O
10	Y	C	H	E	W	X	E	R	T	M	Y	K	X	T	I	N	E	I	W	Q	I
11	U	O	Y	T	C	U	Y	S	E	S	L	Z	I	L	G	J	M	B	N	W	T
12	L	R	F	A	H	B	I	Q	V	Y	R	L	E	I	Y	U	R	S	G	G	O
13	S	T	W	C	L	X	I	W	T	Z	A	B	I	X	N	H	S	O	D	U	M
14	R	Z	B	P	E	H	F	K	V	U	A	R	X	F	R	C	F	W	L	F	E
15	I	M	R	Q	U	N	H	X	T	V	L	D	P	R	L	Y	G	Z	V	N	G
16	R	P	L	N	G	P	Z	I	K	L	X	K	S	Q	P	U	N	S	Q	W	W
17	B	S	W	I	L	R	R	T	B	S	R	F	K	L	D	X	F	O	Y	L	V
18	T	A	V	O	I	I	P	W	N	H	E	R	U	T	A	N	R	O	K	C	J
19	W	M	I	Q	P	D	S	I	N	T	R	O	S	P	E	C	T	I	O	N	G
20	C	N	Y	S	M	C	U	D	T	F	N	K	O	H	M	C	I	S	D	C	R
21	K	I	N	T	E	R	C	O	N	N	E	C	T	E	D	N	E	S	S	Q	

BELIEFS ENLIGHTENMENT INTROSPECTION
BELONGING EXISTENTIAL NATURE
DIRECTION FULFILLMRNT PRAYER
EMOTIONAL INTERCONNECTEDNESS SPIRITUALITY

THE JOURNEY TO A FULFILLING AND MEANINGFUL LIFE

ANSWER

	1	2	3	4	5	6	7	8	9	10	11	12	13	14	15	16	17	18	19	20	21
1	D	F	N	J	A	N	O	I	T	C	E	R	I	D	D	S	L	P	H	W	W
2	M	L	Y	S	M	E	P	W	M	G	E	M	E	H	Y	D	G	R	M	H	F
3	E	N	L	I	G	H	T	E	N	M	E	N	T	Q	V	G	W	N	T	M	Q
4	B	B	B	P	L	W	Z	F	O	B	V	B	Y	B	L	C	Z	G	L	P	T
5	S	E	C	S	V	S	G	D	X	V	H	R	E	A	L	H	S	Y	X	I	E
6	I	Z	U	I	O	Y	U	P	O	E	W	P	I	L	H	R	T	L	R	X	L
7	U	T	T	E	B	L	T	T	D	C	W	T	P	H	O	O	Y	S	S	O	A
8	W	Y	J	Q	Z	I	Z	N	M	I	N	A	A	Q	U	N	F	P	M	Q	N
9	T	W	F	U	L	Z	F	Z	R	E	B	I	D	A	Y	E	G	B	R	J	O
10	Y	C	H	E	W	X	E	R	T	M	Y	K	X	T	I	N	E	I	W	Q	I
11	U	O	Y	T	C	U	Y	S	E	S	L	Z	I	L	G	J	M	B	N	W	T
12	L	R	F	A	H	B	I	Q	V	Y	R	L	E	I	Y	U	R	S	G	G	O
13	S	T	W	C	L	X	I	W	T	Z	A	B	I	X	N	H	S	O	D	U	M
14	R	Z	B	P	E	H	F	K	V	U	A	R	X	F	R	C	F	W	L	F	E
15	I	M	R	Q	U	N	H	X	T	V	L	D	P	R	L	Y	G	Z	V	N	G
16	R	P	L	N	G	P	Z	I	K	L	X	K	S	Q	P	U	N	S	Q	W	W
17	B	S	W	I	L	R	R	T	B	S	R	F	K	L	D	X	F	O	Y	L	V
18	T	A	V	O	I	I	P	W	N	H	E	R	U	T	A	N	R	O	K	C	J
19	W	M	I	Q	P	D	S	I	N	T	R	O	S	P	E	C	T	I	O	N	G
20	C	N	Y	S	M	C	U	D	T	F	N	K	O	H	M	C	I	S	D	C	R
21	K	I	N	T	E	R	C	O	N	N	E	C	T	E	D	N	E	S	S	S	Q

BELIEFS 13:12

BELONGING 4:12

DIRECTION 1:14

EMOTIONAL 14:21

ENLIGHTENMENT 3:1

EXISTENTIAL 14:5

FULFILLMRNT 17:17

INTERCONNECTEDNESS 21:2

INTROSPECTION 19:8

NATURE 18:16

PRAYER 15:13

SPIRITUALITY 20:4

CHAPTER 17
DEVELOPING INNER PEACE

While external events can often feel chaotic or overwhelming, cultivating inner peace allows individuals to navigate life with grace and resilience.

The Bible Says

"These things I have spoken to you while I am still with you. But the Helper, the Holy Spirit, whom the Father will send in my name, he will teach you all things and bring to your remembrance all that I have said to you. Peace I leave with you; my peace I give to you. Not as the world gives do I give to you. Let not your hearts be troubled, neither let them be afraid." **(John 14:25-27)**

"In peace I will both lie down and sleep; for you alone, O LORD, make me dwell in safety." **(Psalm 4:8)**

"And let the peace of Christ rule in your hearts, to which indeed you were called in one body. And be thankful." **(Colossians 3:15)**

"I have said these things to you, that in me you may have peace. In the world you will have tribulation. But take heart; I have overcome the world." **(John 16:33)**

"Great peace have those who love your law; nothing can make them stumble." **(Psalm 119:165)**

"The Lord bless you and keep you; the Lord make his face to shine upon you and be gracious to you; the Lord lift up his countenance upon you and give you peace." **(Numbers 6:24-26)**

"For the moment all discipline seems painful rather than pleasant, but later it yields the peaceful fruit of righteousness to those who have been trained by it. Therefore lift your drooping hands and strengthen your weak knees, and make straight paths for your feet, so that what is lame may not be put out of joint but rather be healed. Strive for peace with everyone, and for the holiness without which no one will see the Lord." **(Hebrews 12:11-14)**

"But the wisdom from above is first pure, then peaceable, gentle, open to reason, full of mercy and good fruits, impartial and sincere. And a harvest of righteousness is sown in peace by those who make peace." **(James 3:17-18)**

"The LORD sits enthroned over the flood; the LORD sits enthroned as king forever. May the LORD give strength to his people! May the LORD bless his people with peace!" **(Psalm 29:10-11)**

"You keep him in perfect peace whose mind is stayed on you, because he trusts in you. Trust in the LORD forever, for the LORD GOD is an everlasting rock." **(Isaiah 26:3-4)**

"O LORD, you will ordain peace for us, for you have indeed done for us all our works." **(Isaiah 26:12)**

"May the God of hope fill you with all joy and peace in believing, so that by the power of the Holy Spirit you may abound in hope." **(Romans 15:13)**

"Rejoice in the Lord always; again I will say, rejoice. Let your reasonableness be known to everyone. The Lord is at hand; do not be anxious about anything, but in everything by prayer and supplication with thanksgiving let your requests be made known to God. And the peace of God, which surpasses all understanding, will guard your hearts and your minds in Christ Jesus." **(Philippians 4:4-7)**

"Now may the Lord of peace himself give you peace at all times in every way. The Lord be with you all." **(2 Thessalonians 3:16)**

"The LORD is my shepherd; I shall not want. He makes me lie down in green pastures. He leads me beside still waters. He restores my soul. He leads me in paths of righteousness for his name's sake. Even though I walk through the valley of the shadow of death, I will fear no evil, for you are with me; your rod and your staff, they comfort me. You prepare a table before me in the presence of my enemies; you anoint my head with oil; my cup overflows. Surely goodness and mercy shall follow me all the days of my life, and I shall dwell in the house of the LORD forever." **(Psalm 23:1-6)**

Introduction

Inner peace is a state of calmness and serenity that transcends external circumstances. It is the foundation of emotional and mental well-being, providing stability in the face of life's inevitable challenges. While external events can often feel chaotic or overwhelming, cultivating inner peace allows individuals to navigate life with grace and resilience. Developing inner peace is not about avoiding challenges or stress, but rather about creating an inner sanctuary that remains unaffected by external turmoil.

In this chapter, we will explore the practices that foster inner peace, including meditation, self-reflection, and emotional release. We will also discuss the importance of letting go of fear and anxiety, and how embracing forgiveness and gratitude can deepen our sense of calm. Inner peace is a journey, not a destination, and it requires ongoing effort and intention. However, with the right practices, it is possible to create an enduring sense of tranquility that enriches every aspect of life.

Life Story

After a decade of juggling a demanding job, raising two children, and managing a bustling household, Myrna often felt as if she was running on empty. The chaos of daily life—school runs, work deadlines, and the never-ending chores—left her feeling stressed and overwhelmed. Despite her accomplishments, she couldn't shake the feeling of anxiety that seemed to follow her everywhere.

One particularly hectic day, Myrna found herself stuck in traffic, late for a meeting and worrying about all the tasks she had yet to complete. Frustrated, she pulled out her phone and started scrolling through social media, seeking a distraction. Instead of solace, she felt even more agitated as she compared her life to the carefully curated images of others. It was then she realized that she was living in a constant state of reaction rather than being present in her own life.

Determined to find a way out of this cycle, Myrna began exploring practices to develop inner peace. She started attending a weekly yoga class, where she learned to focus on her breath and become aware of her thoughts. In these moments of stillness, she discovered the power of mindfulness—realizing that she didn't need to control everything around her to find calm.

Myrna also began to incorporate daily reflection into her routine. Each morning, she would take a few moments to journal her thoughts and express gratitude for the little things in her life. As she shifted her focus from what was missing to what was present, she felt her anxiety begin to fade.

Over time, Myrna noticed a profound transformation. The chaos of life didn't disappear, but her response to it changed. She learned to embrace the moments of stillness amidst the noise, finding peace in knowing that it was okay to slow down and prioritize her well-being.

Through her journey, Myrna discovered that inner peace is not the absence of chaos but the ability to remain centered despite it. Her story serves as a reminder that developing inner peace is a practice—a journey of self-awareness and acceptance that allows us to navigate life with grace and resilience.

Sayings about Developing Inner Peace

Consider these quotes about inner peace.

"There are times when we stop, we sit still. We listen and breezes from a whole other world begin to whisper." — **James Carroll**

"Breath is the power behind all things.... I breathe in and know that good things will happen." —**Tao Porchon-Lynch**

"Peace of mind for five minutes, that's what I crave." — **Alanis Morissette**

"Set peace of mind as your highest goal, and organize your life around it." —**Brian Tracy**

"Peace begins with a smile." —**Mother Teresa**

"I took a deep breath and listened to the old bray of my heart. I am. I am. I am." — **Sylvia Plath**

"Doing something productive is a great way to alleviate emotional stress. Get your mind doing something that is productive." —**Ziggy Marley**

"Give your stress wings and let it fly away." —**Terri Guillemets**

"Love and peace of mind do protect us. They allow us to overcome the problems that life hands us. They teach us to survive... to live now... to have the courage to confront each day." —**Bernie Siegel**

"You'll never find peace of mind until you listen to your heart." —**George Michael**

"Peace is a daily, a weekly, a monthly process, gradually changing opinions, slowly eroding old barriers, quietly building new structures." —**John F. Kennedy**

"It isn't enough to talk about peace. One must believe in it. And it isn't enough to believe in it. One must work at it." —**Eleanor Roosevelt**

"Nobody can bring you peace but yourself." —**Ralph Waldo Emerson**

"Inner peace can be reached only when we practice forgiveness. Forgiveness is letting go of the past, and is therefore the means for correcting our misperceptions."— **Gerald Jampolsky**

"Peace can become a lens through which you see the world. Be it. Live it. Radiate it out. Peace is an inside job." – **Wayne Dyer**

"Weather out the storm in the island of tranquility to find inner peace." —**Ana Monnar**

"When we develop patience, we find that we develop a reserve of calm and tranquility." —**Dalai Lama**

"When you're at peace with your life and in a state of tranquility, you actually send out a vibration of energy that impacts all living creatures." —**Wayne Dyer**

"A happy life consists in tranquility of mind." —**Marcus Tullius Cicero**

"From tranquility emerges power and strength."— **C. Joybell C.**

"Sit quietly – be. May you find tranquility in all the little moments of your day." —**Anonymous**

"Learn to be and you will always be happy."— **Paramhansa Yogananda**

"Nature is the best medicine for serenity. Peace, calmness, stillness. It's good for the heart." — **Karen Madwell**

Source: https://www.seventeen.com/life/a37146311/peace-quotes/

The Practice of Meditation and Reflection

Meditation and reflection are two of the most powerful tools for cultivating inner peace. By turning our focus inward, these practices help calm the mind, reduce stress, and foster a sense of centeredness. Meditation allows us to quiet the noise of daily life, creating a mental space where we can find clarity and peace. Reflection, on the other hand, encourages deep thinking about our experiences, emotions, and values, helping us gain insight and understanding.

Meditation

Meditation is an ancient practice with deep roots in various spiritual traditions, but it has gained widespread popularity in modern times as a tool for reducing stress and promoting mental well-being. At its core, meditation involves focusing the mind on a single point of reference—such as the breath, a mantra, or an image—in order to quiet the constant stream of thoughts. Through regular practice, meditation helps individuals become more aware of their mental and emotional patterns, cultivating a state of mindfulness that can be carried into everyday life.

The benefits of meditation are well-documented, ranging from reduced anxiety and depression to improved concentration and emotional resilience. For those seeking inner peace, meditation provides a space to reconnect with the present moment, free from the distractions and stresses of the outside world. By anchoring our awareness in the present, we learn to let go of past regrets and future worries, which are often the main sources of emotional unrest.

Self-Reflection

Self-reflection complements meditation by encouraging deeper introspection and understanding. While meditation quiets the mind, reflection involves actively thinking about one's experiences, emotions, and actions. By taking time to reflect on our thoughts and behaviors, we gain insight into what drives our feelings of peace or unrest. This practice encourages self-awareness and helps individuals recognize patterns that may be contributing to stress or inner conflict.

Journaling is a common form of self-reflection, allowing individuals to write down their thoughts and feelings in a structured way. This process helps externalize emotions and can provide clarity on difficult situations. Reflection can also be done mentally, through quiet contemplation or guided questions. The goal is to create a habit of looking inward with curiosity and compassion, fostering self-understanding and emotional growth.

Letting Go of Fear and Anxiety

Fear and anxiety are two of the most common barriers to inner peace. They often stem from the need to control outcomes or from uncertainty about the future. While it is normal to feel fear and anxiety at times, holding onto these emotions for too long can lead to chronic stress and emotional imbalance. Learning to let go of fear and anxiety is essential for developing inner peace.

Understanding the Root of Fear

Fear is often rooted in a desire for certainty and control. We fear the unknown, the unpredictable, and the uncontrollable, because they challenge our sense of safety. To cultivate inner peace, it's important to understand that uncertainty is a natural part of life. By accepting that not everything can be controlled, we can begin to release the grip of fear and trust in the process of life.

One way to combat fear is through the practice of mindfulness. Mindfulness teaches us to observe our fears without judgment or attachment, helping us understand that fear is just a temporary emotion, not a permanent reality. Instead of avoiding fear or letting it dictate our actions, we can learn to confront it with openness and courage, reducing its power over us.

Managing Anxiety

Anxiety, like fear, is often rooted in uncertainty about the future. It manifests as worry, nervousness, or unease, and can create a constant state of emotional tension. To manage anxiety and cultivate inner peace, it is important to develop healthy coping mechanisms.

One effective strategy is to focus on what can be controlled rather than what cannot. By breaking down larger worries into manageable tasks, we can reduce feelings of overwhelm. Another approach is to practice grounding techniques, such as deep breathing or progressive muscle relaxation, which help calm the nervous system and bring the mind back to the present moment.

In addition to these strategies, cultivating a mindset of trust and acceptance is key. This involves trusting that challenges can be faced with resilience and that even difficult situations have the potential for growth and learning. By letting go of the need for certainty, we free ourselves from the constant worry about the future and open the door to inner peace.

Embracing Forgiveness and Gratitude

Two of the most powerful practices for cultivating inner peace are forgiveness and gratitude. These emotional states are transformative, allowing individuals to release negativity and cultivate a more positive and peaceful outlook on life. Forgiveness helps us let go of past hurts, while gratitude shifts our focus toward the blessings in our lives, creating a sense of abundance and contentment.

Forgiveness

Holding onto grudges, resentment, or anger creates emotional turbulence that blocks inner peace. Forgiveness is the process of letting go of these negative emotions, freeing ourselves from the pain of the past. It is not about condoning harmful actions or forgetting what happened, but about releasing the emotional hold that past hurts have on our present state of mind.

Forgiveness can be a challenging process, especially when the wounds are deep. However, by practicing empathy and compassion—both for ourselves and for others—we can begin to heal and move forward. Forgiveness brings emotional freedom, allowing us to reclaim our peace and focus on the present rather than being weighed down by past wrongs.

Gratitude

Gratitude is a powerful antidote to negative emotions like fear, anxiety, and anger. By focusing on the positive aspects of our lives, we shift our mindset from one of lack to one of abundance. This shift in perspective is essential for developing inner peace, as it helps us see that there is much to be thankful for, even in the midst of challenges.

A daily gratitude practice, such as writing down three things you are grateful for each day, can significantly improve emotional well-being. Over time, this practice rewires the brain to focus on the positive, creating a more optimistic and peaceful outlook on life. Gratitude helps us stay grounded in the present, appreciating the simple joys and blessings that are often overlooked.

Conclusion

Developing inner peace is a lifelong journey that requires intention, practice, and self-awareness. By incorporating practices like meditation and reflection into our daily lives, we can create a mental and emotional space that fosters calm and clarity. Letting go of fear and anxiety is essential for reducing stress and embracing a sense of trust and acceptance in the face of uncertainty. Additionally, cultivating forgiveness and gratitude allows us to release past hurts and focus on the abundance in our lives.

Inner peace is not about avoiding life's challenges but about facing them with resilience, compassion, and an open heart. It is about creating an inner sanctuary that remains undisturbed by external events, offering a sense of tranquility that can be carried through every aspect of life. With consistent practice, anyone can develop inner peace, transforming both their inner world and their interactions with the world around them.

Exercise

Cultivating Inner Peace

This exercise is designed to help you practice techniques that promote a calm and peaceful state of mind, allowing you to carry inner peace with you through life's challenges.

Step 1: Create a Peaceful Environment

Spend 10-15 minutes setting up a calm and relaxing space for yourself. This could be a quiet corner of your home where you feel safe and comfortable. Consider adding items that promote serenity, such as:

- Candles or soft lighting
- Calming music or sounds of nature
- A comfortable chair or cushion for sitting
- Personal items that bring you peace (e.g., photos, spiritual symbols, or plants)

This space will serve as your personal retreat for practicing inner peace whenever needed.

Step 2: Practice Mindful Breathing

Sit comfortably in your peaceful space and begin a mindful breathing exercise. Focus on your breath as it flows in and out. Practice the following steps for 5-10 minutes:

- **Inhale deeply through your nose for a count of 4.**
- **Hold your breath for a count of 4.**
- **Exhale slowly through your mouth for a count of 6.**

As you breathe, allow your mind to settle. Let go of any thoughts or worries, bringing your focus back to your breath whenever your mind wanders. This exercise can help center you, reduce stress, and promote inner calm.

Step 3: Identify Sources of Inner Conflict

Take a few moments to reflect on any sources of inner conflict, stress, or anxiety in your life. Ask yourself:

- **What are the situations or thoughts that disturb my inner peace?**
- **Are these situations within my control, or are they beyond it?**
- **How can I respond to these situations in a way that supports my peace of mind?**

Write down your thoughts in a journal, identifying the sources of conflict that feel most pressing. This will help you become more aware of the areas in your life that may need peace and resolution.

Step 4: Practice Letting Go

Next, practice letting go of stress and tension related to your identified sources of inner conflict. Try the following visualization exercise:

- Close your eyes and visualize each source of stress as an object (e.g., a heavy rock).
- Imagine placing each object into a flowing river. Watch as the current gently carries it away, freeing you from its weight.
- As you let go of each object, feel the lightness and peace returning to your body and mind.

This exercise encourages you to release things beyond your control and find peace in accepting the present moment.

Step 5: Embrace Forgiveness and Gratitude

Forgiveness and gratitude are essential to inner peace. To practice, follow these steps:

- **Forgiveness:** Think of one person (or yourself) whom you have not fully forgiven. Write down your feelings of hurt or resentment and then write a letter of forgiveness. You don't need to send the letter, but this act of releasing anger can create space for peace.
- **Gratitude:** Reflect on three things in your life that bring you joy and contentment. Write them down and take a moment to feel truly grateful for each. Practicing gratitude regularly can shift your focus from stress to appreciation.

Step 6: Create a Daily Peace Ritual

Commit to a small, simple practice each day to cultivate inner peace. Choose from the following or create your own:

- A morning meditation or breathing exercise
- A gratitude practice (writing down three things you're grateful for)
- Taking 10 minutes in the evening to unwind with a calming activity (e.g., reading, stretching, or listening to music)

Write out your daily peace ritual and start small. Over time, these small habits will build a lasting sense of inner peace.

Step 7: Reflect on Your Progress

After two weeks of practicing these exercises, reflect on how you feel:

- **Do you notice more calmness and clarity in your daily life?**
- **Have any inner conflicts or anxieties diminished?**
- **How has the practice of letting go or forgiveness impacted your peace of mind?**

Write a brief reflection on the progress you've made and identify any additional practices that could support your journey to developing inner peace.

By completing this exercise, you'll begin to integrate practices that lead to a more peaceful and fulfilling life.

THE JOURNEY TO A FULFILLING AND MEANINGFUL LIFE

CHAPTER 17
WORDSEARCH

	1	2	3	4	5	6	7	8	9	10	11	12	13	14	15
1	R	F	S	L	B	U	L	X	U	K	F	K	H	U	Q
2	T	Q	P	S	K	E	H	E	N	X	H	E	L	U	J
3	A	P	P	G	E	K	C	N	N	O	K	T	K	X	Z
4	F	G	Q	A	R	N	S	E	R	E	N	I	T	Y	W
5	C	T	N	N	Y	A	D	I	Y	F	T	Y	Q	F	U
6	A	N	A	X	W	E	T	E	W	G	E	P	N	O	T
7	L	R	Z	I	Z	M	T	I	R	L	L	A	Z	O	Y
8	M	C	R	E	S	V	A	A	T	E	T	O	R	P	X
9	N	R	Y	T	G	Z	C	I	P	U	T	M	U	R	A
10	E	M	Q	Y	C	E	C	Y	E	B	D	N	F	F	Y
11	S	Q	R	V	P	N	Y	M	A	C	O	E	E	K	D
12	S	Y	N	W	P	K	T	Q	C	L	Q	I	Q	C	A
13	H	C	Z	Y	W	S	L	U	E	X	A	G	Y	R	P
14	Q	F	O	R	G	I	V	E	N	E	S	S	W	X	A
15	A	N	O	I	T	N	E	T	N	I	X	H	H	Y	T

ANXIETY FORGIVENESS PEACE
CALMNESS GRACE SERENITY
CENTEREDNESS GRATITUDE
FEAR INTENTION

DEVELOPING INNER PEACE

ANSWER

	1	2	3	4	5	6	7	8	9	10	11	12	13	14	15
1	R	F	S	L	B	U	L	X	U	K	F	K	H	U	Q
2	T	Q	P	S	K	E	H	E	N	X	H	E	L	U	J
3	A	P	P	G	E	K	C	N	N	O	K	T	K	X	Z
4	F	G	Q	A	R	N	S	E	R	E	N	I	T	Y	W
5	C	T	N	N	Y	A	D	I	Y	F	T	Y	Q	F	U
6	A	N	A	X	W	E	T	E	W	G	E	P	N	O	T
7	L	R	Z	I	Z	M	T	I	R	L	L	A	Z	O	Y
8	M	C	R	E	S	V	A	A	T	E	T	O	R	P	X
9	N	R	Y	T	G	Z	C	I	P	U	T	M	U	R	A
10	E	M	Q	Y	C	E	C	Y	E	B	D	N	F	F	Y
11	S	Q	R	V	P	N	Y	M	A	C	O	E	E	K	D
12	S	Y	N	W	P	K	T	Q	C	L	Q	I	Q	C	A
13	H	C	Z	Y	W	S	L	U	E	X	A	G	Y	R	P
14	Q	F	O	R	G	I	V	E	N	E	S	S	W	X	A
15	A	N	O	I	T	N	E	T	N	I	X	H	H	Y	T

ANXIETY 4:4   FORGIVENESS 14:2   PEACE 9:9
CALMNESS 5:1   GRACE 6:10   SERENITY 4:7
CENTEREDNESS 12:14   GRATITUDE 3:4
FEAR 5:10   INTENTION 15:10

CHAPTER 18
THE ART OF LETTING GO

Whether it's releasing the past, surrendering to the unknown, or embracing the reality of impermanence, the art of letting go is essential for inner peace and growth.

The Bible Says

Forget the former things; do not dwell on the past. See, I am doing a new thing! Now it springs up; do you not perceive it? I am making a way in the wilderness and streams in the wasteland. -**Isaiah 43:18-19**

Brothers and sisters, I do not consider myself yet to have taken hold of it. But one thing I do: Forgetting what is behind and straining toward what is ahead, I press on toward the goal to win the prize for which God has called me heavenward in Christ Jesus. -**Philippians 3:13-14**

Therefore, if anyone is in Christ, he is a new creation: The old has gone, the new is here! -**2 Corinthians 5:17**

As far as the east is from the west, so far has he removed our transgressions from us. -**Psalm 103:12**

Then I acknowledged my sin to you and did not cover up my iniquity. I said, "I will confess my transgressions to the Lord." And you forgave the guilt of my sin. -**Psalm 32:5**

If we confess our sins, he is faithful and just and will forgive us our sins and purify us from all unrighteousness. -**1 John 1:9**

And be kind to one another, tenderhearted, forgiving one another, even as God in Christ forgave you. -**Ephesians 4:32**

Bear with each other and forgive one another if any of you has a grievance against someone. Forgive as the Lord forgave you. -**Colossians 3:13**

Then Peter came to Jesus and asked, "Lord, how many times shall I forgive my brother or sister who sins against me? Up to seven times?" Jesus answered, "I tell you, not seven times, but seventy-seven times. -**Matthew 18:21-22**

Trust in the Lord with all your heart and lean not on your own understanding; in all your ways submit to him, and he will make your paths straight. -**Proverbs 3:5-6**

At the end of that time, I, Nebuchadnezzar, raised my eyes toward heaven, and my sanity was restored. Then I praised the Most High; I honored and glorified him who lives forever. His dominion is an eternal dominion; his kingdom endures from generation to generation. All the peoples of the earth are regarded as nothing. He does as he pleases with the powers of heaven and the peoples of the earth. No one can hold back his hand or say to him: "What have you done? -**Daniel 4:34-35**

Do not be anxious about anything, but in every situation, by prayer and petition, with thanksgiving, present your requests to God. And the peace of God, which transcends all understanding, will guard your hearts and your minds in Christ Jesus. -**Philippians 4:6-7**

Humble yourselves, therefore, under God's mighty hand, that he may lift you up in due time. Cast all your anxiety on him because he cares for you. **1 Peter 5:6-7**

You will keep in perfect peace those whose minds are stayed on you, because they trust in you. -**Isaiah 26:3**

Therefore, since we are surrounded by such a great cloud of witnesses, let us throw off everything that hinders and the sin that so easily entangles. And let us run with perseverance the race marked out for us. -**Hebrews 12:1**

But you, man of God, flee from all this, and pursue righteousness, godliness, faith, love, endurance and gentleness. -**1 Timothy 6:11**

Do not love the world or anything in the world. If anyone loves the world, love for the Father is not in them. For everything in the world—the lust of the flesh, the lust of the eyes, and the pride of life—comes not from the Father but from the world. -**1 John 2:15-16**

No one who lives in him keeps on sinning. No one who continues to sin has either seen him or known him. Dear children, do not let anyone lead you astray. The one who does what is right is righteous, just as he is righteous. -**1 John 3:6-7**

Be strong and courageous. Do not be afraid or terrified because of them, for the Lord your God goes with you; he will never leave you nor forsake you. -**Deuteronomy 31:6**

So do not fear, for I am with you; do not be dismayed, for I am your God. I will strengthen you and help you; I will uphold you with my righteous right hand. -**Isaiah 41:10**

For I am the Lord your God who takes hold of your right hand and says to you, Do not fear; I will help you. -**Isaiah 41:13**

I have told you these things, so that in me you may have peace. In this world you will have trouble. Be of good cheer! I have overcome the world. -**John 16:33**

Looking carefully lest anyone fall short of the grace of God; lest any root of bitterness springing up cause trouble, and by this many become defiled. -**Hebrews 12:15**

Get rid of all bitterness, rage and anger, brawling and slander, along with every form of malice. -**Ephesians 4:31**

A soft answer turns away wrath, but a harsh word stirs up anger. -**Proverbs 15:1**

So if you are suffering in a manner that pleases God, keep on doing what is right, and trust your lives to the God who created you, for he will never fail you. -**1 Peter 4:19**

Do not be misled: "Bad company corrupts good character." -**1 Corinthians 15:33**

Walk with the wise and become wise, for a companion of fools suffers harm. -**Proverbs 13:20**

Therefore do not be partners with them. For you were once darkness, but now you are light in the Lord. Live as children of light (for the fruit of the light consists in all goodness, righteousness and truth). -**Ephesians 5:7-9**

Give careful thought, then, how you live—not as unwise but as wise, making the most of every opportunity, because the days are evil. -**Ephesians 5:15-16**

Introduction

Letting go is one of the most profound yet challenging practices in life. It involves releasing control, accepting change, and detaching from the things that no longer serve us. Whether it's releasing the past, surrendering to the unknown, or embracing the reality of impermanence, the art of letting go is essential for inner peace and growth. Holding on too tightly—whether to outcomes, relationships, or material possessions—creates stress and tension, whereas letting go opens the door to freedom, peace, and self-discovery.

In this final chapter, we will explore the deeper aspects of letting go, including surrendering control to life's flow, accepting the inevitability of change, and finding freedom in detachment. Each of these practices contributes to a more peaceful, liberated way of living. By learning to let go, we make room for new possibilities and allow ourselves to fully experience the present moment.

Life Story

Evelyn had always been a creature of habit, finding comfort in the predictable rhythms of her life. For over thirty years, she had held the same job at a local non-profit, dedicating herself to serving her community. Her colleagues admired her dedication, but behind the scenes, Evelyn felt increasingly trapped by her fear of change and uncertainty.

After retiring, Evelyn found herself faced with an unexpected wave of emotions. The routine that had once provided her with stability vanished overnight. She felt unmoored, grappling with an identity that had been so intertwined with her career. While her friends encouraged her to embrace this new chapter, Evelyn found herself clinging to the past, reminiscing about the work she once loved and the relationships she had built.

One rainy afternoon, feeling particularly lost, Evelyn decided to take a walk through her neighbourhood. As she strolled, she came across a small art gallery featuring a local artist's work. Drawn in by vibrant paintings that depicted the beauty of nature, she stepped inside. The artist was there, engaged in conversation with a few visitors, and Evelyn struck up a discussion about the pieces on display.

The artist spoke passionately about the creative process and how letting go of expectations often led to the most beautiful creations. She shared a story about a painting she had destroyed because it didn't match her vision, only to discover that the act of letting go opened new doors for her creativity. Intrigued by this idea, Evelyn began to reflect on her own life and what she needed to release.

That evening, she sat down with her journal, pouring out her thoughts and feelings. She wrote about her fears, her regrets, and the ways she had clung to her past. As she wrote, she realized that her reluctance to let go was holding her back from experiencing the joy of new beginnings. With each stroke of her pen, she began to release the weight of her past, acknowledging that it was okay to move forward.

Over the next few months, Evelyn embarked on a journey of letting go. She began decluttering her home, donating items that no longer served her and simplifying her surroundings. She also explored new interests, taking a pottery class and joining a book club. With each new experience, Evelyn learned to embrace the unknown, allowing herself to be vulnerable and open to what life had to offer.

As time passed, she discovered a profound sense of freedom in letting go. The memories of her past no longer defined her; instead, they became cherished lessons that enriched her present. Evelyn found herself laughing more, connecting with new friends, and embracing life with a renewed spirit.

Through her journey of letting go, Evelyn learned that change is not to be feared but embraced. Her story serves as a powerful reminder that life is a series of transitions, and the art of letting go allows us to create space for growth, healing, and endless possibilities. In letting go, we often find ourselves—more vibrant and alive than ever before.

Sayings about Letting Go

Here are some quotes that might inspire you to let go of things that can hinder you from experiencing a meaningful life.

Some of us think holding on makes us strong but sometimes it is letting go.
— **HERMANN HESSE**

The truth is unless you let go—forgive yourself, forgive the situation, realize the past is over—you cannot move forward.
— **STEVE MARABOLI**

When things start to fall apart in your life, you feel as if your whole world is crumbling. But actually it's your fixed identity that's crumbling. And that's cause for celebration.
— **PEMA CHÖDRÖN**

The sooner we let go of holding on, the sooner we can hold on to the beauty of what's unfolding before us. Nothing was ever meant to stay the same forever.
— **JULIEANNE O'CONNOR**

Seek not that the things which happen should happen as you wish; but wish the things which happen to be as they are, and you will have a tranquil flow of life.
— **EPICTETUS**

It's not a matter of letting go, you would if you could. Instead of 'Let it go' we should probably say 'Let it be'.
— **JON KABAT-ZINN**

It is the same with people as it is with riding a bike. Only when moving can one comfortably maintain one's balance.
— **ALBERT EINSTEIN**

Let go of becoming but never let go of taking action. Stop expecting and start living.
— **MAXIME LAGACÉ**

Breathe. Let go. And remind yourself that this very moment is the only one you know you have for sure.
— **OPRAH WINFREY**

There ain't no way you can hold onto something that wants to go, you understand? You can only love what you got while you got it.
— **KATE DICAMILLO**

To let go does not mean to get rid of. To let go means to let be. When we let be with compassion, things come and go on their own.
— **JACK KORNFIELD**

If you want to fly in the sky, you need to leave the earth. If you want to move forward, you need to let go of the past that drags you down.
— **AMIT RAY**

I don't regret difficulties I experienced; I think they helped me to become the person I am today, I feel the way a warrior must feel after years of training; he doesn't remember the details of everything he learned, but he knows how to strike when the time is right.
— **PAULO COELHO**

To resist change, to try to cling to life, is like holding your breath: if you persist you kill yourself.
— **ALAN WATTS**

Surrender is a journey from outer turmoil to inner peace.
— **SRI CHINMOY**

Growth is painful. Change is painful. But nothing is as painful as staying stuck somewhere you don't belong.
— **MANDY HALE**

Let reality be reality. Let things flow naturally forward in whatever way they like.
— **LAO TZU**

The key in letting go is practice. Each time we let go, we disentangle ourselves from our expectations and begin to experience things as they are.
— **SHARON SALZBERG**

If strength is love, then we weren't strong enough, But if strength is letting love go, we were.
— **JOE BOLTON**

The nearer a man comes to a calm mind, the closer he is to strength.
— **MARCUS AURELIUS**

The ultimate act of power is surrender.
— **KRISHNA DAS**

Vitality shows in not only the ability to persist but the ability to start over.
— **F. SCOTT FITZGERALD**

We must be willing to let go of the life we have planned, so as to have the life that is waiting for us.
— **E.M. FORSTER**

When all is lost, when all is let go of, when all is abandoned, what you are left with is an ocean of bliss.
— **ROBERT THURMAN**

The more anger towards the past you carry in your heart, the less capable you are of loving in the present.
— BARBARA DE ANGELIS

People have a hard time letting go of their suffering. They prefer suffering that is familiar to the unknown.
— THICH NHAT HANH

Source: https://www.verywellmind.com/quotes-about-letting-go-8678775

Releasing Control and Surrendering to Life

One of the most difficult lessons to learn is that we are not in control of everything. While we can influence certain aspects of our lives, much remains beyond our grasp—be it the actions of others, the outcome of our efforts, or the unfolding of life's events. Releasing control and surrendering to life's flow is a crucial step in the art of letting go.

The Illusion of Control

Control is often an illusion. We spend so much time and energy trying to orchestrate events, people, and outcomes in the way we want them to be. This desire for control stems from fear—fear of the unknown, fear of failure, or fear of loss. However, no matter how much we try, life is inherently unpredictable. Trying to control everything creates stress and anxiety, leaving little room for peace or spontaneity.

Surrendering is not about passivity or resignation but about trusting the flow of life. It means accepting that while we may not be able to control every situation, we can always choose how we respond. Surrender is an act of faith—faith in ourselves, faith in others, and faith in the process of life itself. By releasing control, we open ourselves to the natural flow of life, allowing things to unfold in their own time.

The Power of Trust

Trust plays a central role in letting go. To surrender, we must trust that life will unfold as it is meant to, even if the path is unclear or different from what we envisioned. Trusting life means having faith that, no matter the outcome, we will find a way through. It involves trusting our own inner strength and resilience, as well as the wisdom of the universe or higher power.

When we trust that life's twists and turns have their own purpose, we can release the tight grip of control and move with the natural ebb and flow of life. In doing so, we create space for greater peace and flexibility. This act of surrender allows us to let go of expectations, easing the burden of trying to force things to happen according to our plans.

Accepting Change and Impermanence

Change is the only constant in life, yet many of us resist it out of fear of the unknown. Learning to accept change and embrace impermanence is a crucial aspect of the art of letting go. When we resist change, we create suffering for ourselves, clinging to what is familiar even when it no longer serves us. However, when we embrace the reality that everything is in a constant state of flux, we can move more fluidly with the natural rhythms of life.

The Nature of Impermanence

Everything in life is temporary—our circumstances, relationships, successes, failures, and even our physical existence. Impermanence can be frightening because it reminds us of the fleeting nature of life and the inevitability of loss. However, it is also what makes life precious. By accepting that everything is subject to change, we learn to appreciate the present moment for what it is, without clinging to it or fearing its end.

Impermanence teaches us to live in the now. When we fully accept that nothing lasts forever, we can release our attachment to outcomes and embrace whatever comes our way with an open heart. This acceptance of change allows us to let go of fear and anxiety, creating space for joy, love, and inner peace.

Letting Go of Resistance

Resisting change is one of the most common ways we block ourselves from inner peace. Whether we resist changes in our personal lives, careers, or within ourselves, this resistance creates tension and unhappiness. Letting go of resistance doesn't mean we must agree with or like every change that happens, but it does mean acknowledging and accepting that change is an inevitable part of life.

One of the ways to practice accepting change is to focus on flexibility and adaptability. Instead of trying to prevent or control change, we can choose to flow with it, allowing ourselves to grow and evolve through new experiences. By releasing our grip on how we think things "should" be, we open ourselves to new opportunities and possibilities.

Finding Freedom in Detachment

Detachment is a practice of letting go of attachment to specific outcomes, material possessions, or even personal relationships. It does not mean becoming indifferent or unfeeling, but rather maintaining a healthy emotional distance that allows us to experience life without becoming overly attached to its transient aspects. Detachment is about cultivating freedom—freedom from the need for control, from fear, and from the illusion of permanence.

Emotional Detachment

Emotional detachment doesn't mean shutting off emotions or avoiding meaningful connections. Instead, it means recognizing that our happiness and well-being are not dependent on external circumstances. Many of us attach our sense of self-worth and happiness to specific people, outcomes, or material things. When we do this, we give those things power over us, allowing them to determine our emotional state.

Detachment allows us to enjoy life's experiences without becoming enslaved by them. It involves finding joy in the present without clinging to it, and experiencing loss or change without being consumed by it. By practicing detachment, we find an inner freedom that is not tied to the constant ups and downs of life.

Material and Mental Detachment

In addition to emotional detachment, material and mental detachment play crucial roles in achieving inner freedom. Many of us attach ourselves to material possessions, believing they bring us happiness or security. However, material possessions are temporary, and their pursuit often leads to stress and dissatisfaction. Detaching from the need for material wealth allows us to focus on what truly matters—relationships, experiences, and personal growth.

Mental detachment, on the other hand, involves letting go of rigid thinking patterns, expectations, and the need to be right. By releasing these mental attachments, we become more open-minded and flexible, which helps us navigate life's uncertainties with ease.

Conclusion

The art of letting go is a lifelong practice that requires intention, trust, and acceptance. It is about releasing the illusion of control, accepting the inevitability of change, and finding freedom in detachment. Letting go does not mean giving up or becoming indifferent; it means embracing the flow of life with openness and grace.

Through the practices of surrender, acceptance, and detachment, we can cultivate a deeper sense of peace and freedom. By letting go of fear, attachment, and resistance, we create space for growth, new experiences, and true happiness. Ultimately, the art of letting go allows us to live more fully in the present moment, appreciating life for what it is rather than what we think it should be.

As we conclude this chapter and the book, remember that letting go is not about losing anything; it is about gaining freedom—freedom to live authentically, to love without fear, and to find peace in the ever-changing dance of life.

Exercise

Mastering the Art of Letting Go

This final exercise is designed to help you internalize the lessons of the chapter and apply them to your life. Letting go is a lifelong practice that brings freedom, peace, and growth. This exercise will guide you through steps to release control, accept change, and find peace in detachment.

Step 1: Reflect on What You're Holding On To

Take a moment to reflect on one or two things in your life that you are struggling to let go of. These could be:

- A past hurt or disappointment
- An unfulfilled expectation
- A fear of change or the unknown
- A relationship that has shifted or ended

Write down what comes to mind, identifying the specific thoughts or emotions that keep you from letting go. Acknowledge how these feelings affect your peace of mind and overall well-being.

Step 2: Accept the Impermanence of Life

Spend a few minutes contemplating the impermanence of life. Everything—relationships, situations, achievements, and even our emotions—is constantly changing. Reflect on the following questions:

- **What does it mean to accept that life is always in motion?**
- **How can I find peace in the reality that nothing stays the same?**

- **What positive growth or opportunities have come from changes in my life?**

Write a brief paragraph in your journal about your thoughts on impermanence and how accepting this truth could help you move forward in life with more peace and flexibility.

Step 3: Let Go of Control

One of the key aspects of letting go is surrendering control over things we cannot change. Try this simple exercise:

- **List three things in your life that are beyond your control.** These could include someone else's behaviour, a past event, or an unpredictable outcome in the future.
- **Next, for each item, write down how you typically respond.** Do you worry, get frustrated, or try to manipulate the situation?
- **Now, imagine a new response based on letting go of control.** Picture yourself accepting the situation as it is and allowing life to unfold naturally. Write down how this response would change your emotional state and overall outlook.

By visualizing how letting go of control can lead to greater peace, you'll start shifting your mindset toward acceptance.

Step 4: Practice a Letting Go Meditation

Set aside 10-15 minutes for a guided meditation on letting go:

- Sit in a comfortable, quiet space. Close your eyes and take a few deep breaths to center yourself.

- **Visualize the thing you are holding on to**, whether it's a fear, resentment, or desire. Imagine it as a heavy object that you're carrying in your hands.
- As you exhale, **release the object into the air** or place it down on the ground. Watch it drift away or sink into the earth.
- As the weight leaves your hands, feel your body and mind become lighter and more at peace. Allow yourself to embrace the sense of freedom that comes with letting go.

After the meditation, take a moment to write down how you feel. Did you experience a sense of relief or clarity? How can you bring this practice into your daily life when feelings of attachment arise?

Step 5: Embrace Change and New Beginnings

Change is inevitable, but it often brings new opportunities and growth. Think of a time in your life when a significant change (planned or unexpected) led to something positive:

- **What was the change, and how did you initially feel about it?**
- **What new doors opened because of that change?**
- **What lessons did you learn from the experience?**

Now, look at your current life. Identify one area where change is happening or may soon occur. Write about how you can approach this change with an open heart and mind, allowing yourself to embrace it as a new beginning rather than a loss.

Step 6: Find Freedom in Detachment

Detachment doesn't mean indifference, but rather the ability to enjoy life without being overly attached to outcomes. Try this exercise:

- **Choose one goal or desire you have been holding on to tightly.** It could be related to work, relationships, or personal achievement.
- **For one week, practice focusing on the process instead of the outcome.** Put your energy into the journey—whether it's learning a new skill, strengthening a relationship, or achieving better health—without fixating on how things "should" turn out.

At the end of the week, reflect on how detaching from the outcome influenced your experience. Did you feel more at peace? Were you able to enjoy the moment without worrying about success or failure?

Step 7: Celebrate Your Growth

Letting go is not a one-time event but a continuous practice. Reflect on how far you've come on your journey of letting go:

- **What have you learned about yourself throughout this process?**
- **In what areas have you found greater peace and freedom by releasing control or attachment?**
- **How has letting go improved your relationships, mindset, or emotional health?**

Celebrate these successes, no matter how small, and commit to continuing this practice as you move forward. Write a short affirmation or mantra to remind yourself of the peace that comes with letting go, and use it whenever you feel overwhelmed by attachments or fear of change.

By completing this exercise, you will have taken important steps toward mastering the art of letting go and embracing the freedom, peace, and fulfillment that come with it. This final chapter serves as a powerful reminder that true growth and happiness lie not in holding on, but in letting go and trusting the journey.

CHAPTER 18
WORDSEARCH

	1	2	3	4	5	6	7	8	9	10	11	12	13	14	15
1	N	O	I	T	C	A	F	S	I	T	A	S	W	P	U
2	E	E	F	K	O	T	N	M	V	W	M	C	E	A	A
3	C	C	R	B	Y	Q	N	E	A	B	Y	E	A	G	B
4	N	N	E	S	Q	G	F	E	P	T	C	V	L	E	Z
5	A	A	E	U	G	O	N	C	M	N	E	D	T	V	N
6	T	T	D	R	Q	Q	A	I	E	H	O	R	H	Z	G
7	P	S	O	R	X	J	O	N	S	D	C	Y	I	W	J
8	E	I	M	E	F	K	A	V	Q	A	G	A	O	A	J
9	C	S	W	N	N	M	V	V	E	H	E	F	T	X	L
10	C	E	R	D	R	K	O	R	W	A	D	L	D	E	W
11	A	R	J	E	D	K	G	D	P	W	L	F	E	K	D
12	U	G	P	R	C	U	G	A	N	O	P	D	Z	R	N
13	I	M	G	I	V	K	K	K	T	D	D	U	L	Z	Y
14	I	P	F	N	W	C	D	F	J	I	G	A	D	W	N
15	M	Q	B	G	K	P	R	B	T	B	D	V	V	B	M

ACCEPTANCE   MATERIAL   SURRENDERING
DETACHMENT   RELEASING   WEALTH
FREEDOM   RESISTANCE
IMPERMANENCE   SATISFACTION

THE ART OF LETTING GO

ANSWER

	1	2	3	4	5	6	7	8	9	10	11	12	13	14	15
1	N	O	I	T	C	A	F	S	I	T	A	S	W	P	U
2	E	E	F	K	O	T	N	M	V	W	M	C	E	A	A
3	C	C	R	B	Y	Q	N	E	A	B	Y	E	A	G	B
4	N	N	E	S	Q	G	F	E	P	T	C	V	L	E	Z
5	A	A	E	U	G	O	N	C	M	N	E	D	T	V	N
6	T	T	D	R	Q	Q	A	I	E	H	O	R	H	Z	G
7	P	S	O	R	X	J	O	N	S	D	C	Y	I	W	J
8	E	I	M	E	F	K	A	V	Q	A	G	A	O	A	J
9	C	S	W	N	N	M	V	V	E	H	E	F	T	X	L
10	C	E	R	D	R	K	O	R	W	A	D	L	D	E	W
11	A	R	J	E	D	K	G	D	P	W	L	F	E	K	D
12	U	G	P	R	C	U	G	A	N	O	P	D	Z	R	N
13	I	M	G	I	V	K	K	K	T	D	D	U	L	Z	Y
14	I	P	F	N	W	C	D	F	J	I	G	A	D	W	N
15	M	Q	B	G	K	P	R	B	T	B	D	V	V	B	M

ACCEPTANCE 11:1   MATERIAL 2:8   SURRENDERING 4:4

DETACHMENT 11:15   RELEASING 12:14   WEALTH 1:13

FREEDOM 2:3   RESISTANCE 11:2

IMPERMANENCE 14:1   SATISFACTION 1:12

CONCLUSION

Reflecting on the Journey

As we come to the end of this book, it is important to take a moment to reflect on the journey we have taken together. We've explored many facets of what it means to live a meaningful life—from understanding ourselves and our purpose to cultivating deep relationships, practicing gratitude, and learning the art of letting go. Along the way, we've delved into topics like personal growth, spirituality, financial literacy, and inner peace, each contributing to a well-rounded approach to finding fulfillment and purpose.

Life's journey is never a straight path. It is full of twists, turns, and moments of both joy and difficulty. But in reflecting on what we've learned, it becomes clear that the meaning we seek is not found in the external achievements or the milestones we hit but in how we engage with life's experiences. A meaningful life is one lived with intention, one that embraces both the highs and the lows, and one that continually seeks to grow and evolve. Each chapter of this book represents a stepping stone on this journey toward greater fulfillment, deeper understanding, and lasting peace.

As you think about your own journey, consider the ways in which you've already begun to live with more meaning. What changes have you made? What new insights have you gained? Reflecting on these questions will help solidify the lessons learned and create a foundation for the ongoing pursuit of a fulfilling and meaningful life.

Continuous Growth and Lifelong Learning

One of the most important truths about a meaningful life is that it is a continual process. There is no final destination at which we will arrive and say, "Now my life is meaningful, and I am done growing." Instead, life is a series of opportunities for learning, evolving, and refining our understanding of who we are and what we value.

The quest for meaning requires ongoing curiosity and a willingness to embrace change. Whether it's learning a new skill, deepening your spiritual practice, or engaging in self-reflection, growth must remain a constant companion. Each new experience—whether joyful or challenging—offers a chance to expand your perspective, learn something new, and move closer to the person you aspire to be.

Moreover, continuous growth involves understanding that our definitions of success and fulfillment will shift over time. What mattered to you in your twenties may not carry the same weight in your fifties, and that's perfectly okay. Meaning is not a static concept; it is dynamic, adapting to the changes in your life, your priorities, and your values.

Remember that there is no pressure to have everything figured out all at once. Life is a journey, and every small step forward contributes to your overall growth and sense of meaning. Approach each day with an open mind, knowing that the pursuit of a meaningful life is lifelong and filled with opportunities for discovery.

Final Thoughts and Encouragement

As you continue down your own path to a meaningful life, I want to leave you with a few final thoughts and words of encouragement. First, understand that meaning is personal. No one else can define what a meaningful life looks like for you. It is something that you create through your choices, your actions, and the way you engage with the world around you. Trust yourself to know what resonates with you and to follow your own unique path.

Second, remember that challenges and setbacks are part of the journey. There will be times when life feels difficult, when you question your direction, or when you struggle to find meaning in the midst of hardship. But it is often in these moments of challenge that we experience the most profound growth. Embrace the difficult times with grace and patience, knowing that they, too, contribute to the overall richness and depth of your life.

Finally, don't underestimate the power of small actions. A meaningful life is built not only on grand achievements but also on the small, everyday choices we make. The way you treat others, the care you put into your relationships, and the moments of kindness and gratitude you practice—all of these things contribute to a life that is rich with meaning.

As you move forward, I encourage you to live with intention, to continually seek growth, and to embrace the beauty of the present moment. Life is a gift, and every day offers a new opportunity to live it in a way that brings you closer to your highest self. Trust in the journey, and remember that the path to a meaningful life is one that you are always creating, step by step.

May you walk this path with courage, curiosity, and a heart open to all the possibilities that life has to offer.

Riddles

Riddles offer a unique and engaging way to reflect on the deeper truths of life. In *The Journey to a Fulfilling and Meaningful Life*, they serve as both a mental challenge and a metaphor for the journey of self-discovery. Just as one must ponder the clues of a riddle to find its answer, so too must we reflect on our experiences, struggles, and values to uncover life's meaning. Riddles provoke thought, spark curiosity, and encourage readers to pause, think, and appreciate the wisdom hidden in everyday moments, making them a powerful tool for personal growth and introspection.

Riddle 1

Journey without it and you will never prevail, but if you have too much of it you will surely fail.
Answer: Confidence

Riddle 2

Poor people have it. Rich people need it. It can make you or break you.
Answer: Adversity

Riddle 3

Everyone wants more of it to feel special, yet the more you have of it the less special you feel.
Answer: Knowledge

Riddle 4

If you have me, you want to share me. If you share me, you haven't got me. What am I?
Answer: Secret

Riddle 5

You can only have it once you have given it.
Answer: Respect

Riddle 6

Imagine you are in a dark room. How do you get out?
Answer: Stop imagining it

Riddle 7

What is always coming but never arrives?
Answer: Tomorrow

Riddle 8

At night they come without being fetched. By day they are lost without being stolen.
Answer: Doubts and fears

Riddle 9

A prison you feel safe in, yet never quite happy. Whenever you try to leave, it only grows bigger.
Answer: Your comfort zone

Riddle 10

If you break me I do not stop working; if you touch me I may be snared; if you lose me nothing will matter.
Answer: Your heart

Riddle 11

It starts off light and easy to bear, yet the more you carry it with you, the heavier a burden it becomes.
Answer: A guilty conscience

Riddle 12

I do not listen to reason, but I hear every siren's song and will try to steer us towards the rocks if you let me take the wheel. Who am I?
Answer: Ego

Riddle 13

One by one we fall from heaven down into the depths of past, and our world is ever upturned so that yet some time we'll last.
Answer: Dreams and aspirations

Riddle 14

A mile from end to end, yet as close to as a friend. A precious commodity, freely given. Found on the rich, poor, short and tall, but shared among children most of all. What is it?
Answer: A smile

Riddle 15

We hurt without moving. We poison without touching. We bear the truth and the lies. We are not to be judged by our size. What are we?
Answer: Words

Source:
https://www.lifehack.org/articles/communication/answer-these-riddles-and-you-will-find-the-answers-life.html

Glossary of Terms

A

Adaptability – The ability to adjust to new conditions or challenges with flexibility and resilience.

Altruism -- The selfless concern for the well-being of others, often leading to actions that benefit others without expecting anything in return.

Aspiration – A strong desire or ambition to achieve something, often related to personal growth or fulfillment.

Awareness – The state of being conscious of something, including one's own thoughts, emotions, and surroundings.

B

Balance – The practice of maintaining equilibrium in various aspects of life, such as work, relationships, and personal well-being.

Body-Mind Connection – The interplay between physical health and mental/emotional well-being, emphasizing their mutual influence.

Bonds -- Debt securities issued by governments or corporations to raise capital. Investors who purchase bonds lend money to the issuer in exchange for periodic interest payments and the return of the bond's face value upon maturity.

Boundaries – The limits or guidelines set to protect one's emotional, physical, or mental health from being compromised by external influences.

Budget -- A financial plan that outlines expected income and expenditures over a specific period, helping individuals or organizations manage their money and achieve financial goals.

C

Clarity – The quality of being clear and easy to understand, often applied to one's thoughts, goals, or intentions.

Compassion – The ability to empathize with others' suffering and the desire to alleviate it.

Concentration – The mental effort and focus placed on a specific task or thought, avoiding distractions.

Consumer -- An individual or entity that purchases goods or services for personal use or consumption rather than for resale or production.

Contentment – A state of peaceful happiness, often rooted in satisfaction with what one has rather than seeking more.

Creativity – The ability to produce original ideas, often linked to innovation and problem-solving.

D

Decision -- The act of making a choice or conclusion after considering different options, often weighing potential outcomes to arrive at a course of action.

Detachment – The practice of letting go of attachments, often to emotions or outcomes, in order to achieve a sense of inner peace.

Diet – The regular food and drink consumed by an individual, impacting overall health and well-being.

Distractions – External or internal factors that divert one's attention away from the task at hand.

Diversification -- A risk management strategy that involves spreading investments across various asset types, industries, or markets to reduce the impact of losses in any one area.

E

Economics -- The social science that studies the production, distribution, and consumption of goods and services, focusing on how individuals, businesses, and governments make choices to allocate resources.

Emotional Balance – The ability to maintain stability and control over one's emotions, especially during stressful or challenging situations.

Emotional Intelligence – The ability to recognize, understand, and manage one's own emotions, as well as the emotions of others.

Emotion – A complex experience of consciousness, bodily sensation, and behaviour that reflects feelings such as joy, sadness, anger, or love.

Empathy – The ability to understand and share the feelings of another person.

Exercise – Physical activity that improves or maintains physical fitness, health, and overall well-being.

F

Financial Independence – The state of having sufficient income or wealth to cover one's living expenses without the need for ongoing employment.

Forgiveness – The act of letting go of resentment or anger toward someone who has wronged you, promoting emotional freedom.

G

Grace -- The free and unmerited favour or kindness, often associated with divine love or the ability to act with compassion and forgiveness in human interactions.

Gratitude – A feeling of thankfulness and appreciation, often expressed toward others or life circumstances.

Gratitude Practice – The regular habit of reflecting on and appreciating the positive aspects of life, often leading to greater emotional well-being.

Growth Mindset – The belief that abilities and intelligence can be developed through dedication, effort, and perseverance.

H

Habits – Regular practices or routines, often unconscious, that can either support or hinder one's well-being.

Happiness -- A state of well-being and contentment, often characterized by feelings of pleasure, joy, and satisfaction with life.

I

Inflation -- The general increase in the price levels of goods and services in an economy over time, which reduces the purchasing power of money.

Inner Peace – A state of mental and emotional calmness, with no anxiety or worry, often achieved through mindfulness and spiritual practices.

Intention – A deliberate aim or plan to achieve something, typically aligning actions with values and goals.

Interest -- The cost of borrowing money, expressed as a percentage of the loan amount, paid by the borrower to the lender over a specified period.

Interest rate -- The percentage charged on a loan or paid on savings over a specific period, usually expressed as an annual percentage of the principal amount.

J

Joy – A deep and enduring sense of happiness or delight, often resulting from inner contentment or spiritual fulfillment rather than external circumstances.

K

Kindness -- The quality of being friendly, generous, and considerate toward others, often involving actions that contribute to the well-being of others without expecting anything in return.

L

Letting Go – The act of releasing control, attachment, or expectations to attain inner peace and emotional freedom.

Love – A profound and selfless affection or deep emotional bond with someone or something, characterized by care, compassion, and commitment.

M

Market -- A place or system where buyers and sellers interact to exchange goods, services, or financial assets, determining prices based on supply and demand.

Meditation – A mental practice involving focused attention and mindfulness, often used to cultivate relaxation, awareness, or spiritual growth.

Milestones -- Significant events or achievements that mark progress in personal, professional, or financial goals, often used as indicators of success or completion.

Mindfulness – The practice of maintaining awareness of the present moment without judgment, often used to manage stress and enhance focus.

Mindset – The established set of attitudes or beliefs held by an individual, often shaping how he or she perceives and reacts to experiences.

Mortgage -- A loan used to purchase real estate, where the property itself serves as collateral, and the borrower makes periodic payments to repay the debt over time.

Motivation – The inner drive or reason that prompts an individual to take action, pursue goals, or overcome challenges, often influenced by personal desires or external rewards.

N

Nutrition – The process of providing or obtaining the food necessary for health, growth, and vitality.

P

Patience – The ability to endure waiting, challenges, or suffering without frustration or anger.

Perception – The way in which an individual interprets and makes sense of sensory information or experiences.

Personal Finance – The management of an individual's or household's financial resources, including budgeting, saving, and investing.

Personal Fulfillment – A state of happiness and satisfaction derived from achieving one's goals, purpose, or potential.

Physical Health – The overall condition of the body, influenced by factors such as diet, exercise, sleep, and preventive care.

Portfolio -- A collection of financial assets, such as stocks, bonds, and other investments, owned by an individual or institution to achieve specific financial goals.

Presence – The state of fully engaging in the current moment, free from distractions or preoccupations with the past or future.

Purpose -- A clear sense of direction or intention that gives meaning to one's actions and life. It reflects an individual's goals, values, and desires, often guiding decisions and providing motivation to pursue personal fulfillment or contribute to a greater cause.

R

Reflection – The process of thinking deeply about one's thoughts, actions, and experiences, often used for personal growth.

Reframing – The process of changing the way one interprets or thinks about a situation, often to see it in a more positive or constructive light.

Relaxation – A state of rest and calmness, often achieved through practices like deep breathing, meditation, or yoga.

Resilience – The ability to recover from or adapt to difficult situations, challenges, or setbacks.

Routine – A regular, often habitual, set of actions or behaviours performed daily or weekly, which contribute to one's overall well-being.

S

Self-Awareness – The conscious knowledge of one's own character, feelings, motives, and desires, often leading to personal insight.

Self-Care – The practice of maintaining and improving one's health and well-being, often through activities that nurture physical, emotional, or mental health.

Self-Compassion – Treating oneself with kindness, understanding, and care, particularly during times of difficulty or failure.

CONCLUSION

Self-Discipline – The ability to control one's impulses, emotions, or behaviours to achieve long-term goals.

Self-Improvement – The process of actively seeking to enhance one's abilities, knowledge, or character to achieve personal growth.

Service – The act of helping or doing work for others, often as an expression of kindness, compassion, or contribution to the community.

Spiritual Fulfillment – A deep sense of satisfaction and peace that comes from living in alignment with one's spiritual beliefs and values.

Spirituality – A sense of connection to something greater than oneself, often involving a search for meaning, purpose, and inner peace.

Stocks -- Shares of ownership in a corporation, representing a claim on part of the company's assets and earnings, with the potential for returns through dividends and capital appreciation.

Stress – A physical or emotional response to external pressures or demands, often resulting in feelings of tension or anxiety.

Stress Management – Techniques and practices used to reduce or manage stress, including relaxation, mindfulness, and time management.

Surrender – The act of accepting things as they are, letting go of control, and trusting in life's process or a higher power.

T

Thankfulness -- The quality of being appreciative or grateful for the blessings, people, or experiences in one's life, often expressed through positive thoughts or actions.

Time Management – The ability to plan and control how much time to spend on specific activities, often leading to greater efficiency and productivity.

V

Vaccinations – Medical injections that help protect the body from specific diseases, contributing to overall health.

Visualization – The process of creating mental images or scenarios to help achieve specific goals or outcomes.

Vulnerability – The willingness to be open, honest, and emotionally exposed, often in the face of uncertainty or potential criticism, as a means of fostering deeper connections and personal growth.

W

Well-being -- A holistic sense of health, happiness, and prosperity, encompassing physical, emotional, and mental states, as well as an overall sense of balance and fulfillment in life.

Wellness – A holistic approach to health that encompasses physical, mental, emotional, and spiritual well-being.

Wisdom – The ability to make sound judgments and decisions based on knowledge, experience, and insight.

CONCLUSION

Y

Yoga – A physical and mental practice that combines postures, breath control, and meditation, promoting relaxation, flexibility, and inner peace.

www.ingramcontent.com/pod-product-compliance
Lightning Source LLC
Chambersburg PA
CBHW051542010526
44118CB00022B/2546